Caught in the Middle

Caught in the Middle

Korean Merchants in America's Multiethnic Cities

Pyong Gap Min

UNIVERSITY OF CALIFORNIA PRESS

Berkeley   Los Angeles   London

University of California Press
Berkeley and Los Angeles, California

University of California Press, Ltd.
London, England

Library of Congress Cataloging-in-Publication Data

Min, Pyong Gap.
      Caught in the middle : Korean merchants in
America's multiethnic cities / Pyong Gap Min.
            p.   cm.
      Includes bibliographic references and index.
      ISBN 0-520-20488-3 (hardcover : alk. pa-
per). - ISBN 0-520-20489-1 (pbk. : alk. paper)
      1. Korean Americans–New York (N.Y.)
2. Korean American business enterprises—New
York (N.Y.)   3. Korean Americans—California—
Los Angeles.   4. Korean American business enter-
prises—California—Los Angeles.   5. New York
(N.Y.)—Race relations.   6. Los Angeles (Calif.)—
Race relations   I. Title.
   F128.9.K6M56   1996
   305.895'07741—dc20   95-47020

Printed in the United States of America
9   8   7   6   5   4   3   2   1

The paper used in this publication meets the
minimum requirements of American National
Standards for Information Sciences—Permanence
of Paper for Printed Library Materials, ANSI
Z39.48-1984.

Contents

Illustrations and Tables

Acknowledgments

In 1986 I received a grant from the National Science Foundation for a study of Korean immigrants in Los Angeles. I have used the results of the 1986 survey in chapter 4, as well as other chapters. I would like to express my sincere thanks to the National Science Foundation, especially to Dr. Mark Abrahamson, then the director of the sociology program, for having confidence in an unknown sociologist. I am indebted to more than twenty Korean students who served as research assistants or interviewers for the Los Angeles research project. I still remember one student, Sun Young Lee, who, as a senior at UCLA in 1986, helped me with sampling and the training and supervision of interviewers. I also owe thanks to Eui-Young Yu at California State University— Los Angeles, and Ivan Light, Georges Sabagh, and Mehdi Bozorgmehr at UCLA, who helped me in various stages of the NSF project. Don Nakanishi, director of the Asian American Studies Center at UCLA, was kind enough to allow me to use the center's facilities for my research.

A grant from the City University of New York PSC-CUNY Research Award Program supported my 1988 survey of Korean married women in New York City. The data on self-employment of Korean immigrants in New York City presented in chapter 4 are based on the results of this survey. Another grant from the same research program enabled me to interview staff members of major Korean business associations in Los Angeles and New York in 1990 and 1991, respectively, and also made possible reviewing all issues of the *Korea Times New York* published

between 1970 and 1988. These interviews and reviews have provided
data and information indispensable to demonstrating my central thesis.
I would like to acknowledge that the grants from the PSC-CUNY
Research Award Program have been essential to completing this book
and performing my other research activities at Queens College. I owe
special thanks to Brenda Newman and Merriam Korman at the CUNY
Research Foundation and Regina Caulfield at the Queens College Grant
Office for processing my grants as quickly as possible. He Ran Hurh
interviewed Korean women in New York City for the 1988 survey, and
Hyun Sook Kim reviewed stacks of ethnic newspaper articles in 1990.
Edward Chang at UC-Riverside helped me in interviewing Korean business leaders in Los Angeles in 1990 and 1992.

A Ford Foundation Diversity Initiative grant, originally awarded
to Queens College, supported my survey study of Korean merchants in
New York City's Black neighborhoods and of Black and White residents
in 1992. Chapter 6 is based primarily on the results of the survey. An
interracial team of seven students at Queens College conducted telephone interviews and coded data for the Ford Foundation project. I still
remember that three of the students—Mica McCarty, Hyun Sook Kim,
and Andrew Kolody—were very enthusiastic about the project.

Yo Han Choi has helped me more than any other student assistant to
complete this book. Beginning in his freshman year at Queens College
in 1992, he has reviewed every issue of the *Korea Times Los Angeles* and
the *Sae Gae Times* for this book. He proofread several versions of the
manuscript and checked references and tables for the final version. I feel
lucky to have such a reliable assistant. I would also like to acknowledge
that Michael Min, one of my sons, and Irina Shin, proofread the whole
manuscript.

Many colleagues at the Department of Sociology, Queens College,
have helped me in different ways at different stages, some with technical advice in manuscript preparation and others with moral support
and encouragement. I would like to single out the following six colleagues in particular: Dean Savage, Charles Smith, Paul Blumberg,
Lauren Seiler, Robert Kapsis, and Alem Habtu. Of them, I owe the most
to Dean Savage; he has always been with me when I have had a problem
in using department PC facilities. I also owe special thanks to Alem
Habtu, who suggested the main title of this book.

Erica Klusner edited the entire manuscript, Rose Kim edited six
chapters, and Susan Marsden Kapsis and Glenn Omatsu each edited
some chapters. Ivan Light, Roger Waldinger, Rubén Rumbaut, Steve

Gold, and two anonymous reviewers read the entire manuscript and offered critical comments. I feel grateful to these editors and sociologists. I also thank Naomi Schneider, the sociology editor at the University of California Press, for supporting this book project enthusiastically from the beginning. Erika Bűky and Alice Falk at the University of California Press polished the manuscript; Alice Falk, in particular, copyedited the manuscript carefully but quickly. Their work helped me to improve the manuscript greatly.

The unselfish support and cooperation of my wife, Hyun Suk, have been important to my academic achievements and to the completion of this book. Her company on a research trip to Los Angeles enabled me to overcome many difficulties—even an unexpected and intimidating southern snowstorm on our drive back.

Finally, I would like to extend thanks to the Korean business leaders and respondents to my surveys in New York and Los Angeles who provided valuable information and ideas about Korean immigrants' commercial activities, intergroup conflicts, and their own experiences in the United States. This book would have been impossible without their cooperation.

CHAPTER I

Introduction

On April 29, 1992, a predominantly White jury returned a "not guilty" verdict against four White police officers accused of beating an African American motorist, Rodney King, and ignited three days of rioting in Los Angeles that claimed 52 deaths, about 2,400 injuries, and $785 million worth of property damage. The multiethnic character of the riots and the disproportionately large number of Korean stores that were targets of destruction made the riots unique. Approximately 2,300 Korean-owned stores in South Central Los Angeles and Koreatown were burned and looted during three days of rioting. Korean merchants suffered $350 million worth of damage, 45% of the total riot damages. Conflicts between Koreans and African Americans had been the topic of headlines in recent years, yet the targeting of Korean merchants during the Los Angeles riots was a defining moment of Koreans' business-related conflicts with the African American community.

Korean–African American conflicts have been fully covered by the mainstream media. Not so well covered by the media, but sociologically important, is how these conflicts have increased solidarity in the Korean community. The day after the riots ended, thirty thousand Koreans in Los Angeles held a rally for peace and solidarity. Korean Americans from all over the United States contributed more than $5 million to help the Korean riot victims. The Korean 4.29 Riot Victims Association organized daily rallies at the Los Angeles City Hall for over a month, at which an average of two hundred Korean riot victims participated.

The victimization of Korean merchants during the riots also heightened Koreans' political consciousness and second-generation Korean Americans' ethnic identity.

Although Korean–African American conflicts climaxed in the Los Angeles riots, they were occurring in other cities as well. Korean merchants also faced African American protests and boycotts in New York, Baltimore, Atlanta, Philadelphia, and Washington and these conflicts have helped unify those Korean communities. The New York Korean community has encountered a number of long-term Black—African American and Afro-Caribbean—boycotts, and each has enhanced Korean ethnic solidarity. During the much-publicized 1990–91 Brooklyn boycott of two Korean stores, not only merchants but also many other Koreans in New York participated in fund-raising campaigns, collecting approximately $150,000 to help the "victims of Black racism against Koreans." They also supported the store owners by visiting their businesses and sending letters to them. Finally, dissatisfied with Mayor David Dinkins's "lukewarm" effort to terminate the boycott, the Korean community organized a demonstration in front of City Hall that drew approximately seven thousand Koreans.

Korean merchants are in conflict not only with African American customers but also with suppliers, landlords, and government agencies regulating small businesses. Again, the Korean merchants' conflicts with these powerful forces have enhanced their ethnic solidarity and sharpened their political skills. Using collective strategies such as boycotts, Korean merchants have confronted White suppliers and landlords: Korean trade associations in New York have organized a dozen demonstrations and boycotts against suppliers to protect their economic interests. They have also actively lobbied government agencies and politicians for less stringent regulation of small businesses.

Other immigrant groups are also active in small business, though not to the same extent. For example, Chinese immigrants in New York have created their own subeconomy, specializing in restaurants, garment subcontracting, and the retailing of jewelry and other Asian-imported goods (Kwong 1987; Zhou 1992, 95). Cuban immigrants in Miami have developed a high level of business in their enclave (Portes and Bach 1985; K. Wilson and Portes 1980). But neither group has encountered a level of business-related intergroup conflict comparable to that faced by Korean immigrants.

Why is it that Korean merchants have encountered multifaceted intergroup conflicts that have enhanced their ethnic solidarity, whereas these other entrepreneurial groups have not? To answer this question, one needs to pay special attention to the location of major Korean businesses and the nature of their commercial activities. Many Korean immigrants run grocery, liquor, produce, and fish retail businesses, and these businesses are heavily concentrated in minority neighborhoods. Korean merchants rely mostly on White suppliers. Like the Jews in Europe, the Chinese in Southeast Asia, and the Indians in African countries (Eitzen 1971; Palmer 1957; Zenner 1991), Korean merchants in the United States play the role of a "middleman" minority between low-income, minority consumers and large companies, often distributing merchandise made by predominantly White-owned corporations to African American and Latino customers. In this economic role, Korean immigrants encounter a high level of business-related conflicts with both customers and White suppliers. Korean men and women engage in middleman businesses more than any other immigrant group and thus are more likely to be involved in intergroup conflicts and to have developed collective strategies to protect their economic interests.

KOREANS' MIGRATION, SETTLEMENT, AND OCCUPATIONS

Before the early 1970s, Korean immigrant businesses attracted little public attention; what the majority of Americans knew about Korea and Koreans came mainly through their memories of the Korean War and movies such as *M*A*S*H*. It was the Immigration Act of 1965 that brought the mass influx of Korean immigrants to the United States. From 1976 to 1990, an annual average of 30,000–35,000 Koreans immigrated to the United States (see chapter 3 for details). In the 1970s and 1980s, Koreans were the third largest immigrant group, following Mexicans and Filipinos. The prospect of a higher standard of living and a better opportunity for their children's education motivated many Koreans to choose trans-Pacific migration. But military, political, and economic connections between the United States and South Korea were also important factors in explaining why South Korea sent more immigrants to the United States than did other Asian countries, such as India and China, during this period.

As a result of a large influx of new immigrants, the Korean American population increased from 70,000 in 1970 to approximately 800,000 in 1990. Southern California, connecting Los Angeles and Orange Counties, is the largest residential center with approximately 250,000

Koreans. Koreans in Los Angeles have established Koreatown three miles west of downtown. More recently, many immigrants have relocated to suburban areas in Orange County. The New York–New Jersey area, the home of approximately 150,000 Koreans, is the second largest Korean center. In the 1980s, both the Los Angeles–Orange County and New York–New Jersey metropolitan areas experienced higher rates of Korean population growth than did the United States as a whole.

Post-1965 Korean immigrants, like other post-1965 Asian immigrants, are characterized by their urban, middle-class backgrounds and their high preimmigration educational and occupational levels. Yet, despite their education, Korean immigrants have faced problems in the American job market because of the language barrier and their unfamiliarity with American customs. College-educated immigrants from India and the Philippines who spoke English in their native countries have not faced the same obstacles.

In the early 1970s, Korean immigrants found employment as cooks, gas station attendants, garment factory workers, and in other blue-collar positions. Beginning in the mid-1970s, they began opening small businesses as an alternative. By the early 1980s, Korean immigrants in Los Angeles, New York, and other cities had already established footholds in several business specialties: groceries and liquor stores, retail outlets for Asian-imported items, dry cleaners, produce retailers, and garment subcontracting. Recent immigrants have been able to start up their own businesses more quickly than immigrants in the 1970s because they were able to acquire business information and training through their jobs at Korean-owned stores. Most Korean immigrants also bring a significant amount of money from Korea. Big corporations and White merchants are unwilling to invest in low-income minority neighborhoods where the residents' spending capacity is low and the crime rate is high. Korean immigrants, on the other hand, prefer these neighborhoods because they can start businesses with small amounts of capital without encountering competition from established businesses. Thus, certain types of Korean businesses, such as grocery and liquor retail, heavily concentrate in minority neighborhoods, setting the stage for Korean–African American conflicts.

OBJECTIVES AND SIGNIFICANCE

The primary objective of this book is to show how Korean immigrants' middleman economic role has enhanced their ethnic solidarity in New

York and Los Angeles. Middleman minority theory is one of the major theories in the field of race and ethnic relations, with an abundant literature. However, as will be discussed in chapter 2, few researchers have examined in detail how ethnic solidarity is enhanced by a group's middleman economic role (see Bonacich and Modell 1980; Chan and Cheung 1985; Cohen 1969; Gold 1992; Light and Bonacich 1988; Zenner 1982, 1991). In this book, I test the hypothesis that a middleman group's business-related intergroup conflicts enhance ethnic solidarity. The existing middleman literature is based on middleman cases in preindustrial societies. My major findings, which are based on Koreans' middleman role in contemporary America, refine and revise middleman minority theory.

While researchers have used ethnicity, ethnic solidarity, ethnic mobilization, ethnic attachment, ethnic cohesion, and ethnic identity interchangeably, they have applied these concepts to two interrelated but separate social phenomena. One aspect is the degree to which members are culturally, socially, and psychologically attached to the ethnic group. The term "ethnic attachment" seems best to capture this meaning (Hurh and Kim 1984; Miller and Coughlan 1993; Yinger 1985). The other aspect is the degree to which members use ethnic collective actions to protect their common interests. "Ethnic solidarity" seems the most appropriate term here, though many researchers use "ethnic solidarity" to indicate "ethnic attachment" as well.

Ethnic attachment is a precondition for ethnic solidarity and thus the difference between the two is blurred. Nonetheless, the distinction is important for understanding the central focus of this book. Though several studies have shown how the concentration of members of a minority or immigrant group in small business contributes to their ethnic attachment, few have examined the processes by which it enhances their ethnic solidarity. In this book, I show how Korean immigrants' concentration in a limited range of small businesses and their business-related intergroup conflicts have strengthened their ethnic solidarity.

My definition of ethnic solidarity is close to Nielsen's (1985).[1] Like Nielsen, I consider collective goals and ethnic mobilization the central components of ethnic solidarity. I, too, view ethnic solidarity as a particular form of collective action. The following collective actions taken by Koreans are evidence for ethnic solidarity: fund-raising campaigns to help boycotted merchants; meetings with African American leaders and politicians to end boycotts; administrative and political lobbies to moderate small-business regulations; demonstrations to protect Koreans' business interests against politicians, suppliers, and landlords; boycotts against suppliers; and price bargaining and group purchasing to reduce prices of retail items.

My treatment of Korean immigrants as middlemen and my focus on Korean ethnic solidarity are likely to be criticized by those who emphasize class differences and class divisions in the Korean immigrant community (Abelmann and Lie 1995; S. Cho 1993).[2] However, by emphasizing the middleman characteristics of Korean merchants, I never intend to suggest that the Korean immigrant population is socioeconomically homogeneous. I am well aware that there are class gaps and conflicts over economic interest between Korean professionals and merchants, Korean merchants and co-ethnic employees, and even successful entrepreneurs and marginal store owners such as swap meet owners (see chapters 8 and 11). However, despite their diversity in occupations and business types, more than any other immigrant group Koreans concentrate in middleman-type businesses, connecting White-owned corporations and minority customers (see chapter 10). Their concentration in middleman businesses significantly affects their intergroup relations and in-group solidarity. Thus, middleman minority theory is useful to understanding Korean immigrants' overall social adjustments as well as their economic adjustments.

I consider generational divisions a more serious problem than class divisions in the Korean community. Younger-generation Koreans do not agree with Korean immigrants on many issues, particularly regarding conflicts with Blacks. In several chapters, I will expose generational differences in interpreting and responding to Korean-Black conflicts. However, I will document in chapter 8 that Korean-Black conflicts in general and the victimization of Korean merchants during the Los Angeles riots in particular have contributed to overall solidarity in the Korean community, overcoming generational divisions and sensitizing younger-generation Koreans' ethnic consciousness. Therefore, revealing these intergenerational differences in interpreting Korean-Black relations does not weaken the major focus of this book—Korean ethnic solidarity affected by Koreans' business-related intergroup conflicts.

The secondary objective of this book is to examine systematically hostility toward Korean merchants in African American neighborhoods and Korean merchants' reactions to it. My central thesis is that Koreans' middleman role has increased their intergroup conflicts, which, in turn, has enhanced their ethnic solidarity. Korean–African American conflicts represent the most serious form of intergroup friction caused by this middleman economic role. Furthermore, hostility toward Korean merchants in African American neighborhoods has enhanced Korean ethnic solidarity more than any other form of business-related dispute. Therefore, the topic of Korean–African American conflicts is inseparably related to the central thesis of this book. In addition, a systematic examination of Korean–African American tensions is of great theoretical and practical significance. Middleman minority theory is useful to understanding hostility toward Korean merchants in African American neighborhoods; this book also tests several hypotheses based on other theoretical perspectives (see chapter 2).

Traditional theories of race and ethnic relations in the United States focus on White-Black relations. However, the influx of new immigrants from Third World countries since 1965 has considerably complicated these relations in the United States. Several researchers have argued that the traditional theories based on White-Black, majority-minority relations do not capture the dynamics of race in contemporary America (Chang 1990, 1993a; S. Cho 1993; Omni 1993; Omni and Winant 1986; Rumbaut 1991, 1994; Saito 1993; Waldinger 1996). At present, conflicts between minority groups are as serious as majority-minority conflicts (Chang 1990; Johnson and Oliver 1989; Oliver and Johnson 1984). The 1992 riots in Los Angeles involved Koreans, African Americans, Latinos, and Whites as both victims and victimizers, demonstrating the complexity of racial and ethnic relations in the United States today (Abelmann and Lie 1995; S. Cho 1993; Oliver, Johnson, and Farrell 1993; Ong, Park, and Tong 1994). The Korean–African American conflict, which exploded during the Los Angeles riots, is probably the most serious example of minority-minority conflict in the post-1965 period. In addition, Korean merchants depend heavily on Latino immigrant labor for their business operation, which provides the context for Korean-Latino conflicts. Though this book focuses on Korean–African American conflicts, I discuss Korean-Latino tensions in chapter 11. Moreover, in chapter 10 I also touch on economic conflicts between Korean small business owners and Jewish suppliers and landlords, another interesting dimension of the complexity of racial and ethnic relations in contemporary America.

My systematic examination of Korean–African American tensions is also important for public policy. Over the last two decades, several cities, including Los Angeles, New York, Philadelphia, and Atlanta, have witnessed conflicts between Korean merchants and the Black community. County and city human relations commissions, the Department of

Justice, the Federal Bureau of Investigation, civil rights organizations, and Korean and African American ethnic organizations have been actively involved in resolving conflicts and devising preventive measures. To implement programs, we need accurate information about the magnitude and sources of Korean–African American conflicts. Chapters 5, 6, and 7 focus on Korean–African American conflicts and provide insights that will help government agencies and community leaders establish guidelines for reducing tensions between these two communities.

I generally prefer the term "African Americans" to "Blacks" to refer to the non-Hispanic Black population in the United States because it is more neutral and specific. Nevertheless, in this book I have used both terms—"African Americans" and "Blacks"—because Korean merchants in New York have encountered conflicts not only with native-born African Americans but also with Afro-Caribbean immigrants. I have used the terms "African Americans," "the African American community," and "Korean–African American conflicts" far more frequently than the other terms in discussing South Central Los Angeles, where Afro-Caribbean immigrants are very few.

DATA SOURCES

Books that have focused on minority or immigrant groups are usually based on one or two of three types of data sources: independent surveys, public documents, and field study. This book draws on all three conventional data sources as well as ethnic newspaper articles, and I consider use of multiple data sources one of its major strengths. Ethnic newspaper articles in particular provide rich descriptive information about Korean immigrants' reactions to business-related intergroup conflicts, which is hard to get through other sources. Thus this book has methodological advantages not only over previous works on middleman minorities but also over recently published books on immigrant communities in general.

ETHNIC NEWSPAPER ARTICLES

Koreans' business-related conflicts with others in New York have received detailed coverage in Korean language newspapers. The *Korea Times New York* (hereafter *KTNY*) has the most subscribers out of the four major Korean ethnic dailies in the Northeast. *KTNY* started as a weekly in 1968 and became a daily in 1970. A Korean graduate student reviewed every issue of *KTNY* published between 1970 and 1987, finding all articles dealing with Korean intergroup conflicts in the New York metropolitan area. In addition, she selected all articles dealing with Korean immigrants' collective actions against outside groups in the form of boycotts and mass demonstrations. The content of these articles was analyzed in chronological order.

Since 1988, I have subscribed to three ethnic newspapers published in Korean in New York City: the *Korea Times New York,* the *Sae Gae Times* (hereafter *SGT*), and the *Korea Central Daily New York* (hereafter *KCDNY*). Articles from these three dailies provide rich descriptive information on the development of Korean immigrant businesses and relations with other communities. At the beginning of each year, all three carry special reports on Korean businesses in New York and business-related intergroup conflicts. These special reports have been of great importance to this study. In 1988, *SGT* featured a special series about Korean businesses in New York. The series included more than one hundred articles by reporter Illsuk Moon, based on his personal interviews with successful Korean entrepreneurs and business leaders. Moon's articles have been especially useful to understanding the history of Korean businesses and Korean trade associations in New York.

The *Korea Times Los Angeles* (hereafter *KTLA*) is the major Korean ethnic daily on the West Coast. I have been a regular subscriber since August 1990, and my discussion of Korean business patterns and Korean–African American conflicts in Los Angeles in chapters 4 through 8 is based largely on its articles. *KTLA* also published an English edition weekly that provided valuable information for this book, particularly on the aftermath of the Los Angeles riots. Finally, articles published in the *Los Angeles Times,* the *New York Times, New York Newsday,* the *New York Post,* and the *Amsterdam News* have also been used as sources of data.

INTERVIEWS WITH LEADERS OF BUSINESS ASSOCIATIONS

Though ethnic newspaper articles give an overall picture of Koreans' business-related intergroup conflicts and their collective responses, they do not always provide detailed information about a particular Korean business association's specific activities. I conducted interviews with leaders of business associations to gain information about negotiations with different interest groups and about their plans for collective action. The following are the seven major Korean business associations in the New York metropolitan area: the Korean Produce Association, the Broadway Korean Businessmen's Association, the Korean Apparel Contractors Association of New York, the Korean-American Grocers Association of New York, the Korean Dry Cleaners Association of New York, the Korean Fish Retailers Association of New York, and the Korean Small Business Service Center. I personally interviewed the current president and one former president of each of them.

In addition to these business associations organized by occupation, there are several Korean business associations in New York organized by neighborhood. Both specialized and local business associations have been active in resolving business-related intergroup conflicts. I also interviewed the presidents of three local business associations in predominantly Black neighborhoods—the Harlem Korean Merchants Association, the Jamaica Korean Merchants Association, and the Flatbush Korean Merchants Association. In addition, I interviewed the owners of the two produce stores targeted in the 1990 boycott. These interviews were conducted between October and December 1991.

To assess the effects of Korean businesses on ethnic solidarity, I also compared the activities of Korean business associations to those of nonbusiness, professional associations. I compared membership size, number of paid employees, annual budget, frequency of formal meetings, and other organizational activities. To this end, I interviewed the presidents of five major Korean professional associations by telephone in December 1991.

I visited Los Angeles in the summers of 1990, 1992, and 1994. During my 1990 visit, I interviewed a dozen leaders of Korean trade and professional associations. During my 1992 visit, I interviewed the leaders of several trade associations and owners of swap meets. In the summer of 1994, I interviewed staff members of trade associations and Korean American second-generation organizations, including the Korean American Coalition. These interviews provided data on Korean business patterns, Korean–African American tensions, and Koreans' responses to the intergroup tensions in Los Angeles.

SURVEY OF KOREAN MERCHANTS AND BLACK AND WHITE RESIDENTS

To shed light on Korean–African American conflicts, a multiracial team interviewed three New York City subsamples by telephone in the spring of 1992: Korean merchants in Black neighborhoods, Black (African

American and Afro-Caribbean) residents, and White residents. We randomly selected 150 Korean merchants from directories of Korean merchants' associations in three predominantly Black areas in New York City: the Stuyvesant-Flatbush area, Brooklyn; Jamaica, Queens; and Harlem, Manhattan. Ninety-five of them were interviewed by three Korean students. We also randomly selected 500 households from New York City public telephone directories in the three areas that closely matched the addresses of the selected Korean stores. Two Black and two White students successfully completed 151 telephone interviews; 97 respondents were Black and 51 were White. Chapter 6 is largely based on results from this survey.

SURVEY OF KOREAN IMMIGRANTS IN LOS ANGELES AND ORANGE COUNTIES

To investigate the economic and other positive effects of Korean businesses on the Korean community, twenty bilingual Korean students personally interviewed approximately 500 Korean adult immigrants in Los Angeles County and Orange County who worked twenty or more hours per week in the fall of 1986. We utilized the "Kim sampling technique" introduced by Shin and Yu (1984) to survey a representative sample. Approximately 22% of the Korean immigrant population has the surname Kim, which no other nationality is known to have in such significant numbers. We randomly selected 1,020 Kims from eleven Los Angeles County and Orange County public telephone directories. One hundred fifty-two of these originally selected households were not eligible for the interview because they were either interracially married, American born, unemployed, or in nonimmigrant student households. We interviewed 497 (57.3%) of the remaining 868 Korean households. Some data presented in chapters 4, 6, and 10 are based on the results of this Los Angeles and Orange County survey. Further details about this survey are described in Min (1989).

PARTICIPANT OBSERVATION

I have been deeply involved in the New York Korean community since I came to Queens College in 1987. As a Korean immigrant scholar, I have been invited as an observer to meetings of Korean trade associations, where I was introduced to business leaders. I talked informally with these leaders and gained valuable information on Korean business development and the history of trade associations in New York. Several reporters working for Korean ethnic newspapers, with whom I have maintained close relations, have also provided me with useful information about the Korean business community in New York. This book has greatly benefited from the information acquired through my own interactions with the community.

SCOPE AND ORGANIZATION

I first conceived of this book during the 1990–91 boycott of two Korean stores in Brooklyn. Until the 1992 riots, Koreans' business-related conflicts with the African American community were more intense in New York than in any other city. Korean merchants' conflicts with other interest groups and government agencies were also more severe there than anywhere else. For these reasons, I initially decided to focus on Koreans' middleman economic role and their ethnic solidarity in New York.

However, the Los Angeles riots forced me to modify my original plan. Devastated by the riots, the Korean community has undergone significant structural changes. I found that many Americans—scholars, journalists, and lay people alike—were interested in pre-riot Korean–African American conflicts in Los Angeles and the effects of the riots on the Korean community. Thus, I decided to expand my study to cover these areas as well. I incorporated information on the Korean community in Los Angeles in chapters 5, 6, 7, and 8, which examine Korean–African American conflicts and their effects on ethnic solidarity. Chapters 9, 10, and 11 focus on the New York Korean community, as originally planned. At various points, I have compared the two communities in areas such as business structure, levels of intergroup conflict, and degree of ethnic solidarity. The inclusion of the Korean community in Los Angeles and the intercity comparisons strengthen the arguments of the book.

Following this introductory chapter, chapter 2 offers a literature review useful to understanding the small business basis of Korean ethnic solidarity and Korean–African American conflicts. Though several theoretical perspectives are reviewed, middleman minority theory is presented as the approach central to understanding both Korean-Black conflicts and the effects of Koreans' business-related intergroup conflicts on ethnic solidarity. Chapter 3 presents detailed information about Koreans' immigration and settlement, providing useful background on

New York's and Los Angeles's Korean communities. Chapter 4 examines the high self-employment rate of Korean immigrants, the major Korean businesses in New York and Los Angeles, and the degree of Korean businesses' concentration in African American neighborhoods. To demonstrate the effects of Koreans' middleman economic role on Korean ethnic solidarity, we need to show, first of all, that Korean immigrants are economically segregated in terms of the types of businesses and their location.

The next three chapters focus on Korean–Black conflicts. Chapter 5 examines different forms of hostility toward Korean merchants in African American and Afro-Caribbean neighborhoods in New York and Los Angeles. Chapter 6 uses survey data to analyze the level of Blacks' rejection of Korean merchants and then examines several hypotheses to explain hostility toward Korean merchants in Black neighborhoods. Of the three chapters focusing on Korean–Black conflicts, this is the most significant. Chapter 7 examines the New York and Los Angeles Korean communities' efforts to improve relations with African Americans. This chapter provides valuable information for policy makers and community leaders interested in reducing tensions between Koreans and African Americans.

Chapters 8, 9, and 10, which demonstrate how Koreans' business-related intergroup conflicts have intensified their ethnic solidarity, provide the central focus of the book. Chapter 8 examines how hostility toward Korean merchants in Black neighborhoods in New York and Los Angeles has unified the respective Korean communities. Chapter 9 examines Korean merchants' conflicts with suppliers, landlords, and government agencies in New York, as well as their use of collective strategies to protect their economic interests against these forces. The two issues discussed in chapter 10 provide more convincing evidence of the economic basis of Korean ethnic solidarity. First, the major collective actions in the forms of demonstrations and boycotts against other groups by Koreans in New York are shown to have been taken largely in response to business-related intergroup conflicts. Second, in their efforts to resolve business-related intergroup conflicts, Korean trade associations and business leaders are shown to have increased their influence and power in the Korean community in New York.

Some readers may argue that Koreans' concentration in small business causes internal conflicts and thus destroys solidarity by increasing both intragroup business competition and friction between business owners and co-ethnic employees. Chapter 11 examines to what extent this holds true. Chapter 12, the concluding chapter, discusses theoretical implications of major findings concerning the effects of Korean immigrants' middleman role on their ethnic solidarity. It also summarizes major findings concerning causes of Korean–African American conflicts and their policy implications.

CHAPTER 2

Host Hostility and Middlemen's Reactions

This chapter reviews the literature useful to understanding the effects of Korean immigrants' business-related intergroup conflicts on Korean ethnic solidarity and Korean–African American conflicts. While middleman minority theory is central to understanding both, other theoretical perspectives directly or indirectly related to each of the two social phenomena are also considered.

BUSINESS-RELATED INTERGROUP CONFLICTS AND ETHNIC SOLIDARITY

INTERGROUP CONFLICTS AND HOST HOSTILITY

Historically, minority and immigrant groups often have encountered intergroup conflicts and ethnic hostility, which in turn has unified the community. Stressing intergroup conflicts as a causal factor is consistent with the general proposition derived from Simmel (1955) and Coser (1964) that intergroup conflicts increase internal solidarity. If Simmel and Coser are correct, intergroup conflicts should strengthen ethnic solidarity as well as other forms of group solidarity.

A number of studies have proven this to be the case. Based on an analysis of ethnic newspapers in the late nineteenth and early twentieth centuries, Olzak and West (1991) showed that hostility and violence encouraged White immigrants to establish ethnic newspapers. Portes (1984) suggested that host hostility—as shown by antirefugee

campaigns and an antibilingual referendum—contributed to a growing ethnic awareness among Cuban immigrants. Espiritu (1992, chapter 6) elaborated on how anti-Asian violence, which increased significantly in the 1980s, contributed to pan-Asian solidarity. Jews more than
any other group in the world have been subject to violence and host
hostility; Friedman (1967) viewed anti-Semitism as the major force in
the development of Jewish identity and solidarity.

Extreme forms of host hostility toward a particular minority group
greatly increase its ethnic identity and solidarity. For example, the Nazi
extermination of six million Jews during World War II and the establishment of Israel as an independent Jewish state in 1948 strengthened
the group identity of American Jews (Goren 1982, 108–10). The Turk-
ish massacre of Armenians before and during World War I heightened
the ethnic identity of Armenians in the United States (Mirak 1980),
and internment during World War II was a significant historical event
for Japanese Americans. The wartime incarceration not only brought
about a generational transfer of power in the Japanese American community, it also enhanced ethnic identity among native-born Japanese
Americans (Nakanishi 1993). Chapter 8 will explain and illustrate how
the victimization of Korean merchants during the 1992 riots was similarly an important historical event that has awakened the ethnic consciousness of second-generation Korean Americans.

ETHNIC BUSINESS

There are several empirical studies that have focused on the effects of
ethnic business on ethnicity. Previously we distinguished between ethnic attachment and ethnic solidarity. Ethnic business facilitates both
ethnic attachment and ethnic solidarity, as defined in chapter 1. Minority and immigrant merchants depend mainly on family and other co-
ethnic members to operate their businesses. Those in the ethnic subeconomy—business owners and co-ethnic employees alike—are likely to
interact with family and other co-ethnic members more frequently and
to maintain their cultural tradition more successfully than those in the
general economy. Therefore, a group with a higher level of ethnic business development than others is likely to maintain a higher level of ethnic attachment.

Several case studies have shown that concentrating in small business
facilitates ethnic attachment (Bonacich and Modell 1980; A. Cohen

1969; Fugita and O'Brien 1991; Min 1991; Reitz 1980). For example, Bonacich and Modell (1980) showed that Japanese Americans in the ethnic economy maintained stronger ethnic attachment than Japanese Americans in the corporate economy, in terms of maintaining the Japanese cultural tradition and of interacting socially with co-ethnic members. Using a sample of second- and third-generation Japanese Americans in California, Fugita and O'Brien (1991, chapter 7) found that self-employed Japanese Americans were more highly involved in ethnic networks than were those employed by others. Reitz (1980) demonstrated that the Chinese, Eastern European, and Southern European ethnic groups in Canada maintained higher levels of ethnicity than other ethnic groups in terms of retaining the mother tongue and ethnic endogamy, because they were involved in small business.

Minority groups who concentrate in small business experience business-related intergroup conflicts, which, in turn, contribute to ethnic solidarity. Such minority and immigrant groups usually specialize in a narrow range of businesses. For example, Chinese Americans are heavily concentrated in Chinese restaurants and garment subcontracting (Kwong 1987; Waldinger and Aldrich 1990, 69), whereas Greek Americans have specialized in the pizza or restaurant business (Lovell-Troy 1981). When members of an ethnic or immigrant group concentrate in a few business specialties, they have a strong sense of solidarity because their ethnic identity is attached to their economic activities. However, this specialization may not be sufficient in itself to stimulate ethnic solidarity. It also can increase internal solidarity indirectly because minority and immigrant proprietors engaged in the same line or similar lines of business face similar business-related intergroup conflicts.

As noted above, many researchers have shown how ethnic business increases ethnic attachment, but few have paid attention to how ethnic business unifies an ethnic community through intergroup conflicts.[1] Only two studies have examined how members of a trading minority come together in reaction to business-related intergroup conflicts. Bonacich and Modell (1980, chapter 4) showed how Japanese business owners in California encountered conflicts with White business and White labor, and how these business-related intergroup conflicts strengthened their ethnic solidarity. Light and Bonacich (1988, chapter 12) examined how the business restrictions imposed by government authorities increased Koreans' internal solidarity in Los Angeles.

THE MIDDLEMAN MINORITY ROLE

Middleman minority theory is the theoretical perspective most useful to understanding the effects of Korean ethnic business on ethnic solidarity. Middleman minorities concentrate in trading and usually distribute merchandise produced by members of the dominant group to minority customers (Blalock 1967, 79–84; Bonacich 1973; Bonacich and Modell 1980; Eitzen 1971; Turner and Bonacich 1980; Zenner 1991). Jews in Medieval Europe, the Chinese in Southeast Asia, and Asian Indians in Africa are prominent examples of middleman minorities. Middleman minority theory postulates that there are triadic causal relationships between a middleman group's ethnic solidarity, the middleman economic role, and host hostility (Bonacich 1973; Bonacich and Modell 1980; Turner and Bonacich 1980). The solidarity and economic segregation of a middleman group leads to host hostility, and these conflicts only enhance the minority group's solidarity.

Though middleman minority theory explains how business-related intergroup conflicts generate internal solidarity among minority groups, these studies have neglected to examine empirically the effects of ethnic business on ethnic solidarity. Instead, they have focused on host hostility (particularly hostility from minority customers) and the various stereotypical characterizations of middleman merchants (Capeci 1985; Caplan 1970; N. Cohen 1970; Eitzen 1971; Hunt and Walker 1974; Palmer 1957). In fact, Bonacich and Modell's book on Japanese Americans' concentration in production and distribution of fruits and vegetables in California (1980) is the only monograph that has examined in any detail from *the middleman minority perspective* the solidarity of minority entrepreneurs in reaction to host hostility.[2] However, Japanese produce owners in California did not function as middlemen in the movement of goods and services; they served the general population and relied on co-ethnic suppliers. They did not satisfy the most important requirement of middleman minority theory: to play the intermediary role between producers and consumers (O'Brien and Fugita 1982).[3] Japanese produce owners did not encounter conflicts with minority customers or White suppliers, and it is exactly these two types of intergroup conflict that have provided the economic basis of Koreans' ethnic solidarity.

Though many studies have documented the conflicts between middleman minorities and their minority customers, the literature has paid scant attention to conflicts between middleman merchants and suppliers, landlords, or government agencies. Theorists have probably neglected these conflicts with suppliers and government agencies because they viewed middleman merchants as brought to the host society by these powerful groups to serve their interests and thus as generally under their control.

Middleman minorities typically existed in preindustrial societies in which social classes were polarized (Blalock 1967, 79–84; Bonacich 1973; Rinder 1958–59; Shibutani and Kwan 1966, 191–97). Thus, a middleman minority is unlikely to develop in a contemporary industrial society with a large middle-class segment, such as the United States, though Loewen (1971) described Chinese grocers in the Mississippi Delta area as middlemen bridging the status gap between Whites and Blacks. In an effort to explain Korean immigrants' economic role in contemporary U.S. capitalism, Bonacich used the world capitalist system model (Bonacich 1980; Light and Bonacich 1988, part 4). She argued that Korean immigrant entrepreneurs in Los Angeles were being used by White suppliers; that is, big corporations relied on them to distribute products to low-income minority customers. Thus, in her theoretical perspective, Korean merchants again are more or less at the mercy of big corporations, with little power to protect their interests. While my book highlights Korean merchants' conflicts with suppliers, landlords, and government agencies, as well as with African American customers, it also documents how Korean merchants have acted collectively to protect their economic interests against these White interest groups and government agencies.

Middleman minority theorists generally agree that ethnic solidarity, the intermediary economic role, and host hostility are the key characteristics of a middleman minority and that there are circular relations among the three variables, but they do not agree on the underlying causes of the pattern. Most middleman theorists (Blalock 1967, 89–94; Eitzen 1971; Loewen 1971; Rinder 1958–59) considered status gap, discrimination, or both (i.e., structural factors) to be the major causes of the middleman minority pattern. Bonacich (1973), however, viewed sojourning orientation as the main cause. She argued that middleman groups originated as sojourners or temporary residents in host societies and planned to return to their homelands. The economic effects of sojourning included a tendency toward thriftiness to hasten a return home and the concentration in occupations that were easily liquidated and transportable; for example, commerce and trade. The noneconomic effects of sojourning included a high degree of internal solidarity and the maintenance of distinctive cultural traits.

Several researchers have criticized Bonacich's middleman minority theory. Cherry (1989) and Zenner (1980) indicated that the Jews in the United States, whom Bonacich considered a typical middleman minority, were not sojourners. Wong (1985) criticized Bonacich's sojourning theory for stereotyping Chinese and Japanese in the United States as "sojourners," "inassimilable," "aliens," and the like. Both Cherry (1989) and Wong (1985) questioned Bonacich's sojourning theory partly because it gives the impression that Jews or Chinese in the United States entered small business *by choice,* thus ignoring the reality that discrimination and disadvantage forced them to do so. Still other researchers (Aldrich et al. 1983; Ward 1985) showed that sojourners are more likely to prefer employment by another over self-employment.

In this book, I consider Korean immigrants in the United States a middleman minority, but not as defined by Bonacich (1973); that is, Korean immigrants are not sojourners. Therefore, this book is not vulnerable to the criticisms surrounding Bonacich's version of middleman minority theory. Surveys (Min 1988a; Park et al. 1990, 102) have shown that most Korean immigrants plan to remain permanently in the United States, though positive changes in economic, social, and political conditions in South Korea during recent years have led some Korean immigrants to go back to Korea. As detailed in my previous work (1988a, 1988b), and as will be further discussed in chapter 4, I argue that Korean immigrants' problems with the English language and other disadvantages for employment in the general labor market— rather than their sojourning orientation—are the main reasons for their concentration in small business.[4] Moreover, like most other middleman minority theorists, I consider big corporations' unwillingness to invest in low-income minority neighborhoods a major factor that significantly contributes to Korean merchants' concentration in such neighborhoods. In addition, this book focuses on the consequences rather than causes of Korean immigrants' middleman economic adjustment, that is, on their intergroup conflicts (host hostility) and reactive solidarity.

Finally, Cherry (1989), Wong (1985), and others question the characterization of Jewish, Japanese, Chinese, and Korean Americans as middleman minority groups because, in their view, the middleman minority thesis, like the model minority thesis, depicts Jewish and Asian groups as economically successful, thereby excluding them as possible beneficiaries of welfare programs. Yet the two positions are logically distinct. In considering Korean immigrants a middleman minority, I by no means intend to create the impression that Koreans are economically successful or problem free. Instead, I want to emphasize that their disadvantages in the general labor market in contemporary America almost force them into small business, where they must maintain solidarity for economic survival.

KOREAN-AFRICAN AMERICAN CONFLICTS

MIDDLEMAN MINORITY THEORY

Middleman minority theory is useful in understanding the basis of Korean–African American conflicts, as well as the positive effects of such intergroup conflicts on ethnic solidarity among Korean immigrants. Middleman theorists have suggested that the vulnerable economic position of middleman minorities, along with their visibility, cohesion, and outside status, provokes host hostility and scapegoating (Blalock 1967, 79–84; Rinder 1958–59; Zenner 1991, 22–25). Middleman minorities are often hated by both the ruling group and other minority groups in the host society. During periods of economic and political distress, reactions to middleman minorities can include boycotts, riots, expulsions, and genocide.

As previously noted, middleman minority studies neglected to examine empirically the positive effects of middleman merchants' intergroup conflicts on their ethnic solidarity, but many did document the hostility that middleman merchants were subject to. For example, Palmer (1957) showed that Indians in Africa were victims of violent riots and expulsions. Eitzen (1971) documented that Chinese merchants in the Philippines confronted hostile reactions by local residents. Zenner (1991) described the pogroms, expulsions, and genocide suffered by Jews in Europe. Jews in the United States, as merchants filling the gap between the residents of African American and Latino neighborhoods and the dominant classes controlling banks, economic institutions, and the political power structure, were particularly vulnerable to hostility (Porter 1981). Black anti-Semitism was caused partly by the economic role that Jews played in these neighborhoods. Several studies have documented the boycotts and riots that victimized Jewish merchants in African

American neighborhoods (Capeci 1985; N. Cohen 1970; Weisbord and Stein 1970, 45).

THE SCAPEGOAT THEORY

In addition to middleman minority theory, the scapegoat or frustration-aggression theory is useful to understanding hostility toward Korean merchants in African American neighborhoods. This theory posits that members of the dominant group who are not successful in their efforts to achieve desired goals unleash their frustration-produced aggression against the closest suitable group who cannot retaliate effectively (Allport 1958, 330–32; Dollard et al. 1939). Minority members often become the scapegoats. Though the scapegoating theory was proposed to explain anti-Black prejudice and violence on the part of lower-class Whites, it also seems useful in analyzing the anti-Korean attitudes and behavior exhibited by lower-class Blacks. Inner-city Blacks who have been frustrated with their inability to advance economically may blame Korean merchants, who are easy targets of scapegoating because they lack linguistic fluency and political power. Both journalists and scholars have linked Korean–African American conflicts to frustrations of African Americans with their deplorable economic conditions and their motivations for scapegoating (Bonacich 1987; Jo 1992; N. Kim 1992; H. Lee 1993; Liu 1988).

The literature on middleman minorities also indicates that the ruling group faced with frustrated minority customers can use middleman merchants as scapegoats (Blalock 1967, 84; Zenner 1991, 23). Middleman merchants thus are vulnerable to being used as a bulwark to protect the dominant group from possible violence by members of a minority group. This is a plausible hypothesis, as middleman merchants in a socially stratified system lack the political power to protect themselves from either group. Consistent with this theoretical proposition, many Korean Americans, including Korean American scholars (Abelmann and Lie 1995; S. Cho 1993), have claimed that during the Los Angeles riots Korean merchants were used by White people to shield themselves from African Americans' hostility.

BLACK NATIONALISM AS AN ANTI-MIDDLEMAN IDEOLOGY

Korean merchants disproportionately serve African American and Latino customers. However, as will be shown in chapter 5, Korean mer-

chants in Latino neighborhoods have not encountered the overt hostility to which Korean merchants in African American neighborhoods
have been subject. Why have these two groups of customers responded
to Korean middleman merchants in such different ways?

A closer look at the role anti-middleman ideologies play in provok-
ing host hostility helps explain the difference. In response to Bonacich's
article on middleman minorities (1973), Stryker (1974) pointed out
that in some societies middleman minorities faced neither host hostility
nor hatred. According to Stryker, antagonism toward them developed
in the context of a particular political configuration. He noted that
these minorities were persecuted in societies in which ideologies associated with "emergent nationalism" developed.[5] In his recent book on
middleman minorities, Zenner (1991) argued that anti-middleman ideologies played a critical role in spawning hatred toward middleman minorities. Thus, in his view, "Anti-Semitism fits the nationalist concep-
tion that the nation must control its own economy and sees danger in
letting important sections fall under the control of strangers such as
Jews" (49).

Black nationalism has served as an anti-middleman ideology against
outsiders' commercial activities in African American neighborhoods
in the United States. Black nationalism is too diverse to allow coher-
ent generalization, but one important idea that has been consistently
emphasized by Black nationalists is community control of educational,
social, economic, and political institutions (Carmichael and Hamilton
1967; Turner 1973). This stress on the economic autonomy of the Black
community clearly bears on Black boycotts of Korean stores. Black nationalists of the 1960s, such as Malcolm X, claimed that their liberation
from economic control by Jewish, Italian, and other White business
owners was essential to overall community control. Not only politically
oriented Black nationalists of the 1960s but also earlier Black intellectuals embraced the ideology of economic nationalism: in their view,
businesses in Black neighborhoods should be owned by Blacks. For example, in *Black Metropolis,* originally published in 1938, Drake and
Cayton (1945, 430–32) reported that Black pastors and writers in Chicago preached the "Double Duty Dollar" doctrine. A dollar spent in
a Black-owned store not only served the duty of buying merchandise
for the Black consumer but also contributed to the economic prosperity
and autonomy of the Black community. Carlos Cook took the same position when he launched the "Buy Black" campaign in Harlem in 1941
(Tait 1988).

THE IMMIGRANT HYPOTHESIS

The influx of large numbers of immigrants to urban labor markets ele-
vated the level of conflicts between native-born and immigrant workers
(Light 1983; Olzak 1986, 1989; Piore 1979). Regardless of whether the
influx adversely affected the labor market or not, native-born workers
blamed the immigrants for their economic woes. Thus, new immigrants
have often become targets of racial violence, particularly in times of
economic hardship. Various sources report that anti-Asian violence has
increased recently (Espiritu 1992, chapter 6; U.S. Commission on Civil
Rights 1986). The real or perceived economic competition between
Asian immigrants and American natives has been indicated as a major
source of these anti-Asian hate crimes (Desbarats 1985; U.S. Commission on Civil Rights 1986).

Various forms of hostility toward Korean merchants in African
American neighborhoods, including boycotts, may be viewed as the nativist reaction to Korean immigrants' economic activities. One study
has seriously considered this: in an attempt to explain the Korean–African American conflict in Los Angeles, Cheng and Espiritu (1989) proposed the "immigrant hypothesis." Since in Los Angeles many Mexican
as well as African American neighborhoods contain Korean stores, they
would appear to pose an equal potential for conflict. However, Mexicans have not shown the kinds of overt hostility toward Korean merchants that African Americans have shown. Cheng and Espiritu (1989)
noted that whereas immigrants constituted high percentages of Mexicans and Koreans in Los Angeles, an overwhelming majority of the
population in African American neighborhoods was native born, and
they argued that this difference largely explained the different reactions
to Koreans' business activities. In their view, many African American
residents were angry because "they perceive Koreans as foreigners who
take advantage of Blacks" (Cheng and Espiritu 1989, 528). Mexican
immigrants, in contrast, were sympathetic to Korean merchants because they shared the immigrant emphasis on hard work and the view
of America as the land of opportunity.

SOCIOPSYCHOLOGICAL FACTORS

Cultural differences and mutual prejudice were found to contribute
to ethnic conflicts and discrimination (Allport 1958; Myrdal 1944;
Noel 1968). A number of studies showed that White Americans were

prejudiced against Blacks, American Indians, and Jews, as measured by ethnic stereotypes and social distance (Allport 1958; Bogardus 1968; Gilbert 1951; Katz and Braly 1933). Before the arrival of Korean immigrants, Jews in the United States played a middleman economic role in African American neighborhoods and suffered similar intergroup conflicts. Many researchers showed strong anti-Jewish attitudes among American Blacks (e.g., Forster and Epstein 1974; Silberman 1985).

Disputes and altercations between African American or Afro-Caribbean customers and merchants in Korean-owned stores were partly caused by cultural differences between the two groups and mutual prejudice. Newspaper articles often suggested that these were the main sources of Korean–African American conflicts (Banks 1985; Karwatch 1990; Njeri 1989). In particular, they emphasized Korean immigrants' language barrier and unfamiliarity with American customs. Several researchers viewed these cultural difficulties as partly responsible for Korean–African American conflicts, though usually not a fundamental cause (Chang 1990, 168; Jo 1992; H. Lee 1993; Ong, Park, and Tong 1994). Jo (1992), however, explained Korean–African American conflicts mainly in terms of Korean immigrants' prejudice against African Americans. In chapter 6, we will examine the extent to which cultural differences, language barriers, and mutual prejudice contribute to Korean–African American conflicts.

A major proposition of conflict theory is that members of a group tend to be united when they encounter threats from the outside world, and a number of studies did indeed show that intergroup conflicts and host hostility enhanced a particular ethnic group's solidarity and ethnic consciousness. Both the general proposition from conflict theory and empirical studies documenting the effects of ethnic conflicts on ethnic solidarity provide a broad theoretical framework for understanding how Korean merchants' intergroup conflicts have increased their ethnic solidarity. Several studies showed how ethnic business increased ethnic attachment, but only two studies—one by Bonacich and Modell (1980) and the other by Light and Bonacich (1988)—examined how ethnic business contributed to ethnic solidarity. Such solidarity, as well as high levels of business-related intergroup conflict, is found among minority and immigrant business owners who engage in middleman businesses that connect producers and minority customers. Thus, middleman minority theory is most useful to understanding how ethnic business enhances ethnic solidarity. However, neither of the above two studies tested the hypothesis regarding the effects of middleman merchants' business-related intergroup conflicts on ethnic solidarity systematically and empirically.

Middleman theorists suggested that the vulnerable economic position of middleman minorities provoked host hostility and scapegoating by both the ruling group and minority customers in the host society. This middleman proposition helps us understand hostility toward Korean merchants in African American neighborhoods as well as the government inaction in protecting Korean merchants during the Los Angeles riots. Middleman theorists also pointed out that middleman merchants were subject to rejection and violence when strong anti-middleman ideologies were present. Black nationalism, which emphasizes the economic autonomy of the Black community, can be considered one such important anti-Korean ideology. In addition, two other theoretical perspectives are relevant to understanding Korean–African American conflicts. One view interprets hostility toward Korean merchants in African American neighborhoods as nativist reactions to immigrants' economic activities; the other emphasizes sociopsychological factors, such as cultural differences, language barriers, and mutual prejudice, as contributing to Korean-Black conflicts. We will examine each of these perspectives in chapter 6.

CHAPTER 3

Korean Communities

New York and Los Angeles

Before addressing this book's central focus, the middleman role of Korean immigrants in New York and Los Angeles, a brief description of the New York and Los Angeles Korean communities is needed. The first section of this chapter examines the influx and characteristics of Korean immigrants since the Immigration Act of 1965 (which was in full effect by 1968), and the second section briefly describes their residential distribution. The third and fourth sections provide overviews of the Los Angeles and New York Korean communities while the fifth section examines major ethnic networks in both.

POST-1965 IMMIGRATION

From 1903 to 1905, approximately 7,200 Korean laborers came to Hawaii to work on sugar plantations, creating the first wave of Korean immigration to the United States. About 2,000 more Koreans moved to the United States from 1906 to 1924, before the "Oriental Exclusion Act" barred all further Asian immigration. Whereas more than 90% of the pioneer immigrants between 1903 and 1905 were men, the majority of the Koreans who came to the United States from 1906 to 1924 were "picture brides," invited by the Korean male laborers. These later immigrants also included a large number of students and political refugees who had been involved in anti-Japanese movements, most of whom eventually returned home when Korea was liberated from Japanese colonial rule in 1945.[1]

As a result of racist immigration laws,[2] the number of Korean immigrants to the United States became virtually nil between 1924 and 1949: ten or fewer Koreans entered each year. However, Korean immigration resumed in the 1950s because of the close military, political, and economic relations established between the United States and South Korea during the Korean War. The cold war that followed further strengthened the ties between the two countries. According to the Immigration and Naturalization Service (1950–1964), about 15,000 Koreans were admitted to the United States as immigrants between 1950 and 1964. Korean wives of U.S. servicemen stationed in South Korea and Korean orphans adopted by American citizens constituted the vast majority of Korean immigrants during this period.

In 1965, the U.S. Congress passed a new immigration law that abolished discriminatory immigration quotas based on national origin. The Immigration Act of 1965 significantly modified American immigration patterns. White Europeans constituted the vast majority of immigrants before 1965, but their numbers have since steadily decreased, with a concomitant increase in the number of immigrants from Asia, Latin America, and the Caribbean Islands. For example, nearly 70% of immigrants in the 1950s were from European countries but in the 1980s the proportion dropped to 13% (Rumbaut 1994). In contrast, the proportions of Latino and Asian immigrants increased from 22% and 6% in the 1950s to 47% and 37%, respectively (Rumbaut 1994).

The new immigration law significantly affected Korean immigration. Though annual Korean immigrants numbered a few thousands annually in the early 1960s, their numbers gradually increased in the late 1960s and the early 1970s, reaching the 30,000 mark in 1976, as indicated in table 1. Korea maintained an annual flow of over 30,000 in the 1980s; during that decade, only Mexico and the Philippines had more immigrants to the United States.

Post-1965 Korean immigrants, like other Asian immigrants, are primarily economic migrants who have crossed the Pacific seeking a higher standard of living. However, the close connections between the United States and South Korea during and after the Korean War and the American cultural influence in South Korea have also contributed greatly to a large influx of Korean immigrants to the United States (H. Kim and Min 1992; I. Kim 1987).

Table 1 shows that Korean immigration peaked in 1987 at about 36,000, but it has gradually fallen since 1988, the year of the Seoul Olympic Games. In 1993, the number of Korean immigrants dropped

TABLE 1.

KOREANS WHO IMMIGRATED AND
NATURALIZED (1965–93)

Year	Total U.S. Immigrants	Total Korean Immigrants	Korean Immigrants as % of U.S. Immigrants	Koreans Naturalized
1965	296,697	2,165	0.7	1,027
1966	323,040	2,492	0.8	1,180
1967	361,972	3,356	0.9	1,353
1968	454,448	3,811	0.8	1,776
1969	358,579	6,045	1.7	1,646
1970	373,326	9,314	2.5	1,687
1971	370,478	14,297	3.9	2,083
1972	387,685	18,876	4.9	2,933
1973	400,063	22,930	5.7	3,562
1974	394,861	28,028	7.1	4,451
1975	386,194	28,362	7.3	6,007
1976	398,613	30,830	7.7	6,450
1977	462,315	30,917	6.7	10,446
1978	601,442	29,288	4.9	12,575
1979	460,348	29,248	6.4	13,406
1980	530,639	32,320	6.1	14,073
1981	596,600	32,663	5.5	13,258
1982	594,131	30,814	5.2	13,488
1983	559,763	33,339	6.0	12,808
1984	543,903	33,042	6.1	14,019
1985	570,009	35,253	6.2	16,824
1986	601,708	35,776	6.0	18,037
1987	601,516	35,849	6.0	14,233
1988	643,025	34,703	5.4	13,012
1989	1,090,924	34,222	3.1	11,301
1990	1,536,483	32,301	2.1	10,500
1991	1,827,167	26,518	1.5	12,216
1991	1,827,167	26,518	1.5	12,216
1992	973,977	19,359	2.0	8,297
1993	904,292	18,026	2.0	9,611

Sources: Immigration and Naturalization Service, *Annual Reports*, 1965–1978 and *Statistical Yearbook*, 1979—1993.

to approximately 18,000, about half the number in 1987. The improved economic, social, and political conditions in South Korea are largely responsible for the recent gradual reduction of Korean immigration. The standard of living in South Korea has risen greatly, as reflected by the per capita income of over $10,000 in 1995. Most middle-class households in Seoul and other large cities now have their own cars. Moreover, social and political insecurity, which pushed many Koreans to the United States in the 1970s and the early 1980s, has been reduced substantially. South Korea had a popular presidential election at the end of 1987, putting an end to the sixteen-year military dictatorship. At the same time that conditions have improved significantly, the South Korean people are increasingly well informed of the difficulties of Korean immigrants in adjusting to the United States.[3] Therefore, at present middle-class Koreans generally do not hold it an attractive prospect: a survey conducted in Seoul indicates that lower-class Koreans, rather than middle-class Koreans, show a strong preference for emigration to the United States (Yoon 1993). It is also noteworthy that in recent years many Korean immigrants have returned to Korea permanently, giving up their "American dream."

The Korean population in the United States before 1970 was insignificant in size. Though a great number of Koreans were overlooked in the 1970 census (69,130 were counted), the number at that time probably fell short of 100,000. However, more than 600,000 Koreans immigrated from 1970 to 1993, resulting in radical growth in the Korean American community. The 1990 census estimated the Korean population to be close to 800,000 (U.S. Bureau of the Census 1993a, table 23), but this also seems to be low. Taking into consideration Korean students, visitors, illegal residents, and children born since 1970, we may put the Korean population at close to one million in 1990.

Post-1965 Korean immigrants, like other Asian immigrants, generally represent the middle-class strata of their home country. The 1990 census indicated that 34% of Korean immigrants who were twenty-five or older had completed four years of college, and that 80% had completed high school (U.S. Bureau of the Census 1993d, 84).[4] In contrast, 20% of the U.S. population had received a college education and 75% had completed high school (U.S. Bureau of the Census 1993d, 72). Consistent with their high educational level, most post-1965 Korean immigrants held professional and white-collar jobs before they immigrated, as evidenced in several case studies. For example, nearly 50% of Korean respondents in Chicago indicated their preimmigration occupations had been professional, administrative, managerial, or technical, whereas only 7% said they had held blue-collar jobs (Hurh and Kim 1988). My survey of Korean immigrants in the Los Angeles–Orange County area revealed similar occupational backgrounds. Fifty-four percent of the respondents who were working in Korea at the time of their immigration had held jobs classifiable as professional, administrative, executive, or managerial, and only 4% had been employed in blue-collar occupations

(Min 1989). As previously noted, as a result of the great improvement in economic conditions in South Korea, more lower-class Koreans have immigrated to the United States since the late 1980s than before. This means that the Korean community is no longer socioeconomically homogeneous.

Recent Asian immigrants are also characterized by their urban background (B. Kim 1978), in contrast to earlier peasant immigrants, and this is probably most marked among Koreans. Approximately 1,800 of the prospective Korean immigrants in 1986 were interviewed at the U.S. Consulate in Seoul at the time of their visa interview. Though only one-fourth of all Koreans live in the capital city, more than half the respondents in this predeparture survey reported that they resided there (Park et al. 1990, 31). The survey also indicated that more than three-fourths of the respondents lived in one of the five largest cities in Korea at the time of their interview. While many residents in Seoul and other large Korean cities previously migrated from rural areas, they quickly became familiar with the Korean urban lifestyle before departing for the United States.[5] Thus, the interurban migration of Koreans to American cities could have lessened the sense of panic, isolation, and alienation experienced by earlier White European immigrants (Thomas and Znaniecki 1927).

Recent Korean immigrants were also a select group in terms of their disproportionately Christian background. Though less than 25% of the Korean population is affiliated with Christian churches (Park and Cho 1995), the majority of Korean immigrants practiced Christianity in Korea. For example, in a survey of the 1986 cohort of Korean immigrants conducted in Seoul (Park et al. 1990, 60), 54% of the respondents reported that they were affiliated with Protestant (41.6%) or Catholic (12.3%) churches. A Chicago survey similarly indicated that 52.6% of Korean immigrants had been Christians in Korea (Hurh and Kim 1990). This heavily Protestant background clearly separates Korean immigrants from other Asian immigrant groups.[6]

Three major factors appear to have contributed to the overrepresentation of Christians among Korean immigrants. First, Christianity is most commonly practiced by urban, middle-class people in South Korea, and Korean immigrants have been largely drawn from this segment of the population. Second, many Christians fled from North Korea to South Korea before and during the Korean War, and North Korean refugees, with no strong kin and regional ties in South Korea, have been more likely to immigrate to the United States than the Korean general population. Moreover, for these refugees immigration offers the only possibility of visiting their relatives in North Korea.[7] One survey showed that Koreans born in North Korea made up more than 20% of Korean immigrants in Los Angeles, though North Korean refugees constituted less than 5% of the population in South Korea (Yu 1983). Third, Korean Christians were more likely than Buddhists, Confucians, or those not affiliated with a religion to have immigrated to the United States because they knew it would be easier to maintain their religion and lifestyle in America.[8]

DISTRIBUTION OF POST-1965 IMMIGRANTS

Table 2 shows the growth of the Korean population from 1980 to 1990 in states with a major Korean population. Overall, there was a 125% increase during the ten-year period. The Northeast witnessed a higher growth rate than the United States as a whole, with dramatic gains in New York and New Jersey in particular. The rate of increase in California was also higher than in the United States as a whole. These findings suggest that Korean Americans tend to congregate in two major areas: Southern California (encompassing Los Angeles and Orange Counties) and the New York–New Jersey metropolitan area.

Of all states with sizable Korean populations, New Jersey experienced the most growth (200%) in the 1980s. Many Koreans who had originally settled in New York City eventually moved to New Jersey, probably in search of better housing and schools. This migration reflected the suburbanization of Korean immigrants. New immigrants usually settled in Korean enclaves in New York City, such as Flushing and Elmhurst in Queens, where they could find employment in Korean-owned stores, speak the Korean language, and obtain Korean food. As they achieved economic mobility and some level of cultural assimilation, they moved to suburban areas in Long Island and New Jersey where there were lower crime rates and better schools. Similarly, Orange County in California witnessed an astounding 217% growth in the Korean population, substantially higher than Los Angeles County (149%).

Interestingly, the Korean population in Hawaii proportionately decreased over the years. In 1990, only 3% of Korean Americans settled in the state of Hawaii. Honolulu, the center of earlier Korean immigration, is no longer an important Korean enclave. In the 1970s and the early 1980s, Chicago was the third largest Korean center, follow-

TABLE 2.

DISTRIBUTION OF KOREANS BY REGION AND
STATE (1980 and 1990)

State	1980		1990		Increase	
	N	%	N	%	N	%
Northeast						
Total	68,151	19.2	182,061	22.8	113,910	167.1
New York	34,157	9.6	95,648	12.0	61,491	180.0
New Jersey	12,845	3.6	38,540	4.8	25,695	200.0
Pennsylvania	12,502	3.5	26,787	3.4	14,285	114.3
Midwest						
Total	62,214	17.5	109,087	13.7	46,873	75.3
Illinois	23,989	6.8	41,506	5.2	17,517	73.0
Michigan	8,714	2.5	16,316	2.0	7,602	87.2
Ohio	7,257	2.0	11,237	1.4	3,980	54.8
South						
Total	70,381	19.9	153,163	19.2	82,782	117.6
Maryland	15,089	4.3	30,320	3.8	15,231	100.9
Virginia	12,550	3.5	29,697	3.7	17,147	136.6
Texas	13,997	3.9	31,775	4.0	17,778	127.0
Georgia	5,968	1.7	13,275	1.7	7,307	122.4
West						
Total	153,847	43.4	354,538	44.4	200,691	130.4
Washington	13,083	3.7	29,697	3.7	16,614	127.0
California	103,845	29.3	259,941	32.5	156,096	150.3
Hawaii	17,962	5.1	24,454	3.1	6,492	36.1
U.S. Total	354,593	100.0	798,849	100.0	444,256	125.3

Sources: U.S. Bureau of the Census (1983, table 63; 1993a, table 276).

ing Los Angeles and New York. During the most recent years, however, Chicago has become less attractive to Korean immigrants. The Korean population in Illinois increased only by 73% in the 1980s, compared to 180% in New York.

THE LOS ANGELES COMMUNITY

In 1970, the Los Angeles–Long Beach metropolitan area already had 9,395 Koreans, a larger population than that of Honolulu (8,938; see U.S. Bureau of the Census 1972, table 48). Since then the Korean popu-

TABLE 3.

KOREANS IN CALIFORNIA AND
LOS ANGELES (1990)

Area	N	% of Koreans in CA
LA City	72,970	28.1
LA County	145,431	55.9
Orange County	35,910	13.8
LA and Orange Counties	181,341	69.8
California	259,941	100.0

Source: U.S. Bureau of the Census (1993b, 26, 28, 29).

lation in Los Angeles has rapidly increased; moreover, it has expanded
into Orange County, making Southern California the second largest
overseas Korean center (after Yanbian, China). As shown in table 3,
about 73,000 Koreans settled in Los Angeles City in 1990, making up
28% of all Koreans in California. Fifty-six percent of Koreans in California resided in Los Angeles County and 70% in Los Angeles and Orange Counties.

In the 1970s and 1980s, the Korean population grew more quickly
in Los Angeles and Orange Counties than in the United States as a
whole. Every year, increasingly higher proportions of Korean immigrants chose to settle there. There is also evidence that Korean immigrants who originally settled in other cities relocated to Los Angeles.
For example, in my 1986 survey of Korean immigrants in Los Angeles
and Orange Counties, 26% of the respondents reported that they had
moved to Southern California from another U.S. city. The thriving Korean ethnic economy in Southern California attracted both immigrants
from Korea and Koreans living in American cities. The development of
Los Angeles's Koreatown as a commercial, social, and cultural center
also encouraged more and more Korean immigrants to cluster in Southern California. In addition, the mild weather, the prestigious universities in the University of California system, and the presence of many
other Asian immigrants all seem to have contributed to this concentration of Korean immigrants. Los Angeles has been a mecca not only for
Korean but for all post-1965 immigrants. The area has accommodated
the immigrants of the 1980s and 1990s to a greater extent than New
York accommodated the immigrants of the 1910s (Waldinger and
Bozorgmehr 1996).

Other Asian groups show even higher levels of concentration in California than do Korean Americans. For example, in 1990, 50% of Filipino Americans, 46% of Vietnamese Americans, and 43% of Chinese Americans resided in California, in comparison to 33% of Korean Americans (U.S. Bureau of the Census 1993b, 26, 28, 29). Japanese, Chinese, and Filipino Americans in Los Angeles County each outnumber Korean Americans by a large margin. Yet Koreans are more highly concentrated in Los Angeles County than any other Asian group in California. Sixty percent of the Koreans in California settled in Los Angeles County in 1990 in comparison to 42% of the Japanese, 35% of the Chinese, and 30% of the Filipinos (U.S. Bureau of the Census 1993b, tables 62, 69). No other Asian ethnic group, with the exception of the Chinese in New York, shows as high a concentration in one city as do Koreans in Los Angeles.

A unique aspect of the Los Angeles Korean community is the development of a physically segregated community known as Koreatown; located about three miles west of downtown Los Angeles, it covers approximately twenty square miles. In the early 1960s, Whites made up more than 90% of the residents of this working-class neighborhood. However, the influx of Hispanic and Asian immigrants since 1965 and the concomitant flight of Whites drastically altered the racial composition of the Koreatown area. According to a *New York Times* analysis of the 1990 census, the majority of the population in Koreatown was Latino and more than one-third was Asian (Barringer 1992). Almost all the Latinos in Koreatown are recent Mexican immigrants. Despite the name, Koreans probably make up less than 15% of the residents.

Many new Korean immigrants with language difficulties have settled in Koreatown, drawn by the availability of ethnic foods and other ethnically oriented services, as well as by the potential for employment in Korean-owned stores. Koreatown attracts the Korean elderly who there can enjoy Korean foods, various services based on ethnic tastes, and social interactions with co-ethnic elder people. During the daytime, they gather at Admore Park and play traditional Korean games such as *janggi* and *badook*. Koreatown also attracts a large number of temporary visitors and illegals from Korea, who can find employment in Korean restaurants, gift shops, garment factories, and travel agencies located inside or near Koreatown. Even some Korean Chinese illegals visit Koreatown to find employment in Korea-owned stores.

However, most Korean immigrants consider Koreatown, which has exceptionally high poverty and crime rates and low-quality schools, a place of temporary residence. Once they have become adjusted to

American society, many of them move to suburban areas. In my 1986 Los Angeles Korean community survey, 28% of Koreatown respondents reported that they had been in this country for three years or less, in comparison to 13% of respondents in other areas of Los Angeles and Orange Counties. Yu (1985) also reported that 89% of the Koreans who had lived in Koreatown in 1972 left the area by 1977.

Koreatown is not only a residential but also a commercial center for Koreans in Los Angeles. As of April 1992, approximately three thousand Korean-owned businesses with Korean language signs were located there. The 1986 survey showed that Koreatown Koreans were less likely to be self-employed than other Koreans, suggesting that many of Koreatown's businesses were not locally owned. In fact, the study indicated that the majority (59%) of Korean-owned businesses in Koreatown were owned by Koreans who lived somewhere else. Most Korean businesses in Koreatown are located in small shopping centers, often called mini-malls. As of October 1991, there were twenty-seven such shopping centers in the heart of Koreatown, and 95% of the businesses housed there were owned by Koreans (*KTLA*, October 23, 1991).

The vast majority of Korean businesses in Koreatown serve Koreans their native cuisine, groceries, books and magazines, and so on and provide services for other distinctively Korean cultural tastes (see Min 1993, table 9.2). According to my 1986 survey, approximately 73% of Korean businesses in Koreatown primarily or exclusively served Koreans, in comparison to only 21% of those in other areas of Southern California. In contrast, Chinatown businesses largely depend on nonethnic customers.[9] Visitors from Korea are another important source of customers for Koreatown businesses, particularly during the summer (*KTLA*, August 9, 1991). But the number of such visitors has declined since the 1992 riots.

Korean immigrants with language difficulties depend on Koreans for professional services. Korean business owners rely on Korean accountants to handle their bookkeeping, and most Korean accounting firms are located in Koreatown. Korean lawyers and physicians also largely depend on Korean customers, and their offices are often located inside or close to Koreatown. Insurance and real estate agencies are professional services that depend even more heavily on a Korean clientele, and thus the concentration of these two businesses in Koreatown is quite natural. Koreatown also houses a large number of businesses associated with Korean cultural traditions.

Koreatown has also become the community's social and cultural center. The Korean Federation of Los Angeles, which is the umbrella organization for the Los Angeles Korean community, and all eight major Korean business associations, including the Koreatown Development Association and the Korean Chamber of Commerce of Los Angeles, have their offices in Koreatown. The Korean American Coalition, the Korean Youth and Community Center, the Korean Family Legal Counseling Center, and other social service organizations are also located there. Most of the Korean ethnic newspapers and magazines published in Southern California, including all three ethnic dailies, have their central offices in Koreatown. Korean business associations, social service organizations, alumni associations, and other social and cultural clubs hold regular seminars, meetings, and parties at offices and restaurants in Koreatown. Many Korean families in other parts of Southern California often come to Koreatown restaurants for a wedding reception, a birthday party, a New Year dinner, or other family affairs. Koreatown holds its annual "Koreatown festival" in October. This ethnic festival introduces traditional Korean dances, songs, dresses, games, and food to non-Korean residents and visitors. There are several Korean-owned hotels and motels in Koreatown, and almost every month one or another of them hosts a Korean professional convention on the national level. The Koreatown hotels also accommodate visitors and entertainers from Korea.

THE NEW YORK COMMUNITY

As of 1994, approximately 150,000 Koreans resided in the New York–New Jersey metropolitan area, 100,000 of them in New York City. Koreans are the third largest Asian group in New York City, after the Chinese and Indians. Table 4 shows the distribution of Koreans and other Asians in the city's five boroughs based on the 1990 census. Nearly half the Asian Americans in New York City reside in Queens, and among its Asian ethnic groups Korean Americans show the highest level of concentration (70%). They concentrate in several areas: Flushing, Jackson Heights, Elmhurst, Woodside, Bayside, and Little Neck. Many Asian Americans, particularly Chinese Americans, have moved to the same areas of Queens. The number 7 subway travels from Times Square to Long Island City, Sunnyside, Elmhurst, Jackson Heights, and Flushing, where many Korean and other Asian Americans live. The train is very often referred to as the "Oriental Express" because of its large number of Asian American passengers.

TABLE 4.
KOREAN AND ASIAN POPULATIONS IN
NEW YORK CITY BOROUGHS

	Korean		All Asian and Pacific Islanders	
Borough	N	%	N	%
Queens	49,088	70.4	238,336	46.5
Brooklyn	6,608	9.5	111,251	21.7
Manhattan	6,183	8.9	110,629	21.6
The Bronx	4,908	7.0	35,562	6.9
Staten Island	2,931	4.2	16,941	3.3
Total	69,718	100.0	512,719	100.0

Source: U.S. Bureau of the Census (1993c, table 55).

Another "overseas Seoul" has been forming in Flushing, New York, since the late 1980s. Though this Koreatown is much smaller in scale than the one in Los Angeles, it possesses many characteristics of a typical ethnic ghetto. First of all, it is an area where many Koreans reside. Counting Kims, the most common Korean surname,[10] listed in the 1992 New York City public telephone directories, I found that almost one-quarter of the city's Koreans and more than one-third of those in Queens resided in Flushing. They are heavily concentrated within a dozen blocks, with its core at the intersection of Roosevelt Avenue and Union Street. Several apartment complexes located along Roosevelt Avenue between Union and 147th Streets house many Korean families, including elderly Koreans who often remain in Flushing when their adult children move to Long Island or New Jersey in search of better schools for their own children. Elderly Koreans prefer to live where they can enjoy their native food and language, and can interact with other elderly Koreans.

In Flushing's Koreatown, as in other ethnic ghettos, there are many restaurants and stores that cater to ethnic tastes. A significant proportion of Korean restaurants, bakeries, beauty salons, barber shops, nightclubs, ethnic presses, ethnic book stores, and real estate companies are located in downtown Flushing. A large number of Korean ethnic stores with Korean language signs are found along Union Street between Northern Boulevard and Roosevelt Avenue. Koreans refer to this area as "Union Hanin Sanga" (the Union Street Korean Business District). Flushing's Koreatown also houses a dozen Korean service organizations, including the Flushing Korean Association, the Korean YMCA and YWCA, the Korean Youth Center, the Korean-American Senior Citizens Center of Greater New York, and the Korean Family Counseling Center. Also, some sixty Korean churches are located there.

Manhattan was the center of the earlier New York Korean community, yet relatively few Koreans currently reside there: only 9% of New York City Koreans settled in 1990 (see table 4). This Korean population is composed largely of U.S.-born Korean Americans and longtime immigrants. There is, however, one place in Manhattan where Koreans are highly visible—the so-called Broadway Korean Business District, a rectangular ten-block area from 24th to 34th Streets between Fifth and Sixth Avenues. The intersection of 32nd Street and Broadway is considered its center. In October 1995, the city named the district "Koreatown" and posted official signs at the intersection.

Approximately four hundred Korean import and wholesale companies with Korean language signs are located in this area. The businesses import wigs, hats, leather bags, clothing, toys, and other manufactured goods from South Korea and other Asian countries and then distribute them to Korean retailers all over the country and to other retailers in the Northeast. Also located in this Broadway area are a large number of Korean professional businesses such as accounting firms, law firms, real estate offices, and travel agencies that serve mainly Korean importers and wholesalers. There are about twenty Korean restaurants, several nightclubs, two bakeries, a few bookstores, and other businesses catering to Korean customers. There is one Korean-owned motel, mainly serving Korean tourists from Korea and other parts of the United States, in the Broadway Korean Business District.

In the 1960s, before Korean importers started their businesses, the Broadway area was a decaying commercial area. Although it contained some Jewish and Indian wholesalers specializing in hats, leather bags, clothing, and India-imported carpets and jewelry, many buildings in the area were unoccupied. The Korean Product Company, the first Korean wholesale company in the area, was established in 1969 to distribute Korean-imported wigs to Korean retailers and peddlers (Korean Businessmen's Association of New York 1987, 77). Following the Korean Product Company, several Korean wig import and wholesale companies opened along Broadway in the early 1970s. Although the wig business has declined since then, more and more Korean immigrants have established import and wholesale businesses in the Broadway area, dealing in other items such as hats, leather bags, jewelry, and toys from Korea and other Asian countries. Korean importers in the Broadway area have developed it into a bustling business district.

ETHNIC NETWORKS IN KOREAN COMMUNITIES

Based on his observations in the 1970s, Illsoo Kim (1981) argued that the New York Korean community maintained a nonterritorial community. Since the mid-1970s, however, the New York Korean community has experienced substantial changes. As noted in the previous section, Koreans have chosen increasingly to reside in Flushing and several other sections of Queens. Most Korean families who have settled in these areas seem to live in the same apartment complex or at least on the same block as other Korean families. Yet the vast majority of Koreans in the New York metropolitan area live not in a territorial community but in a nongeographical community that is based on ethnic networks. This is also true of the majority of Koreans in Los Angeles. Therefore, Kim's conclusion basically remains valid even today for both the New York and Los Angeles Korean communities.

The Korean community, more than any other Asian American community, has a large number of ethnic organizations that provide services, facilitate social interactions among Koreans, or both. These include ethnic churches, alumni associations, ethnic media, various social service agencies, cultural organizations, recreational associations, occupational associations (professional and trade), political organizations, and several surname and provincial associations. I will focus on three major mechanisms of ethnic networks: ethnic churches, ethnic media, and alumni associations.

ETHNIC CHURCHES

As noted previously, the majority of Korean immigrants attended Christian churches in Korea, though Christians constituted only 25% of the Korean population. In addition, many Korean immigrants who did not practice Christianity in Korea have joined a Korean church upon arriving in America. Thus, nearly 75% of Korean immigrant families are affiliated with Korean churches (Hurh and Kim 1990; Min 1989, 1991). The majority of Korean Christians in the United States are Protestants; a little more than one-fourth are Catholics (Hurh and Kim 1990). Nearly half the Korean Protestant churches are Presbyterian, with Methodists forming the second largest denomination. These proportions reflect the denominational distribution in Korea.

In 1976, I. Kim (1981, 192) identified only seventy-two churches in the New York metropolitan area. However, the 1992-93 *Korean Churches Directory of New York* (Council of Korean Churches of Greater New York 1992-93) listed 230 churches in New York City and 385 in the tristate area. Since some are not listed in the directory, the number of Korean churches in the New York area may have exceeded 450 in 1992. The 1990-91 *Korean Directory of Southern California* (Keys Ad. and Printing Company 1990) listed 635 Korean churches in Southern California.

As expected, nearly all the Korean churches in Los Angeles and New York have been established since 1970, with the vast majority started in the 1980s. Before 1970, there were just ten Korean churches in Los Angeles, and only two of them (Robertson Korean United Methodist Church and Los Angeles Korean United Presbyterian Church) were established before 1910 by the pioneer immigrants. Only five Korean churches in New York were established before 1970, and only one (the Korean Church and Institute) was established by the earlier immigrants. Korean immigrant churches are generally small, yet there are some large Korean congregations in Los Angeles and New York. The Oriental Mission Church, established in 1970 and located inside Los Angeles's Koreatown, is the largest Korean congregation in the United States, with 6,250 affiliated members as of 1990. Young-Nak Presbyterian Church of Los Angeles, created in 1973, had 4,500 affiliated members as of 1990. Thirty other Korean churches in Southern California had a membership of 2,000 or more as of 1990. Eleven Korean churches in New York had 2,000 or more affiliated members as of 1992.

Most Korean Christians may attend church for religious purposes. However, if religion were their only motive for going to church, Korean immigrants need not establish their own. As analyzed elsewhere (Min 1992b), Korean immigrant churches serve several practical social functions for Korean immigrants, and that is why almost all churchgoing Koreans attend Korean churches. Perhaps most important, they are places where new immigrants can meet and interact socially with other Koreans. Separated from their relatives and friends in Korea, the immigrants need new networks to cope with the sense of alienation they face in the larger, foreign environment. Korean immigrant churches serve as such networks for social interactions; all have a fellowship hour after Sunday service. At that time, refreshments are served and church members exchange greetings and socialize with fellow Koreans. More than one-fourth of the Korean churches in New York were found to serve a full lunch or dinner after Sunday service (Min 1992b).

Another major social function of Korean immigrant churches is to provide various kinds of information and services that new immigrants need for their initial orientation and adjustment to this country. The head pastor and other religious leaders help church members informally by offering information and counseling on employment, business, housing, health care, social security, children's education, and so forth. They also assist by visiting hospitalized members, interpreting and filling out application forms for those with serious language difficulties, and acting as witnesses in court for congregants with legal problems. Korean immigrant churches, particularly the larger ones, provide additional services through a number of formal programs such as after-school activities or instruction, health clinics, and seminars.[11]

Korean immigrant churches also help Koreans maintain their cultural tradition, supporting both language and customs in various ways. Korean pastors give sermons in Korean in almost all adult services. Even the children's services are conducted more in Korean than in English. Indeed, most Korean churches offer language classes for children on Saturdays or Sundays; this is key for the younger generation to retain the Korean language. Furthermore, all Korean churches celebrate traditional Korean holidays such as Choo Seok (the Korean Thanksgiving Day) and the lunar New Year. Many churchgoers wear traditional dress on important Korean holidays and share a variety of Korean foods.

ALUMNI ASSOCIATIONS

Chinese and Japanese immigrants in the nineteenth and early twentieth centuries organized ethnic associations largely based on clan ties and locality of origin (Kitano 1976, 94; Lyman 1974, 32–27). However, clan and provincial ties in Korea are unimportant for Korean immigrants' ethnic networks, which often center instead on the school one attended in Korea. Though less significantly than Korean churches, alumni associations play an important role in tying Korean immigrants together. The 1990–91 *Korean Directory of Southern California* (Key Ad. and Printing Company 1990) listed 144 alumni associations. Forty two of them were college-based associations while the others were high school–based. Of the forty-two college alumni associations, only four were derived from U.S. colleges; the others were for graduates of Korean colleges. The 1992–93 *Korean Business Guide of New York* listed forty-five middle or high school and twenty-five college alumni associations in the New York metropolitan area (Canaan Publishing Company 1992).

Alumni associations usually hold outdoor picnics in the spring and fall; the gatherings feature Korean food, and alumni and their family members enjoy recreational activities. All alumni associations have a major party for members and their families at the end of the year, usually held in a hotel ballroom. Several university alumni associations in New York have recently prepared year-end parties for children of alumni members who are attending colleges. The main objective of such parties is matchmaking: they provide young men and women with an opportunity to get together. Each alumni association is further divided into subgroups based on the year of graduation. Members of each subgroup often maintain strong friendships and go beyond the formal activities of the organization in mutually aiding one another (I. Kim 1981, 215). They hold monthly meetings at each other's homes and organize rotating credit associations for their mutual benefit. They usually give preferential treatment to alumni members when hiring employees, transacting business, and making private loans. Many Korean alumni associations have established scholarship funds for their schools in Korea.

ETHNIC MEDIA

We have already noted that Koreans in Los Angeles and New York maintain a nonterritorial community based on social networks. The ethnic media play a central role in integrating geographically dispersed Korean immigrants by keeping them informed of what is going on in the local community. The media also draw attention to their homeland by supplying daily news from Korea. There are three Korean-language dailies in Southern California and four dailies in the New York metropolitan area. All of the newspapers, as branches of major dailies in Korea, duplicate articles published out of their headquarters in Seoul. They also include a Korean American section that carries news about the Korean community and the larger American society. In addition, the many ethnic weekly and monthly magazines published in Southern California (thirty) and the New York metropolitan area (fifteen) exert a powerful cultural influence on Korean immigrants.

There are five UHF and cable television stations in Los Angeles and four in New York. Two of them in each community broadcast Korean programs for twenty hours a day, providing news edited by the Korean Broadcasting Station in Seoul via satellite at nine in the evening. Thus, Korean immigrants in Los Angeles and New York have access to news from Korea on the same evening it is broadcast in Korea, even though it airs fourteen hours later because of the time difference. Korean television stations also present Korean movies and TV programs videotaped in Korea, approximately three weeks after they were originally aired. Consequently, Koreans in New York and Los Angeles can watch nearly all TV programs seen in Korea.[12] Watching Korean videotapes is a major recreational activity for many elderly Korean immigrants.

There are three Korean radio stations in New York. One of them, Radio Korea New York, is a general radio channel that broadcasts twenty hours a day (from 6 A.M. to 2 A.M.). Since it was established in July 1993, the station has had a powerful impact on the ethnic attachment of Koreans in New York. The vast majority of Korean immigrants have difficulties with English and thus depend on the Korean media, and Radio Korea New York greatly appeals to them because they can listen to it anywhere at any time. It provides news from Korea at regular intervals several times a day and also supplies all kinds of practical information that assists Korean immigrants in successfully adjusting to life in America. In addition, the station helps Koreans sell, purchase, and exchange used merchandise, furniture, and pets. The vast majority of Koreans in New York seem to enjoy the station's various programs.

The Los Angeles Korean community has four general Korean radio channels. Radio Korea Los Angeles, established in 1989, broadcasts twenty-four hours a day. During the Los Angeles riots, the station helped save the lives of many Korean merchants in Black neighborhoods by giving detailed information about rioting and calling for volunteers to assist Korean merchants who were surrounded by angry rioters. Radio Korea Los Angeles also helped draw a large number of Korean participants to a peace rally held in Koreatown after the riots.

When I. Kim (1981) emphasized how the Korean ethnic media had helped to establish Korean networks in New York in the early 1970s, he focused mainly on the three Korean dailies that existed at that time. Great advances in technology and communication since then have made the ethnic media an even more important tool for maintaining cultural traditions and identity in a nonterritorial community (Min 1995). In particular, the same-day news broadcasts from Korea and the availability of new Korean movies and TV programs on videotape, along with the convenience of air travel to and from Korea, have brought Seoul and cities in the United States much closer together. Furthermore, the influence of Korean ethnic media is enhanced because Koreans use only one language. In contrast, because Indian and Filipino immigrants speak several dialects, English is used in their ethnic media.

Korean immigrants were the second largest Asian immigrant group in the 1970s and 1980s, after Filipino immigrants. Like the Philippines, South Korea maintained close military, political, and economic relations with the United States during this period, and these linkages between home and host countries explain the large influx of Korean immigrants. Southern California, more particularly Los Angeles and Orange Counties, is the area of the largest Korean concentration in the United States, and the New York–New Jersey area is second. Koreans in Los Angeles have created Koreatown, their residential, commercial, and sociocultural center. Koreans in New York, too, are heavily concentrated in one neighborhood: Flushing, where another overseas Seoul is in formation. However, the majority of Koreans in both Los Angeles and New York live in a nongeographical community, tied together by ethnic networks that rely principally on Korean churches, alumni associations, and ethnic media.

CHAPTER 4

Korean Immigrants' Economic Segregation

Korean immigrants most often work in small business. Furthermore, Korean merchants heavily concentrate in particular business specialties. In addition, Korean-owned businesses are overrepresented in low-income African American and Hispanic neighborhoods. These three conditions related to Korean immigrants' economic segregation provide the context for their intergroup conflicts and ethnic solidarity. This chapter examines in detail their economic segregation in a limited range of small businesses in New York and Los Angeles, particularly in minority neighborhoods, examining each condition in turn.

SELF-EMPLOYMENT IN SMALL BUSINESS

The visibility of Korean-owned stores in many neighborhoods in New York, Los Angeles, and other cities, along with the mainstream media's depiction of Koreans' commercial activities, creates the impression that Korean immigrants are business-oriented people. Public documents and survey data support the validity of this general perception. The 1990 census data (U.S. Bureau of the Census 1990) indicated that 34.5% of foreign-born Koreans 25–64 years old in the Los Angeles metropolitan area were self-employed (Light and Roach 1996). Korean immigrants showed the highest self-employment rate among all minority and immigrant groups in Los Angeles, exceeding even the native-born Whites of Russian ancestry (23.4%), most of whom were likely to be Jewish.

Compared to other native-born Whites, foreign-born Koreans were, according to adjusted odd ratios, 3.5 times more likely to be self-employed (Light and Roach 1996). The same data also revealed that 29.8% of foreign-born Koreans 25–64 years old in the New York metropolitan area were either self-employed or were unpaid family workers.

Census surveys, based on respondents' self-reports, underestimate the self-employment rate of the population (Light and Bonacich 1988, 159; Light and Rosenstein 1995, 33–55). There are three major factors that contribute to such underestimation by census surveys (see Light and Rosenstein 1995, 33–55). First, family members of self-employed persons often do not report their work at family stores to the surveys. Second, people who engage in both self-employment and employment usually report themselves only as being employed. Third, those who peddle with no business licenses and those who run illegal businesses do not report their businesses. Errors included in census data seem to affect Korean immigrants to a greater extent than the general population, especially because many Koreans who work for family businesses are not likely to report their self-employment. Surveys conducted in Los Angeles and New York reveal a much higher self-employment rate of Korean immigrants than the 1990 census data suggest.

Table 5 presents two sets of data to show the degree to which Korean immigrants in Los Angeles and New York are self-employed and economically segregated. The left panel of the table indicates the self-employment rate of Koreans in Los Angeles and Orange Counties based on the 1986 survey. The majority of Korean male respondents and more than one-third of female respondents in the two Southern California counties were self-employed. Forty-five percent of Korean workers in Los Angeles and Orange Counties (the respondents, their spouses, and other working family members) were self-employed. The 1986 survey revealed that 53% of the represented households owned at least one business.

The right panel of table 5 presents the self-employment rate of Koreans in New York City based on interviews with randomly selected married women. Nearly half of Korean wives and 61% of their husbands in the city were self-employed in 1988. As a whole, 56% of married Korean workers were self-employed. Unmarried, younger Korean workers, many of whom received a college education in the United States, were likely to show a much lower self-employment rate. Therefore, our sample overestimated the self-employment rate of Koreans in New York City. Moreover, Korean immigrants in the northwestern part

TABLE 5.
SELF-EMPLOYMENT RATES OF KOREAN IMMIGRANTS IN NEW YORK CITY AND LOS ANGELES, BY SEX

Job Type	LA and Orange Counties						New York City					
	Male	(%)	Female	(%)	Total	(%)	Husbands	(%)	Wives	(%)	Total	(%)
Self-employed	179	(53.0)	57	(35.8)	236	(47.5)	172	(61.4)	102	(48.8)	274	(56.0)
Employed in Korean firms	88	(26.0)	49	(30.8)	137	(27.6)	69	(24.6)	76	(36.4)	145	(29.7)
Employed in non-Korean firms	71	(21.0)	53	(33.3)	124	(24.9)	39	(13.9)	31	(14.8)	70	(14.3)
Total	338	(100.0)	159	(100.0)	497	(100.0)	280	(99.9)	209	(100.0)	489	(100.0)

Sources: The 1986 survey of Korean immigrants in Los Angeles and Orange Counties; the 1988 survey of married Korean women in New York City.

of New Jersey, who represented a higher socioeconomic group than New York City Koreans, included a larger proportion of professionals working for the general economy. Thus the self-employment rate of Koreans in the New York–New Jersey metropolitan area was likely to be substantially lower than 56%. Nevertheless, it might have been close to 45%, the self-employment rate of Korean immigrants in the Los Angeles area.

Another 36% of married Korean women and 25% of their husbands in New York City were employed in Korean firms. Such employees consisted largely of recently arrived immigrants who had little facility with the English language, and most of them intended to start their own businesses (Min 1989). As a whole, only 14% of married Korean workers in New York City were employed in non-Korean firms in 1988. Typically, these employees were more highly educated and had been in the United States for a longer period of time than other Koreans (see Min 1989, table 4.2).

Few Korean immigrants who came to the United States in the late 1960s and the early 1970s intended to open their own businesses here. They expected to obtain white-collar and professional positions in fields that they were originally trained for. However, because of the language barrier and other disadvantages for employment, most of these immigrants had to switch to low-level, blue-collar occupations (Min 1988a). They reluctantly turned to small business as an alternative to these undesirable jobs. They were unprepared to establish their own businesses quickly, and, accordingly, it took a long period of time for them to accumulate start-up capital and to train themselves on how to start a business.

Recent Korean immigrants are better prepared to start their own businesses than those who came in the 1970s, since they are informed in Korea that self-employment is the only option for most of them: thus, they usually expect to run small businesses in the United States. For example, in one predeparture survey study conducted in Seoul in 1986, 61% of all respondents (71% of male respondents) reported that they would go into business when they came to the United States (Park et al. 1990, 86). In the early 1970s, many Korean immigrants attended language and vocational schools in Korea to improve their qualifications for employment in the American labor market. In contrast, most prospective Korean immigrants these days try to bring enough money with them to establish their own businesses as quickly as possible. Once they arrive here, Korean immigrants easily acquire business information and training through their employment in Korean-owned businesses.

Consequently, recent Korean immigrants can start their own businesses much more quickly than the Korean immigrants of the 1970s. The 1986 Los Angeles survey showed that it took earlier immigrants (those who immigrated through 1979) longer than recent arrivals (those who immigrated after 1979) to establish their first business. Forty-seven percent of recently arrived immigrants started their first business during their first year here, whereas only 31% of their predecessors were able to do so.

Another way of measuring Korean immigrants' strong tendency to run small business is to compare the Korean community with other Asian communities in the number of firms per capita and the average firm size. The U.S. Bureau of the Census takes a survey of minority-owned businesses every five years. The most recent survey, conducted in 1987, shows that there were 17,165 Korean-owned businesses in the Los Angeles–Long Beach metropolitan area (see table 6). They accounted for 25% of Korean-owned firms in the United States, although only 18% of Korean Americans were settled in this area in 1990. The average annual gross receipts of Korean firms in the Los Angeles–Long Beach area ($145,138) was substantially larger than the average gross receipts of all Korean firms in the United States ($110,854).

Table 6 also compares the four largest Asian ethnic groups in the region by the number of firms per 1,000 persons and their average gross receipts. Since the number of firms in 1987 is compared to the number of people in 1990, the table underestimates the number of Korean firms in Los Angeles in proportion to the population. Nevertheless, the statistics make possible useful comparisons. In relation to their population, the Los Angeles Korean community had more businesses than any other Asian group. Though the Korean population was only 66% of the Filipino population, there were almost two and a half times as many Korean-owned as Filipino-owned firms.

Not only did the Korean community in Los Angeles have more firms in proportion to its population, it also had firms that were on average larger than those of the other major Asian communities. The Japanese, Chinese, and Filipinos each had a much longer history of settlement in Los Angeles than the Koreans and would therefore appear more likely to own some large corporations. Nevertheless, Korean-owned firms in Los Angeles were the largest in their average gross receipts (indeed, far exceeding Japanese- or Filipino-owned firms). Thus, results of the cen-

TABLE 6.

ASIAN BUSINESSES IN THE LOS ANGELES–LONG
BEACH AREA (1987)

	Korean	Chinese	Japanese	Filipino
Total number of businesses in 1987	17,165	16,049	11,086	7,059
Number of people in 1990	145,431	245,033	129,736	219,053
Number of businesses per 1,000 persons	118.0	65.5	85.5	32.2
Total annual gross receipts ($1,000)	2,491,288	1,963,424	926,134	310,021
Average annual gross receipts per business ($)	145,138	122,339	83,541	43,919

Source: U.S. Bureau of the Census (1991, 75–76).

TABLE 7.

ASIAN BUSINESSES IN THE
NEW YORK–NEW JERSEY AREA (1987)

	Korean	Chinese	Indian
Total number of businesses in 1987	6,160	10,864	5,744
Number of people in 1990	74,632	246,817	107,270
Number of businesses Per 1,000 Persons	82.5	44.0	53.5
Total annual gross receipts ($1,000)	548,243	781,947	720,300
Average annual gross receipts per business ($)	89,000	71,976	125,400

Source: U.S. Bureau of the Census (1991, 79).

sus small business survey suggested that the Los Angeles Korean community in the late 1980s was far more entrepreneurial than other Korean communities in the United States and other Asian communities in
Los Angeles.

Table 7 compares the entrepreneurial activities of the Korean, Chinese, and Indian communities in New York based on the 1987 census survey of minority-owned businesses. Korean-owned businesses in
the New York–New Jersey metropolitan area numbered 6,160 in 1987.
Though there were more Chinese-owned businesses than Korean-
owned businesses in the New York metropolitan area at that time, the
New York Chinese community in 1990 had a population that was close
to three and a half times larger than the Korean population. Thus, the
New York Korean community had far more businesses per capita than

the Chinese community even in 1987. Moreover, since the number of Korean-owned businesses in the New York metropolitan area has significantly increased since 1987, it may have equaled the number of Chinese-owned businesses by the mid-1990s.[1] Korean-owned firms had a larger average gross receipt than Chinese-owned firms, although surprisingly their average was lower than Korean firms generally in the United States. The Indian firms in New York had the highest average gross receipts of these three groups, probably because medical offices constituted a large proportion of their businesses.

My 1982 survey in Atlanta showed that the vast majority of Korean merchants considered self-employment in small business to be suitable only for the immigrant generation whose language difficulties and other disadvantages hindered their employment in the general labor market. They did not want their children to engage in small business; rather, they wanted their children to succeed in high-status professions (Min 1988a, 61). Compared to their parents, American-born Koreans not only are advantaged for employment, but they also are not motivated to work the long hours necessary for survival in small business. These factors suggest that few native-born Korean Americans would be interested in opening up their own businesses, a surmise supported by 1990 census data. Only 11% of native-born Koreans in the Greater Los Angeles area were self-employed,[2] a rate lower than even that of native-born White Americans (13%) and much lower than that of Korean immigrants (35%; see Light and Roach 1996). Whereas the annual number of Korean immigrants is likely to be further reduced, the native-born Korean workforce will continue to grow. This implies that the self-employment rate of Korean Americans will continue to decrease and their occupations will be increasingly diversified.

BUSINESS SPECIALTIES

We noted in the previous section both that Korean immigrants in New York and Los Angeles are highly self-employed and economically segregated and that the two Korean communities are more active in small business than other Asian communities in their respective cities. While these observations point to the possibility of a Korean subeconomy in both cities, the task of demonstrating its existence falls to this section, which shows that Korean-owned businesses in Los Angeles and New York concentrate in several business specialties.

To examine the extent of such concentration, we need to estimate both the number of all Korean businesses in each Korean community and the number of businesses in each specialty. The 1987 U.S. census greatly underestimated the total number of all small-scale businesses, including those that are Korean owned (Light and Bonacich 1988, 159). Korean business leaders in each city can provide more accurate information. In addition, the president and staff members of Korean trade associations can roughly estimate the number of businesses in each business specialty, though they tend to exaggerate.

Korean business leaders estimated that in 1987 there were approximately 9,000 Korean-owned businesses in the New York metropolitan area and that, as of December 1991, the number had increased to 15,000. Interviews with leaders of major Korean trade associations and the Korean Small Business Service Center enabled me to estimate the number of business establishments for the major Korean business lines in the region. Produce and grocery retail, fish retail, wholesale and retail of Asian-imported merchandise, dry cleaning, and nail services are major Korean businesses in New York. We should note not simply the large number of Korean immigrants engaged in each business category but also their virtual monopoly over each business type. According to leaders of the two trade associations, Koreans control nearly 60% of all independent retail produce and 50% of manicure/pedicure salons. In some businesses, the proportions are more impressive than they first appear. For example, in April 1991 the neighborhood Cleaners Association reported that 27% of its members were Korean (*KTNY*, April 8, 1991). However, the Korean Dry Cleaners Association discredited these statistics, claiming that many Korean dry cleaners were not affiliated with the American trade association. Thus, the dominance of Koreans in the dry cleaning business was underestimated.

Similar methods were used to estimate the total number of Korean businesses and the numbers in each major specialty in Southern California, as of August 1994. Though Korean businesses in Southern California are more diversified than those in New York, they too exhibit a high level of concentration in certain areas. Nearly half of the businesses concentrate in fourteen business specialties. Retail groceries, dry cleaners, wholesale and retail outlets of merchandise imported from South Korea and other Asian countries, and garment subcontracting are major Korean businesses in Los Angeles as well as in New York. Though greengroceries, fish shops, and nail salons are among the major Korean businesses in New York, they do not figure importantly in the Los Angeles Korean community. Instead, the Los Angeles Korean com-

TABLE 8.

MAJOR KOREAN BUSINESSES IN NEW YORK AND SOUTHERN CALIFORNIA

New York (December 1991)

	N	%
Produce retail	1,800	12.0
Grocery/liquor retail	1,850	12.3
Produce and grocery/ liquor retail	2,950[a]	19.7
Fish retail	720	4.8
Jewelry retail	350	2.3
Wholesale of Asian- and Korean-imported items	500	3.3
Retail of Asian- and Korean-imported items	2,200	14.7
Dry cleaners	1,500	10.0
Nail salons	1,400	9.3
Garment manufacturing	350	2.3
Total	9,970	66.5
Other businesses	5,030	33.5
Estimated total Korean businesses	15,000	100.0

Southern California (August 1994)

	N	%
Grocery/liquor retail	3,500	11.7
Wholesale of Asian- and Korean-imported items	600	2.0
Retail of Asian- and Korean-imported items	3,500	11.7
Garment industry	700	2.3
Gas stations	600	2.0
Dry cleaners and laundries	2,000	6.7
Construction	400	1.3
House painting	1,000	3.3
Korean restaurants	300	1.0
American fast food	550	1.8
Real estate agencies	600	2.0
Insurance agencies	350	1.2
Total	15,340	51.1
Other businesses	14,660	48.9
Estimated total Korean businesses	30,000	100.0

Sources: Interviews with leaders of Korean business associations in New York and Los Angeles; Korean Central Daily Los Angeles (1994).

[a]Those 700 Korean-owned stores selling both greengroceries and general groceries are included in both produce retail and grocery categories. Therefore, the total number of stores engaged in produce or grocery retail is 2,950 rather than 3,650, the sum of the two subtotals.

munity has developed other types of businesses: liquor stores, gas stations, building maintenance firms, swap meet retail stores, and American fast-food franchises. Overall, Koreans in New York are more highly represented in middleman-type retail businesses and less represented in service businesses than Koreans in Los Angeles (see table 8). These differences in business patterns between the two communities have contributed to the differential in use of collective strategies, an issue that will be examined in detail in chapter 10.

As we have just noted, Korean-owned businesses in New York and Los Angeles cluster around several business specialties. Because each specialty developed differently and because some serve minority customers to a greater extent than others, it is useful to look at the major business specialties individually.

ASIAN-IMPORTED MERCHANDISE, WHOLESALE AND RETAIL STORES

Many Korean immigrants in Los Angeles, New York, and other cities sell wigs, handbags, jewelry, toys, and other such manufactured goods. They depend mainly on Korean suppliers who import these items from South Korea, Taiwan, China, and other Asian countries. The growth of international trade between the United States and Asian countries provided Korean immigrants with an advantage in this type of business (Chin, Yoon, and Smith 1996; I. Kim 1981; Min 1984b).

In the 1960s, the South Korean president, Chung Hee Park, took advantage of cheap labor and tried to develop an export-oriented economy (I. Kim 1981, 81–85; Light and Bonacich 1988, 68–70). South Korea's exports to the United States substantially increased in the early 1970s, just as a massive immigration of Koreans to the United States was beginning. Taking advantage of sharing their suppliers' language and ethnic background, many Korean immigrants were able to establish import businesses dealing in Korean-imported merchandise. New York and Los Angeles have had more active trade relations with South Korea than other cities in the United States. There are approximately six hundred Korean-owned import businesses in the Los Angeles– Long Beach area and about five hundred in the New York–New Jersey metropolitan area. Most Korean import businesses in Los Angeles are located in downtown Los Angeles, and over three-fourths of those in New York are located in Manhattan's Broadway Korean Business District.

Korean importers in New York and Los Angeles supply Korean- and Asian-made consumer goods mainly to other Korean wholesalers, who in turn distribute mainly to Korean retailers.[3] Korean immigrants, as a result, have virtually monopolized wig and several other businesses. Korean importers claim that there are more than 2,200 Korean-owned retail businesses dealing in Korean- and Asian-imported items in the New York metropolitan area, a number that is greatly increased when peddlers and flea market merchants are included. Broadway-based Korean wholesale suppliers also serve a large number of Hispanic retailers. In the Los Angeles–Long Beach area, the number of Korean-owned retail and swap meet stores that sold merchandise imported from Korea and other Asian countries numbered over 3,500, as of 1994.

The wig business was the first line of Korean business in both Los Angeles and New York. Since the majority of wigs bought in the United States are manufactured in Korea, Korean immigrants have exercised a near monopoly in selling wigs (Chin, Yoon, and Smith 1996; I. Kim, 1981).[4] Every American metropolitan city has several wig stores and the owners are usually Koreans. When I need to find a Korean restaurant in a strange city, I usually visit a wig store in the central business district to get information about restaurants from the Korean owner. In the late 1960s and the early 1970s, the wig business was very profitable as a result of the African American cultural movement and the youth movement in the United States (I. Kim 1981, 121–22). Some Korean wig peddlers in New York City earned several hundred dollars per day in the late 1960s. This lucrative business provided many Korean immigrants with financial resources to open other types of businesses such as gift shops, men's wear stores, stationery stores, grocery stores, small supermarkets, and dry cleaning establishments (Chin, Yoon, and Smith 1996; I. Kim 1981, 142).

The demand for wigs drastically declined in the mid-1970s when Black hairstyles changed and an economic recession associated with the oil shock started (Korean Businessmen's Association of New York 1987, 72–74). Wig importers and wholesalers in the Broadway Korean Business District responded to the decline in the demand for wigs by carrying other fashion items, such as clothing, hats, leather bags, jewelry, and eyelashes, as well as toys. Wig manufacturers in Korea also began to diversify their products.

The increase in South Korean labor costs and a steady devaluation of the U.S. dollar since the 1988 Seoul Olympic Games have made it unprofitable for Korean immigrants to import merchandise from South

Korea. However, South Korea has established trade relations with China, Russia, eastern European countries, and even North Korea since the 1988 summer Olympics. Furthermore, since 1988 the new unification policy adopted by the South Korean government has allowed Korean Americans to visit Russia, China, and North Korea. These changes have led many Korean immigrant importers to develop business relations with Taiwan, Hong Kong, and China and to forsake their ties with manufacturing companies in South Korea. According to the Broadway Korean Businessmen's Association, the majority of the merchandise that Korean importers handle now comes from other Asian countries; Korean-made items constitute only 30%.

GROCERY AND LIQUOR STORES

Grocery retail is the single largest business enterprise among Koreans in the United States. Yang Il Kim, the president of the National Korean-American Grocers Association (KAGRO) estimated that there were approximately 25,000 Korean-owned grocery stores in the United States and Canada as of December 1991. Koreans in Los Angeles, Atlanta, Philadelphia, Washington, Seattle, Toronto, and Ontario, in particular, heavily concentrate in retail groceries, and KAGRO exercises great power and influence in these communities. Local Korean grocers' associations established the national association in 1989. As will be discussed in detail at the end of this chapter, Korean-owned grocery and liquor stores heavily concentrate in Black neighborhoods. The grocery retail business is a prototype of how Korean merchants act as middlemen, distributing merchandise manufactured by U.S. corporations to minority customers. In all of the major Korean communities, Korean grocers acting as middlemen have encountered conflicts with minority customers and White suppliers.

Grocery and liquor stores constitute the largest single type of businesses among Koreans in Los Angeles and Orange Counties. KAGRO of Southern California published a booklet that provided data on Korean grocery and liquor stores in Southern California (KAGROSC 1990). According to the booklet, in 1990 there were 2,101 Korean-owned beer/wine (Type 20 licenses) or beer/wine/liquor (Type 21 licenses) stores in Los Angeles County and 295 such stores in Orange County. Korean-owned stores accounted for 34% of all grocery and liquor stores in Los Angeles County, 23% in Orange County. According to recent interviews with KAGROSC, the number of Korean grocery and liquor stores in Southern California had grown to 3,500 by August 1994. KAGROSC, along with the Korean Chamber of Commerce, is a major power in the Los Angeles Korean community. The National KAGRO has its main office in Orange County.

Korean-owned grocery stores in New York had not received much attention until very recently. Yet sheer numbers make it clear that grocery retail is an important business among Koreans in New York, as well. Many Korean produce stores recently have begun to sell other groceries, besides fruits and vegetables, to attract more customers. It is therefore very difficult to estimate how many Korean-owned produce or grocery stores are in New York. KAGRONY was established in 1986, much later than the other major Korean trade associations in New York, but has used collective strategies actively to protect the economic interests of its members.

Prices of grocery and liquor stores in major American metropolitan cities have risen astronomically since the early 1970s. According to the Korean-American Grocers Associations in New York, Los Angeles, and Atlanta, strong competition among Korean immigrants to buy these stores has been mainly responsible for this price inflation. Korean realtors who are familiar with Korean immigrants' pursuit of the grocery and liquor business offer high prices as they attempt to persuade White store owners to sell their businesses. They then sell these stores to Korean immigrants for even higher prices. Many immigrants who have brought with them large amounts of money from Korea are ready to invest in a grocery retail business because they have a good chance for surviving in a medium-sized grocery or liquor business. In this way Korean immigrants in many American cities have monopolized the grocery and liquor retail business since the late 1970s, and thus intragroup transfers of grocery and liquor stores among Korean immigrants are exceptionally high. As early as 1975, 80% of Koreans selling liquor stores in the Hollywood section of Los Angeles found Korean buyers (Light and Bonacich 1988, 239).[5]

DRY CLEANERS

Dry cleaning service is another major business among Koreans in several communities. Koreans in Philadelphia and Chicago, in particular, heavily concentrate in this business. According to the Korean Dry Cleaners Association of Southern California, about 10,000 Korean-owned dry cleaning shops existed in the United States in 1990. The mailing list of the Korean Dry Cleaners Association of Southern California included 1,628 businesses, but the actual number may have been closer to 2,000 (*KTLA*, August 17, 1991). Korean Dry Cleaners Associations were established in twenty-one cities, and the national union was created in 1988. The Korean Dry Cleaners Association of New York identified 1,100 Korean-owned dry cleaners in the New York metropolitan area, as of April 1991, accounting for about 27% of all such businesses in the area (*KTNY*, April 8, 1991). However, it estimated the total number of Korean-owned dry cleaners at about 1,500, many more than the reported figure.

Korean immigrants are attracted to the dry cleaning business for two reasons. First, it is suitable as a family business involving both husband and wife. Most Korean-owned dry cleaners are operated by such a team, even though some include other employees. Second, it requires fewer hours of work and less physical exertion than the produce or fish retail business. Many Korean produce or fish retailers switch to running dry cleaners because of these advantages. However, because the business is a low-status occupation in Korea, few Korean immigrants have any experience in the field. Many Korean dry cleaners in New York received training and experience by attending a ten-week night school operated by the Neighborhood Cleaners Association (the major dry cleaners' association in the Northeast).

Like other businesses in New York, the dry cleaning industry was controlled by Jewish and Italian Americans before the 1970s. In that decade, Koreans in New York began to buy dry cleaning stores in predominantly White middle-class areas from these White ethnics. In addition, many Koreans have bought or newly opened dry cleaning stores in all parts of the New York metropolitan area since 1980. Although Korean-owned dry cleaners still heavily concentrate in middle-class White areas, many stores have been established recently in Black middle-class areas such as Inglewood in Los Angeles. Korean immigrants who experienced difficulties in other types of business have opened up dry cleaners, contributing to strong intra-ethnic competition.

GARMENT MANUFACTURING

Garment manufacturing is one of the major Korean businesses in Los Angeles and New York. There are approximately 700 Korean-owned garment factories in Los Angeles and about 350 in New York. There are about 150 additional Korean businesses in Los Angeles and 70 in New

York that support Korean-owned garment businesses: truck drivers delivering garment pieces to White manufacturers, merchants supplying threads for Korean garment owners, and brokers cashing checks for garment owners.[6] My interviews reveal that almost all Korean garment factory owners in Los Angeles and New York (more than 95%) subcontract work from big manufacturers, the majority of whom are Jewish. Not only Korean but also Chinese and Hispanic immigrant garment entrepreneurs in New York City largely subcontract to perform work for White manufacturers (Waldinger 1986).

Immigrants have an advantage for operating garment businesses, because they can use family and co-ethnic members as sources of cheap labor. Seven hundred Chinese-owned garment factories in New York depend mainly on new immigrants from China and Hong Kong who are ready to work for low wages in poor working conditions (Kwong 1987). This dependence on family and co-ethnic members also characterizes Hispanic garment entrepreneurs in New York (Waldinger 1986). However, Korean garment entrepreneurs in New York depend largely on immigrants and illegals from Mexico and South American countries for garment production. According to the Korean Apparel Contractors Association of New York, about 70% of the employees in Korean garment factories are Hispanic. Korean garment manufacturers in New York have recently begun to hire legal and illegal immigrants from mainland China, India, and South American countries. In Los Angeles, the Korean factory owners depend more heavily on Hispanic workers than do their counterparts in New York (Light and Bonacich 1988, 306–8; Min 1989), mainly because a large number of Mexican immigrants and illegals settle in the Los Angeles downtown area where many of these garment factories are located.

Approximately 40,000 Korean immigrants have settled in Brazil. The majority of Korean families in Brazil engage in garment manufacturing or in wholesale or retail sales of garment products (Yeon 1986). The Korean garment subcontractors' associations in Los Angeles and New York indicate that many Koreans working in the business are remigrants from Brazil and other South American countries. Minority groups who remigrated from a third country, such as Chinese immigrants from Vietnam and Indian immigrants from Uganda, are referred to as "twice minorities" (Bhachu 1993; Espiritu 1989). Twice minorities usually maintain strong ethnic solidarity, even in the early stage of their settlement, because they have already established strong ethnic networks prior to migration; this is true of Korean remigrants from Brazil. The Korean garment manufacturers who came from Brazil maintain strong ties by establishing rotating credit associations and helping each other in times of financial difficulty.

PRODUCE STORES

Produce retail is probably the best-known Korean business in New York. Several Korean immigrants opened produce stores in the early 1970s, and most of them were remigrants from South American countries who had run produce retail stores there. By the early 1980s, produce retail had become the dominant business among Koreans in New York. Korean immigrants were able to start produce stores with a small amount of money, since the cash turnaround was very quick. They were also ready to work long hours and had access to cheap labor: that is, loyal family members and co-ethnic employees. Korean greengrocers regularly go to Hunts Point Market as early as 4 A.M. to buy fruits and vegetables and keep their stores open until late at night. Few nonimmigrants would be motivated to work this hard.

Though Korean immigrants in other cities share the readiness to work long hours and their access to cheap labor, they have not developed the produce business as a major Korean business. This suggests that the concentration of Koreans in New York City's retail produce stores has to do with urban patterns that are unique. Because of the scarcity of space in New York, residential and commercial zones are pressed up against each other. Many people in the city buy fruits and vegetables on their way home from bus stops and subway stations; in other cities, suburban residents live so far away from commercial zones that it is not convenient for them to drop by a fruit and vegetable store on their way home.

Many Koreans bought produce stores from retiring Jewish and Italian American owners in Queens and Manhattan. This shift in ownership is a good example of ethnic succession within a business. Many Jewish and Italian produce store owners reached retirement age in the 1970s when Korean immigrants were just entering the retail business; they were willing to sell their stores for significant amounts of cash. Concurrently, many Koreans have opened new produce stores, often close to other Korean-owned stores. Thus, the market in New York City became saturated, and a fierce competition was waged among Korean store owners.

In the 1970s, Koreans established produce stores primarily in Manhattan and high-income White neighborhoods in Queens. However, Korean-owned produce stores gradually spread into nearly every neighborhood in New York City, including low-income Black neighborhoods, in the early 1980s. Currently, in proportion to the population, more Korean produce stores are located in Black neighborhoods than in middle-class White neighborhoods. As will be shown in chapter 5, these Korean-owned stores have been the targets of Black boycotts.

In the mid-1970s, several Koreans established trucking companies that delivered merchandise from Hunts Point Market, the largest farmers' market in New York, to Korean produce retailers. At present, their number has increased to about seventy. Though most Korean trucking companies involve just one truck and no paid employee, other companies operate with eight or nine trucks. There are about 150 Korean truck drivers delivering fruits and vegetables to Korean produce retailers in the New York metropolitan area, and they recently established their own association. The emergence of Korean trucking companies has been a great convenience to Korean produce retailers, allowing them to concentrate on selling their merchandise.

FISH SHOPS

The first Korean fish retail store in New York opened in 1974, and their number had increased to forty by 1977, when the Korean Fish Retailers Association was established (*SGT,* October 25, 1988). By 1990, there were 700 Korean fish retailers. The business was suitable for Korean immigrants because, like retail produce, it required a small amount of starting capital and had a quick cash turnaround. Also like retail produce, the fish retail business has become popular among Koreans only in New York.

The fish retail business in New York City was similarly monopolized by Jewish and Italian Americans before Koreans arrived. Many of the first Korean fish retailers bought ongoing businesses from these White store owners. However, many other Korean fish retail stores, particularly those located in Black neighborhoods, were newly established. My interviews with the Korean Fish Retailers Association revealed that Korean fish retailers preferred Black neighborhoods to White neighborhoods because Black customers tended to buy whole fish (not filleted) and ate fried fish. Korean immigrants innovated by selling fried fish in a corner of the store. Well-informed Korean fish retailers told me that more than half of their stores in New York City and two-thirds of those in Black neighborhoods sell both raw and fried fish. Some Korean fish retailers specialize in distributing fish to Korean restaurants that serve Japanese sushi.[7]

NAIL SALONS

Approximately 1,500 Korean-owned nail salons exist in the New York–New Jersey metropolitan area, controlling 50% of all such businesses in the area. The concentration of Koreans in manicure services is unique to New York's Korean community. The nail salon business in large cities has long been dominated by disadvantaged immigrant groups; Russian Jewish immigrants preceded the Koreans. Wurdinger suggests that Koreans in New York concentrate in the manicure business for the same reasons as earlier immigrant groups: the unimportance of language skills, the small amount of start-up capital necessary, and the lack of required professional skills (Wurdinger 1992). Koreans can rent the second, third, or basement floor of a building for relatively little and need only make a few purchases to open a nail salon. In addition, the traditionally service-oriented attitudes of Korean women may make them inclined toward the manicure business.

Korean women initially began nail salons, but Korean men have entered this female business in large numbers over the last several years, as the business has been touted as a source of profit for Korean immigrants.[8] According to a survey conducted by the Korean Nail Salon Owners Association, approximately 35% of Korean-owned nail salons were owned by men as of December 1990 (SGT, February 6, 1991). A Korean male owner often has several nail salons and hires Korean women as managers to run the business. Female managers usually get commissions for the total amount of sales. As the number of Korean-owned nail salons rose dramatically during the 1980s, the price for a manicure in New York City fell to such extent that low-income women can now afford to have the service.

SWAP MEET STORES

Another business that has become increasingly popular in the Los Angeles Korean community in recent years is the swap meet. There are two kinds of swap meet: outdoor and indoor (Chang 1990). The outdoor swap meet, commonly known as the flea market, usually sells bargain goods at a designated location on weekends. The indoor swap meet, which evolved from the outdoor version, sells extremely cheap goods at a leased booth on a daily basis. Recently arrived immigrants with little money are attracted to the swap meet business because they can start it with a small amount of capital and with no business experience. Many Korean immigrants can gain extra income by operating a weekend swap meet, which does not interfere with a full-time job. In addition, Korean immigrants have an ethnic advantage for starting and operating a swap meet business, because they sell items supplied largely by Korean importers and wholesalers.

As a result of these factors, the number of Korean swap meet operators in Los Angeles has mushroomed over the last several years. According to the California (Korean) Swap Meet Sellers Association, approximately 100 of 130 indoor swap meets in Southern California were owned by Koreans as of July 1992; more than 5,000 Koreans in Southern California were operating swap meet businesses, with the vast majority of their stores located in African American and Mexican areas.[9] Many Korean-owned swap meets were burned during the Los Angeles riots, but most of these were subsequently reestablished. Korean swap meet owners usually lease their booths to Korean merchants through their advertisements in Korean ethnic media. As a result, 80% of merchants retailing goods in Korean-owned swap meets are Korean. These owners exploit co-ethnic swap meet sellers by asking new merchants for "key money" and by raising rents. Korean swap meet sellers in Southern California created an association in 1992 partly to protect their interests against Korean swap meet owners.

PROFESSIONAL BUSINESSES

The 1994–95 *Korean Business Directory of Southern California,* published by the *Korea Central Daily Los Angeles,* listed 200 Korean-owned accounting firms, 200 legal firms, 410 medical offices, and 230 dental offices. It also listed 600 real estate businesses, 350 insurance agencies, and 125 travel agencies. The 1991 *Korean Life Guide,* a New York Korean directory, listed 240 Korean-owned medical offices, 90 law firms, and 58 accounting firms in the New York–New Jersey metropolitan area. The major clientele of these professional and semiprofessional businesses are Koreans. My 1986 Los Angeles–Orange County survey showed that 75% of six major Korean professional and semiprofessional businesses (law firms, medical or dental offices, accounting offices, and insurance, real estate, and travel agencies) in Los Angeles and Orange Counties had Koreans as the majority of their customers, in comparison to only 24% of nonprofessional Korean businesses.

Self-employed professionals primarily serve co-ethnic customers because there is a great demand for their services. Because of the language barrier, Korean immigrants, especially recent arrivals, tend to prefer fellow Koreans for transacting professional services. For example, Korean immigrant patients can more easily explain their medical problems and feelings to a Korean than to a non-Korean physician. Thus, Korean professional businesses depend on a "protected market" for business activities (Auster and Aldrich 1984; Min 1987; Waldinger, Ward, and Aldrich 1985). Taking advantage of this dependence, some Korean professionals have exploited their co-ethnic customers.

Many Koreans engage in one of three semiprofessional businesses: real estate, insurance, and travel agencies. Although these businesses do not require as much professional education as medicine or law, Koreans engaged in them have received a higher level of education and can often speak English better than nonprofessional, blue-collar business owners. They depend almost entirely on Korean customers, and accordingly, these businesses are often located in the areas where Korean immigrants concentrate and are often advertised on Korean language signs.

CONCENTRATION IN MINORITY NEIGHBORHOODS

A middleman minority bridges two groups in a stratified society by distributing the products made by the ruling group to the consuming masses. Korean merchants in the United States draw customers from three groups: White, African American and Hispanic, and Korean. Yet they depend heavily on low-income minority customers, particularly Blacks.

It would be an exaggeration to say that Korean stores overwhelmingly concentrate in African American neighborhoods, since more Korean-owned stores are located in White neighborhoods than in minority neighborhoods. However, Korean merchants serve a much larger proportion of African American customers than allowed for by chance. Blacks make up approximately 12% of the U.S. population, but they constitute a much larger percentage of customers of Korean-owned stores.

Korean merchants in New York depend heavily on African American/Afro-Caribbean and Hispanic customers. In the city, Koreans residentially concentrate in Queens; less than 10% reside in Brooklyn or the Bronx. However, according to Korean business leaders, about 3,000 Korean-owned stores are located in Brooklyn and 2,000 in the Bronx. They constitute respectively 33% and 22% of Korean-owned businesses in the city (which total approximately 9,000). The vast majority of Korean-owned stores in Brooklyn are located in Black neighborhoods where immigrants from Haiti, Jamaica, and other Caribbean islands dominate the population. More important, at least one-third of small businesses in many Black neighborhoods in Brooklyn are owned by Korean immigrants. For example, in April 1990 when the Brooklyn (Church Avenue) boycott was in progress, twenty-three of sixty-seven small businesses within five blocks of Church Avenue were found to be owned by Koreans (H. Lee 1993, 64). Almost 35% of the nearly two million Hispanics in New York City live in the Bronx, and Korean businesses in the Bronx heavily concentrate in their neighborhoods. Also, Korean-owned businesses are highly visible in three major African American areas: Harlem (Manhattan), Jamaica (Queens), and Lefrak City (Queens). In addition, more than six hundred Korean peddlers and flea market store owners in the New York metropolitan area serve primarily Black and Hispanic customers.

Before examining the commercial activities of Koreans in African American neighborhoods in Los Angeles, we need to note differences in residential and segregation patterns among Blacks in New York City and Los Angeles. In New York City, Black neighborhoods are found in different parts of the city, even though the population is heavily concentrated in Brooklyn. In contrast, the Black population in Los Angeles is gathered in one area: South Central Los Angeles. Furthermore, whereas the Black population in New York City consists of both native-born African Americans and Caribbean immigrants, Black residents in South Central Los Angeles are overwhelmingly African American. Since the Black population in Los Angeles lives in one area, race relations involving Blacks can be more explosive there than in other cities.

The majority of businesses in South Central Los Angeles are owned by Koreans. For example, at the end of 1991 when Korean–African American tensions heightened in Los Angeles because two Blacks were shot to death in Korean-owned stores, the *Korea Times Los Angeles* published its own study focusing on the concentration of Korean businesses in South Central Los Angeles. According to the report, in addition to 1,000 Korean swap meet stores, there were approximately 600 grocery and liquor stores, gas stations, and other Korean-owned stores in South Central Los Angeles, which connects Inglewood and Compton, and they accounted for about 80% of all businesses in the African American area (*KTLA*, January 1, 1992). These 1,600 businesses in the Inglewood-Compton African American neighborhoods constituted a little more than 10% of the estimated total Korean businesses in the Los Angeles–Long Beach metropolitan area; however, the fact that the vast majority of the businesses located in South Central Los Angeles were owned by Korean immigrants could have heightened the perception that Koreans were invading the African American community.

Though a variety of Korean-owned stores are located in African American and Hispanic neighborhoods, two types of Korean businesses are especially prevalent in minority neighborhoods: produce/grocery/liquor stores and shops selling fashion items. Though the Korean domination of produce retail stores is unique to New York City, the grocery/liquor and fashion retail businesses are the two most popular among Koreans in all cities with a large Korean population, and they are heavily concentrated in African American and Hispanic areas. A close examination of the nature of each of these businesses helps us understand why both types of businesses are overrepresented in minority areas.

Predominantly White neighborhoods have plenty of chain supermarkets and do not need small grocery stores. Few chain grocery stores exist, however, in low-income African American neighborhoods. Because of the residents' low spending capacity, the neighborhoods' high crime rates, and vandalism, large grocery chains have been unwilling to invest in these areas (Light and Bonacich 1988; Min 1988a, 73). A survey conducted by the New York City Consumer Affairs Department showed that in Manhattan's Upper East Side, a predominantly White upper-middle-class area, there is one supermarket for every 5,762 persons, whereas in the Williamsburg area of Brooklyn, a poor Black area, there is one for every 63,818 persons (*SGT,* June 8b, 1992). Therefore, independent Korean grocery stores in African American neighborhoods do not have to compete with supermarket chains, as they would have to do in White, middle-class neighborhoods. Also, Korean immigrants can start a grocery business with a smaller amount of capital in a African American neighborhood, where rents are lower.

My research in Atlanta demonstrated the advantages that Korean grocers have in African American neighborhoods. Korean-owned grocery stores in White neighborhoods were usually located at the intersections of busy streets, and they sold soft drinks, cigarettes, and other miscellaneous grocery items to passing customers. In contrast, Korean grocery stores in low-income African American neighborhoods often provided major grocery items, including meat, to residents. Korean grocers in African American neighborhoods in Atlanta were more successful than those in White neighborhoods (Min 1988a, 72, 73, 117, 118). The preceding discussion suggests that urban residential patterns of racial segregation have created small business niches in low-income Black areas, which have been filled by Korean and other immigrant merchants.

The other major Korean business in minority areas is the fashion business. Korean fashion stores deal largely in Korean- and Asian-imported merchandise, such as wigs, handbags, hats, clothing, jewelry, and shoes. Korean store owners have the advantage of easy access to Korean suppliers and importers. Whereas American buyers distribute these Asian-imported manufactured goods to department stores, Korean importers provide them directly to Korean retailers (Chin, Yoon, and Smith 1996). A large number of Korean merchants, particularly Korean swap meet owners in Southern California and Korean flea market owners in New York, sell fashion items directly to African American and Hispanic customers, whereas in White areas department stores sell such merchandise. Korean owners of fashion stores, like Korean small grocers, have competitive advantages over large chain stores in selling merchandise in minority areas. Korean owners of swap meet and flea market stores can provide merchandise more cheaply than department stores, because they buy directly from Korean importers and because they can significantly undercut a store's operating cost.[10]

In addition, independent Korean store owners can respond more quickly than department stores to fashion changes. In the contemporary postindustrial economy, fashion cycles are relatively short (Waldinger 1986). Whereas large department stores must go through several intermediaries to obtain merchandise, independent Korean store owners can get the hottest items within a day or two directly from Korean suppliers. Korean swap meet store owners in Los Angeles and Korean flea market store owners in New York usually go early in the morning to Korean suppliers in downtown Los Angeles and Manhattan's Broadway Korean Business District to purchase their merchandise, then open their stores at about 10 or 11 A.M. The restructuring of the U.S. economy in the late 1970s and the early 1980s has thus created the opportunity for independent business owners to compete successfully against large department stores in low-income minority areas (Chang 1990). The first Korean indoor swap meet in Los Angeles was held in a former Sears building in 1985 in the African American neighborhood of Compton.

The reluctance of large chain stores to invest in low-income minority areas (or their disinvestment from these areas) and the Koreans' monopoly of Korean- and Asian-oriented international trade contributed to the concentration of Korean merchants in minority areas. Many Korean merchants in African American neighborhoods may not know that these structural factors have encouraged their Black-oriented businesses. Instead, most of these merchants seem to attribute their business advantages to so-called Black consumption patterns. In a survey of Korean business owners in Atlanta, I asked respondents who had African Americans as the majority of their customers what the advantages and disadvantages were of operating businesses in Black neighborhoods. Interestingly, 90% of them reported that Black customers were less choosy in selecting items, more often involved in "accidental shopping," and "less sensitive to prices" than White customers. According to the respondents, these consumer behaviors made business transactions easier than with Whites (Min 1988a, 72, 73). In my 1992 survey of Korean business owners in Black ghettos of New York City, a lower proportion but still the majority of Korean respondents (67%) referred to similar consumer habits as being an advantage of operating a business in a Black neighborhood.

Cultural stereotyping is always dangerous. As a social scientist, I question the validity of Korean merchants' generalizations about African American consumer behaviors. However, we can make sense of how Koreans have overgeneralized consumer behaviors without our falling into cultural stereotypes of disadvantaged, African American customers. What Korean merchants considered to be "Black consumer behaviors" seem to have been determined structurally by the low incomes and the limited choices of shopping that exist in African American neighborhoods. In this sense, large structural forces are underlying causes of Korean merchants' concentration in African American and Hispanic neighborhoods.

Whereas Korean merchants in low-income minority neighborhoods have the advantages described above, they also contend with frequent shoplifting, the risk of armed robberies, and the lower spending capacity of customers. The majority of Korean merchants sampled in New York and Atlanta cited these three problems as the major disadvantages of running businesses in low-income, African American areas (Min 1988a, 72–73). Armed robbery is the major hazard confronting Korean merchants in urban, predominantly minority areas, and every year, many Korean merchants are killed or injured as a result. Twenty Kore-

ans in Los Angeles County were murdered by African Americans during the five-year period from 1987 to 1991, according to the *Korea
Times Los Angeles*'s analysis of its own coverage (*KTLA,* October 30,
1991). Most of the business owners or employees were shot inside their
stores.[11] This analysis focused on Koreans murdered by African Americans; when Koreans murdered by robbers of other ethnic backgrounds
are included, the number of Koreans murdered during the same five-
year span should be higher.

Because of the physical danger, Korean merchants do not intend to
stay in African American neighborhoods for a long period of time. Most
plan to leave as soon as they are financially able to start other businesses
in more desirable areas. However, it is not easy for these merchants to
save a large amount of money within a short period of time. Thus, most
of them operate their businesses for much longer than they had originally expected. My 1992 survey of New York Korean merchants in African American neighborhoods revealed that, on average, they had been
running their business for six years.

Before Korean immigrants came to this country in large numbers,
Jewish merchants concentrated in African American neighborhoods;
they were the main targets of the urban riots that swept major American cities in the late 1960s. For example, Jews controlled businesses in
Watts, Los Angeles, in the early 1960s and were the major victims of
the 1965 Watts riot (N. Cohen 1970). However, after being victimized
by the race riots in the 1960s, Jewish merchants gradually moved out
of African American neighborhoods. Korean merchants in Los Angeles
suffered even more damage almost thirty years later, in the 1992 riots.
It is interesting to consider whether Korean immigrants, like Jewish
Americans in the 1960s, are getting out of African American neighborhoods after enduring riots.

On May 14, 1992, two weeks after the Los Angeles riots, the city's
Korean community leaders met with Jewish leaders to learn how Jewish
Americans had responded to the 1965 Watts riot. Jewish speakers emphasized that Jewish merchants quickly departed African American
neighborhoods after the riot and that Korean immigrants should do the
same. They suggested that Korean immigrants should try to establish
corporations through partnerships in White areas (*KCDNY,* May 20,
1992). However, this advice may not be sound. The vast majority of
contemporary Jewish Americans are descendants of eastern European
immigrants who came to this country from 1880 to 1924. Most Jewish
merchants in African American neighborhoods in the 1960s were sec-

ond- and third-generation Americans. Jewish merchants in the 1960s, who had no serious language problems and who were familiar with American customs, thus had options other than operating small businesses in African American neighborhoods and may have been able to move quickly out of African American neighborhoods. However, current Korean immigrants have fewer alternatives: the vast majority of Koreans have come to this country over the last twenty years and thus experience serious language barriers. Even before the Los Angeles riots, many Korean merchants in African American neighborhoods had been murdered or seriously injured during armed robberies. Though Korean merchants were well aware of this physical danger, they chose small businesses that served minorities because they had no other alternative.[12] In view of this situation, Korean merchants are likely to take a much longer period of time to move out of minority neighborhoods.

Nevertheless, some Korean riot victims have already moved to other areas and many more are planning to move in the near future. Data released by Korean moving companies in Los Angeles in October 1992 indicate that the number of Koreans moving out of the Los Angeles area significantly increased, as of June 1992, and that most of these Koreans were riot victims (*SGT*, October 24, 1992). Their most frequent destinations were Seattle, a few cities in Oregon, and New York City. In a survey conducted by the Neighborhood Opportunity Center, nearly half of the Korean riot victims who planned to reestablish their businesses reported that they would open businesses at other sites (*KTLA*, December 11, 1992). They indicated that the physical danger connected with robbery and the possibility of another riot were the major reasons for wanting to move out of African American neighborhoods. Many of those respondents who intended to go back to their old locations said that they had to reopen businesses in African American neighborhoods against their will, so as not to lose money. These findings suggest that, at least in the Los Angeles area, more and more Korean merchants are going to depart low-income, African American neighborhoods in the future.

Though many immigrants had high educational and occupational levels before leaving Korea, they had difficulties in finding professional and other desirable white-collar occupations because of their language difficulties and because of other labor market disadvantages. They have turned to self-employment in small business rather than seek employment in blue-collar occupations. Korean immigrants in the 1970s came to the United States poorly prepared to start their own businesses, so it took them a long time to accumulate start-up capital and gain business information and training. But more recent Korean immigrants usually have come to the United States with the money and information necessary for establishing small businesses. They also can get business training easily through their employment in Korean-owned businesses. Thus, they can start their own businesses quickly. As a result, Korean immigrants' self-employment rate has gradually increased to such an extent that the majority of Korean immigrants in New York and Los Angeles are self-employed.

Korean-owned businesses in the United States are highly segregated into several business specialties: liquor and grocery retail, wholesale/retail of Asian-imported manufactured goods, dry cleaning service, and garment subcontracting. In proportion to their population, more Korean businesses are located in low-income minority neighborhoods than in middle-class White neighborhoods; particularly common are liquor and grocery retail stores and those selling Asian-imported manufactured goods. Korean immigrants find niches for these businesses in low-income minority neighborhoods from which corporate chain grocery and department stores have disinvested because of the residents' low spending capacity and the neighborhoods' high crime rates. Korean-owned businesses are highly visible in many African American/Afro-Caribbean neighborhoods in New York and Los Angeles, and this visibility provides the context for the intergroup conflicts that the next three chapters examine.

CHAPTER 5

Hostility toward Korean Merchants in Black Neighborhoods

Korean merchants in African American and Afro-Caribbean neighborhoods have encountered hostility and rejection in the form of boycotts,
arson, physical violence, looting, and attacks in the press. This chapter summarizes major instances of such hostility in New York and Los
Angeles from 1970 to 1994. The sections covering New York consider cases of hostility toward Korean merchants in non-Black as well
as Black neighborhoods in New York City; the sections covering Los
Angeles focus on South Central Los Angeles before the riots, as well as
examining how Korean merchants in Los Angeles were victimized during the three days of riots in 1992. This chapter relies largely on Korean
newspaper articles to provide descriptive information, but the information it supplies about patterns of hostility will be useful to analyzing
that hostility's causes in chapter 6.

NEW YORK: BLACK AREAS

The damages suffered during the 1992 riots in Los Angeles were the
greatest ever inflicted upon a Korean community because of their business-related conflicts with the Black community. Yet Koreans in New
York have experienced business-related conflicts with Blacks for far longer
than their counterparts in Los Angeles. By the time two long-term boycotts of Korean stores started in Los Angeles in 1991, the Korean community in New York had already experienced five such boycotts. This

section describes some of the major boycotts of Korean stores in Black
neighborhoods and the other expressions of hostility that Korean merchants in Black neighborhoods in New York City have experienced.

THE 1981 BOYCOTT IN JAMAICA, QUEENS

The first major Black boycott of a Korean store in New York City
occurred in Jamaica, Queens, at the end of June 1981 and lasted approximately five weeks (*KTNY*, July 30, August 4 and 6, 1981). It
started over an altercation between a Korean produce store employee
and an African American female customer charged with shoplifting, a
scenario repeated in future boycotts. The customer claimed that she
was injured by the employee when he reached into her shopping bag to
retrieve allegedly shoplifted merchandise. Sonny Carson, the Black ac-
tivist who was later responsible for organizing boycotts against Korean stores in Brooklyn in 1988 and 1990, was also responsible for this
boycott. According to my interview with a Korean merchant who operated a business in Jamaica at that time, Black demonstrators picketed
not only the Korean store involved in that particular altercation but
also another Korean store across the street. Initially, many African American residents in Jamaica joined the picket line. But as the boycott
stretched on, fewer residents participated. Later on, five or six so-called
professional boycotters maintained the line. The boycotters demanded
that the store owner fire the employee who "beat" the African American woman, that the Korean-owned stores in Jamaica lower their commodity prices, and that they hire more Black employees.

Initially, the Korean Association of New York and the Korean Produce Association of New York negotiated with boycott leaders in the
hopes of bringing the conflict to an end. Later, Korean merchants in Jamaica formed the Jamaica Korean Merchants Association to address the
boycott and to promote positive relationships with the Black neighborhoods in Jamaica. This association approached local police, Black political leaders, and boycott organizers. A Korean-Black friendship meeting in which nearly one hundred Black community leaders and Black
and White politicians participated brought an end to the boycott.

THE 1984–85 HARLEM BOYCOTT

Though anti-Korean posters were seen in Harlem as early as in 1982
(*KTNY*, June 29, 1982), the first major boycott of Korean stores oc-

curred in October 1984 at Ike Grocery (*KTNY*, October 31, December 13, 1984; *KCDNY*, February 16, 1985). The boycott began after the police arrested a African American male customer, who allegedly had beaten both the Korean store owner's wife and a White female police officer. The boycott was organized by the African Nationalist Pioneer Movement, which had also initiated the "Buy Black" movement. It eventually spread throughout Harlem, shutting all Korean stores in the area for six months. At first, the Harlem Korean Merchants Association intervened in an attempt to end the boycott. Later, the Korean Produce Association and the Korean Association of New York became involved in negotiations with boycott organizers, the Uptown Chamber of Commerce, New York City government officials, and federal government agencies. The boycott stopped in February 1985 when the Federal Bureau of Investigation intervened and after African American political leaders began criticizing boycott organizers.

Korean merchants in New York City's Black areas encountered three more long-term boycotts between 1988 and 1990—one in Harlem, another in the Bedford-Stuyvesant area of Brooklyn, and a third in the Flatbush section of Brooklyn. As in the previous two incidents, Korean produce retailers were the targets, and each boycott began after a similar scuffle between a Korean store owner or employee and a Black customer. The Harlem boycott, which started in September 1988 and lasted for more than a year, passed unnoticed even by the Korean media, since the owner of the boycotted store did not want the Korean community to intervene (*KCDNY*, April 10 and October 27, 1989; *SGT*, April 8, 1989). Yet the other two Brooklyn boycotts, described below, received national media attention.

THE 1988 BROOKLYN BOYCOTT

The boycott of Tropic Fruit Market, a produce store in the Bedford-Stuyvesant area, started at the end of August 1988 after a sixty-nine-year-old woman, Ivy King, and her daughter, both Guyanese natives, refused to allow the wife of the store owner to search their shopping bags where they had allegedly put three stolen dried fish (*KCDNY*, August 31, 1988). A fight ensued, as the two customers pushed her and the store employees tried to get the shopping bags. Ivy King claimed that they were punched and that the store owner, Woo Yang Chung, threatened them with a knife. Chung, however, claimed that the Black women had attacked his wife and were stealing merchandise. Sonny Carson

and other leaders of the December 12th Movement organized the boycott, widely distributing a pamphlet that described how the two Black
women were beaten severely by the Korean owner (*SGT*, September 9,
1988). During the first week, all Korean stores in the Bedford-Stuyvesant area were shut down by angry protesters. Leaders of the December
12th Movement also organized several peddlers, called "the People's
Farmers Market," to sell fruits and vegetables on weekends in front of
Korean produce stores in the Bedford-Stuyvesant area (*SGT*, December
2a, 1988).

Korean and Black negotiation teams trying to settle the conflict met
several times. At one point, the Black community negotiation team,
headed by state Assemblyman Albert Vann, made the following five demands: (1) that the Korean store owner publicly apologize to the Black
media for beating two Black elderly customers, (2) that the store owner
turn over the ownership of the store at issue to the Black community,
(3) that Korean merchants in Black neighborhoods use Black-owned
banks, (4) that the Korean community make its financial resources
available to Blacks for establishing businesses, and (5) that Korean merchants teach business skills to young unemployed Blacks (*SGT*, October
6, 1988).

On December 21, 1988, Koreans and Blacks signed an agreement to
stop the boycott that had stretched on for four months. In the pact,
Koreans promised that they would use a Black-owned bank (the Free-
dom National Bank), share their entrepreneurial skills with Black residents, donate money to community organizations, and trade with Black
businesses (F. Lee 1988). Though eleven Korean store owners in the
Bedford-Stuyvesant area opened their business accounts with the Free-
dom National Bank immediately after the accord (*SGT*, December 29,
1988), the agreement to share entrepreneurial skills with Blacks was
never implemented. Sung Soo Kim, director of the Korean Small Business Service Center, who represented the Korean negotiating team, and
an African American assemblyman, Albert Vann, were the architects of
this agreement. After the accord, Kim was criticized by many Korean
merchants for having made too many concessions. On the other hand,
Sonny Carson and other boycott organizers were critical of Vann's
effort to negotiate such agreements with Korean merchants (Jamison
1988; F. Lee 1988). As will be discussed in detail in chapter 6, the African American boycott leaders believed that the basic issue was who
should control businesses in Black neighborhoods, not whether Korean
merchants should help Black neighborhoods economically.

Though the boycott ended in December 1988, the People's Farmers Market continued to stay open on weekends in the Bedford-Stuyvesant area. Tropic Fruit Market, the target of the boycott, never recovered from its radical drop in sales, even after the boycott was over. Chung, unable to pay his rent, eventually closed his store, and as of July 1992, he was driving a taxicab to support his family. Four other Korean-owned stores in the Bedford-Stuyvesant area also closed in 1989 because of their financial difficulties (*SGT*, August 26, 1989). Black peddlers, organized in the name of the People's Farmers, caused enduring problems for Korean produce retail stores in Brooklyn and Harlem.

THE 1990–91 BROOKLYN BOYCOTT

The longest and most agonizing Black boycott of Korean stores in New York City occurred in the Church Avenue–Fulton Street area in Brooklyn. It started in January 1990 after a scuffle between Giselaine Fetissante, a forty-eight-year-old Haitian immigrant, who paid only two dollars for a three-dollar item, and Bong Ok Jang, the Korean manager of the Family Red Apple, who allegedly beat the customer. The Korean manager told the police that the Haitian woman intentionally fell down on the floor. When residents saw the Haitian woman being carried out of the store on a stretcher, they quickly gathered in front of the store and began picketing. A few days later, boycotters picketed Church Fruits, Inc., another Korean store across the street. The owner of the Church Fruits had hidden in his store a Korean employee who was being pursued by angry Black customers on the day of the altercation. The employee had missed a van that would have given him a safe ride home.

Immigrants from Haiti and other Caribbean islands constitute the majority of Black residents in the Church Avenue–Fulton Street area. At the beginning of the boycott, many participated in the rally because they had heard a rumor that the Haitian woman had died from the beating. In its first week, approximately 150 Blacks, many of whom were not local residents, participated in the rally that led to the closure of many Korean stores in the Church Avenue–Flatbush area. The Haitian Economic Development Association, a local Black community organization, originally organized the boycott (*SGT*, February 8, 1990). Later, Sonny Carson, president of the December 12th Movement, made it long-term by guaranteeing that a dozen demonstrators were on duty almost every day (*SGT,* January 30, 1990). During the first two or three months, a few police officers were stationed in front of every store in the area because of the threat of racial violence. All Korean-owned stores in the area suffered a significant reduction in sales during most of the boycott.

The Brooklyn borough president, the New York City government, the Federal Bureau of Investigation, and the Department of Justice (the Community Relations Bureau) intervened in the Church Avenue–Fulton Street area boycott. The boycott also led to court battles between boycott leaders and the Korean store owners, who were supported by the Korean community. Jang, the brother of the owner, was charged with third-degree assault for beating the Haitian woman. A Brooklyn judge reinstated a restraining order requiring that boycotters stay fifty feet away from the stores being picketed, but the police did not enforce it. New York City Mayor David Dinkins was severely criticized by the mainstream media, politicians, and White citizens for not taking any effective action to bring an end to the boycott.[1]

On September 21, 1990, after a large demonstration mounted by Koreans in front of City Hall, Mayor Dinkins made a symbolic visit to the boycotted stores and purchased some fruits (Purdum 1990). In January 1991, Bong Ok Jang, the store manager who had been accused of severely beating the Haitian woman and who also had been charged with a third-degree assault, was declared innocent by a Brooklyn grand jury (*SGT,* February 1, 1991). The grand jury's decision greatly weakened the efforts of Sonny Carson and others; after it, few Black residents participated in the boycott. The boycott ended in May 1991, after Bong Jae Jang sold his business to another Korean. The Department of Justice helped him get a $500,000 Small Business Administration loan to open a business in a White area (*SGT,* March 16, 1991).

RACIAL VIOLENCE AGAINST KOREAN MERCHANTS

In the latter half of 1990 when the Church Avenue–Fulton Street boycott drew national media attention, many Korean stores in Brooklyn and Manhattan and their owners became targets of racial violence, threats, and verbal attacks by Blacks. On February 1, 1990, two weeks after the boycott had begun, Eun Ha Park, the wife of the owner of one of the two boycotted stores, was beaten inside her own store by a picketer (*SGT,* May 24, 1990). She was pregnant at that time, and because of her injuries she had to have an abortion. On May 13, 1990, a Vietnamese young man who lived three blocks away from the Church Avenue–Flatbush Street boycott site was mistaken for a Korean and severely beaten by about ten Black youths (*KCDNY*, May 16, 1990).

On August 4, 1990, a Korean produce store owner in Brooklyn, He Jin Lee, was robbed of his day's sales ($2,600) and beaten by about thirty Blacks after he had an argument with a Black girl, who he claimed ate cherries without paying (*KCDNY*, August 8, 1990). Two days later, a shot was fired into his store and one of his employees (a Mexican) was beaten by Black youths. The produce store, R & N Fruits, was transferred to another Korean in mid-August. The new owner received a warning from Sonny Carson that his store would be boycotted, and about forty Blacks picketed the store in late August, which forced the store to close for several days (*KCDNY*, August 28, 1990).

On August 21, 1990, Bong Jae Jang, the owner of the store that was the main target of the boycott, was spat upon inside his store by a picketer. On his way home from the store, he was also beaten up by about twenty young Blacks (*SGT*, August 23, 1990). In addition, several other Korean store owners in Brooklyn and Manhattan were either physically or verbally attacked inside their stores by Blacks during the summer of 1990.

ARSON

Hostility toward Korean merchants in Black neighborhoods has also taken the form of arson. In New York as in other cities, several Korean-owned stores in Black neighborhoods have been destroyed by arsonists. A recent victim, Tong Kwang Kim, opened his produce store in a Black neighborhood in Brooklyn in January 1990. He had had numerous conflicts with the residents until his store was burned to the ground in February 1992. After the fire, a pamphlet stating "We Won a Victory. Let Us Boycott All Korean Stores" was distributed in the neighborhood by young Black men. This suggests that arson was involved (*KTNY*, February 29, 1992).

Prior to the fire, Kim and his wife had an altercation with the Black owner of a neighboring store, were the target of a boycott, and were physically attacked by several masked men (Tabor 1992). The brutal attack came after the couple fired a Black employee whom they had hired to meet the demands of boycotters from the previous year; the employee was dismissed for allegedly helping one of his friends break into the store at night. The store owner's wife was severely injured during the attack, requiring twelve stitches on her head (*KCDNY,* December 13, 1991).

The Kims, like many other Korean small business owners, did not have fire insurance; thus, the accumulation of several years of hard work turned literally into ashes. Unable to afford their apartment rent, the Kims have lived separately since the fire. Ok Sun Kim works as a salad bar attendant in a Korean store in Queens and lives with two other Korean women, while her husband lives with a friend on Long Island. Though several Korean and Asian American organizations have helped the Kims by pushing city government officials and police to investigate, the case is still open. Korean business leaders have been reluctant to help the couple, because they fear that the publicity would only worsen tensions with the Black community.

NEW YORK: NON-BLACK AREAS

A MANHATTAN DELI

Though this chapter focuses on hostility toward Korean merchants in Black neighborhoods, it may be useful to consider similar incidents in non-Black neighborhoods in New York City. There has been only one minor attempt in the city to boycott a Korean store in a White neighborhood. In March 1984, Kyu-Sung Choi, a Korean immigrant, tried to remodel a closed flower shop at Park Avenue and 75th Street, in an overwhelmingly White residential neighborhood in midtown Manhattan, into a delicatessen that sold fruits and vegetables (Geist 1985). Some residents were opposed to the deli on the grounds that it would spoil the community's reputation as a upscale neighborhood. In order to block the opening of the store, residents picketed the building and influenced city officials to threaten Choi with a lawsuit, claiming that he was in violation of zoning codes and could not open a deli there.

Many neighborhood residents and several city politicians, however, supported the Korean merchant, as did the mainstream White media, including the New York Times. With the backing of the residents, some politicians, and the media, Choi finally succeeded in opening a food store in the predominantly White upper-middle-class area. In this episode, which attracted much media attention, White residents were rejecting not a Korean immigrant merchant but his food store, which they feared would ruin the quality of their exclusive residential neighborhood.

KOREAN-LANGUAGE COMMERCIAL SIGNS

Hundreds of Korean stores serving exclusively Korean customers are located in the Flushing, Woodside, and Elmhurst neighborhoods in Queens, where many Korean immigrants live. Almost all of these stores write their primary business signs in Korean. Though most also have English language signs, these are usually too small to read. Of course, Korean immigrants are not alone in using "foreign language" signs. Chinese and Hispanic immigrants in Flushing and other parts of Queens also rely on signage in their native languages. This exclusive use of foreign languages for commercial signs has been the subject of complaints and criticisms by White residents. Some in Flushing and other Queens neighborhoods, particularly many White elderly women, have complained that these signs confuse them because they do not know whether they are at a store or a "whorehouse" (SGT, November 3, 1990). They have pointed out that using only foreign language signs is bad for business, since English signs might attract American customers.[2]

The White residents' frequent complaints about Chinese and Korean language signs in Flushing led the Networks of Intergroup Harmony, a Flushing-based nonprofit organization created to improve intergroup harmony, to get involved. In March 1989, they advised Flushing's Chinese and Korean merchants associations to take measures to begin using English signs (KCDNY, April 14, 1989). In April 1989, anti-Korean sentiment among the residents of Woodside and Sunnyside was expressed in a local English newspaper, the Sunnyside News: Koreans' exclusive use of Korean language signs was cited as one of the major complaints (KCDNY, April 12, 1989).[3]

Julia Harrison, a longtime city councilwoman representing the Flushing–College Point area, made a political issue out of the use of foreign language signs. Her office is located at Union Street and 40th Avenue, where there is a heavy concentration of Korean stores with Korean language signs. Responding to White residents' complaints, in 1990 Harrison proposed a bill requiring all stores to have English signs (KCDNY, November 3, 1990; SGT, November 3, 1990). Hearings on this issue were held at City Hall and at Community Board No. 7. The proposed bill was severely criticized by Korean and Chinese representatives. Arguing on behalf of Korean merchants in the Flushing area, Sung Soo Kim, director of the Korean Small Business Service Center, said that Korean and other immigrant merchants should be persuaded through informal discussions to adopt English signs rather than being compelled to do so by a law. The bill did not win support in the local media and was eventually dropped.

THE WASHINGTON HEIGHTS RIOTS

North of Harlem in Manhattan and throughout all of the Bronx, Hispanics constitute a large proportion of the population. Most Hispanic residents in the area are Puerto Ricans or recent immigrants from South and Central American countries. Particularly along Broadway north of 125th Street, a large number of Korean-owned stores sell general merchandise, clothing, fruits and vegetables, and fast food, mainly to Hispanic customers.

On July 6, 1992, the shooting death of an immigrant boy from the Dominican Republic by a White police officer ignited a race riot in the Washington Heights area. Thousands of Hispanic youngsters participated in the riot, which lasted two days, injured twenty-eight people, and caused one death (SGT, Jul y 9, 1992). Three buildings were burned, and rioters destroyed and looted many stores. Three Korean stores in Washington Heights were targets; the owners were not compensated for their losses by any government agencies, but the Minority Business Development Agency, under the Department of Commerce, helped them to get large Small Business Administration loans to reestablish their businesses (KCDNY, July 18, 1992; SGT, August 15, 1992). One American citizen who did not disclose his or her name contributed $25,000 through the mayor's office to Hwa-Eun Hong, a Korean victim of the Washington Heights riot, to rebuild her store (KCDNY, August 10, 1992).

SOUTH CENTRAL LOS ANGELES

In the 1980s, the Korean community in Los Angeles had a better relationship with African Americans than did the one in New York. Though several small-scale conflicts were reported between Korean merchants and African American customers, the store owners in Black neighborhoods were not systematically targeted. As the number of Korean-

owned stores in African American neighborhoods dramatically increased, however, Korean–African American tensions escalated.

THE MEDIA IN THE 1980s

As the number of Korean-owned stores increased in South Central
Los Angeles in the mid-1980s, tensions mounted between Koreans and
African Americans; the Black media led the attack against the city's
Korean merchants. Two major Black dailies in Los Angeles, the *Los Angeles Sentinel* and *Money Talks News,* carried several articles and edi-
torials in the early 1980s that criticized Korean merchants for economically exploiting African Americans. In August 1983, the *Los Angeles
Sentinel* published a series of articles attacking Korean and Asian merchants under the title "Black Agenda." For example, in an editorial of
August 25, 1983, James Creaver, the executive editor, argued (Creaver
1983):

> There is no question that there has been a substantial increase of Asian
> businesses in the Black community over the past decade. There can also be
> no question that some of the businesses, while not all, have been abusive and
> even condescending to the Black community.
> But this does not have to be. This is something we can attack and change
> almost as fast as the twinkling of an eye.
> First of all, it becomes necessary that we accept some facts, although they
> may not be palatable to all of this community. One of those facts is that we
> make the determination as to whether these businesses stay in our commu-
> nity or are forced to look elsewhere for their livelihood.

Though the Black media initially referred to "Asian merchants" (probably because they could not distinguish between Koreans and other
Asians), they later specifically named them as Korean. Many of the articles that were published reflected the complaints of African American
residents against Korean merchants, but they also reflected a bias particular to these newspapers.

Korean–African American relations in Los Angeles, nevertheless,
were not yet as bad as those in New York. Four major, long-term Black
boycotts against Korean stores took place in New York City in the
1980s; in Los Angeles, there were only a few short-term boycotts, last-
ing a matter of days. Three major factors may explain why the Korean
community in Los Angeles maintained better relations with the Black
community than their counterpart in New York. First, Black national-

ists, who usually were responsible for organizing boycotts against Korean businesses, did not wield as much influence in Los Angeles as they did in New York. Second, the mayor of Los Angeles during most of the 1980s was Tom Bradley, a Black politician, who was able to influence African American leaders and moderate Korean–African American conflicts; by contrast, New York's Jewish mayor, Ed Koch, lacked any influence with Black leaders. Third, the Black-Korean Coalition, established in 1986 (see chapter 7), helped to mediate Korean–African American conflicts in Los Angeles. This biracial coalition served as a channel of communication between Korean and African American communities at times of racial tension. No similar interracial organization existed in New York City.

SOUTH CENTRAL LOS ANGELES IN 1990

While the national media was focusing on the boycott of two Korean stores in Brooklyn in the summer of 1990, many incidents that reflected hostility toward Korean merchants were reported locally in Los Angeles. For example, a Korean man was beaten and shot by two Black youths in an African American neighborhood in South Central Los Angeles on July 17, 1990. The police classified the incident as an anti-Korean hate crime, because the attackers did not rob the victim but taunted him as a "Yellow Monkey" (*SGT*, June 19, 1990). The same summer, several Korean swap meet owners in this area were attacked by Black gang members in their stores (*SGT*, August 16, 1990). In addition, anti-Korean pamphlets calling for the eradication of Korean merchants from the Black community were widely distributed (*SGT*, August 18, 1990). In late 1990 and early 1991, two Korean stores in South Central Los Angeles were destroyed by arson. The police agreed with the owners that Black gangs were responsible (*SGT*, January 31, 1991).

THE FATAL SHOOTING OF LATASHA HARLINS

Two events at two separate Korean stores in South Central Los Angeles escalated racial tensions between Korean and African American communities in 1991. On March 16, 1991, a fifteen-year-old Black girl, Latasha Harlins, was shot to death by a Korean store owner, Soon Ja Du, while struggling over an unpaid bottle of orange juice. Du claimed that she grabbed the gun only after the girl punched her four times and knocked her to the ground twice. Before the fatal shooting, Black gang members had terrorized the Du family for several months with shoplifting, vandalism, and physical violence.

The morning following the incident, a meeting was held by representatives of the Black-Korean Coalition, the Los Angeles chapter of the NAACP, the Los Angeles Mayor's Office, the Los Angeles County Human Relations Committee, the Korean Chamber of Commerce, the Korean-American Grocers Association, and other civil rights organizations; the group eventually issued a statement, emphasizing that the shooting was not racially motivated and asking people to remain rational (*KTLA*, March 20, 1991). Nonetheless, the incident immediately increased tensions. The Empire Liquor Market, the store where Latasha Harlins was shot, was closed at once. Yet, two days later, about 150 African Americans picketed in front of the store. The demonstration was organized by Danny Bakewell, president of the Brotherhood Crusade, a Black nationalist organization, and the Reverend Edgar Boyd, pastor of the Bethel African Methodist Episcopal Church, which was located in the same neighborhood as the Empire Liquor Market.

A week later, leaders of the Brotherhood Crusade announced that they would identify Korean grocery and liquor stores in South Central Los Angeles whose owners and employees were rude to customers, including the Empire Liquor Market, and assume their operation (*KTLA*, March 28, 1991). Following the shooting, several area Korean merchants became targets of verbal and physical assaults by African American residents (*KTLA*, March 22 and 30, 1991). In one case, a male customer slapped a female store owner in the face and said, "Go back to Korea" (*KTLA*, April 11b, 1991).

As in the later Rodney King case, the court decision angered the African American community more than the incident itself. Du, after being convicted of voluntary manslaughter (second-degree murder), was sentenced to five years of probation by Los Angeles Superior Court Judge Joyce Karlin (*KTLA*, November 17, 1991). This action of a White judge gave African Americans the impression that Koreans were being protected by a White institution, and activists and demonstrators strongly protested. Led by Bakewell, African Americans picketed outside the criminal court building for several days following the decision, asking for the resignation of Judge Karlin (*KTLA*, November 23, 1991). The demonstrators also threatened to boycott all Korean stores in South Central Los Angeles to protest the "unfair" court decision.

Charles Lloyd, the African American defense attorney who successfully defended Du, also received many threats from his co-ethnics.
Later, the Los Angeles County Bar Association's Criminal Section
named Lloyd their trial lawyer of the year (S. Kim 1992b; *SGT,* April
28a, 1992). After the Los Angeles race riots, Du paid $300,000 to the
parents of the victim as an out-of-court settlement in a civil suit filed
against her (*SGT,* July 11, 1992). The insurance company that insured
her grocery store (Allstate) reportedly covered the entire amount.

Five months later, a jury found innocent the four White police officers accused of beating an African American motorist, Rodney King,
sparking the riots in Los Angeles. African American rioters easily
equated the Rodney King case and the shooting of Harlins, especially
since the media recalled and recapitulated both throughout the riots.
Thus, it was not mere coincidence that Korean stores were targeted selectively. The Los Angeles Riot Special Investigation Committee held
a hearing at a high school in South Central Los Angeles in September 1992. Most African American participants in the hearing cited Du's
"unfair" sentence as a reason for targeting Korean merchants during
the riots, as well as blaming it for contributing to the overall animosity
of African Americans toward Korean merchants (*SGT,* September 12,
1992).

Large numbers of Koreans from Los Angeles, other American cities,
and even Korea had submitted letters of petition to Judge Karlin, asking
for a light sentence for Soon Ja Du (*KTLA,* October 26, 1991). When
the news of Du's five-year probation was released, many Koreans considered it a victory for their community. Probably none of them suspected that a court decision favoring a Korean defendant would contribute to the victimization of Korean stores in riots five months later.
Judge Karlin may have given Du a lenient sentence partly to promote
racial harmony (*KTLA,* November 17, 1991), not suspecting that it
would make African Americans more antagonistic to Koreans.

A ROBBER'S DEATH AND A BOYCOTT

Korean–African American relations were worsened by another unfortu-
nate incident in a Korean store in South Central Los Angeles in the summer of 1991. On June 4, 1991, a Korean liquor store owner shot and
killed an African American robber. The robber had beaten the wife of
the owner; though he had no gun, he then threatened to shoot her. Prose-

cutors ruled that the shooting was justified as an act of self-defense. The decision caused African Americans to picket and boycott John's Liquor Store for three and a half months (*SGT,* June 26, 1991). The boycott organizers, Danny Bakewell and the Reverend Edgar Boyd, announced that they would continue picketing until the store was shut down.

Korean community and business leaders maintained that the store should not be closed, arguing that the death of one African American shot committing a holdup was insignificant compared to the large number of Korean merchants murdered by Black robbers. They decided to create a fund to support the store owner should the protest turn into a long-term boycott, such as the one the year before in New York. The boycott prompted a group of young Koreans to organize Korean American Racial Equality, an organization that sought to improve Korean–African American relations and to serve as a voice for the Korean community. Many Koreans in Los Angeles and other cities participated in fund-raising campaigns to support the "victim of the Black boycott," and nearly $50,000 was raised in the first three months.

When Black boycott leaders learned about the Korean community's financial support of the targeted store owner, they took the community's reaction as a collective challenge. Boycott leaders threatened to boycott all Korean stores in the area. In the middle of August 1991, demonstrators launched a boycott against two other Korean stores that were close to the John's Liquor Store (*KTLA,* August 17, 1991). Korean–African American tensions in Los Angeles reached a fevered pitch on August 17 when fire bombs partially destroyed John's Liquor Store and Empire Liquor Market (*KTLA,* August 19, 1991). Later, the association of Los Angeles County African American government employees announced that it supported Danny Bakewell and the boycott of the Korean liquor store that he had organized (*KTLA,* September 27, 1991).[4]

The newly created Korean American Racial Equality played a central role in resolving the boycott. It collected money donated by Korean individuals and groups to help the owner of the boycotted store. Members of KARE were generally young, American-educated 1.5-generation Koreans—those who were born in Korea but who immigrated to the United States at early ages. Their viewpoint on racial issues was more liberal than that of Korean immigrant merchants. KARE members concluded that further financial support of John's Liquor Store by the Korean community would only harm relations with African Americans. Thus, the organization decided to stop supporting the store as of September 30 and let it be shut down (*KTLA*, September 13, 1991). However, first-generation Korean merchants were very critical of the decision to stop supporting the store. In the face of these strong objections, KARE members later abolished the organization, stating that "we cannot work with first-generation Koreans" (*SGT*, October 11, 1991). This episode reflects a generational clash in the Los Angeles Korean community about how to respond to Korean–African American conflicts.

Mayor Bradley meanwhile sought to end the boycott by meeting personally with the boycott leaders. After a series of behind-the-scene talks, Bradley's aides helped African American and Korean leaders reach an agreement in early October. The agreement provided (1) that the boycott would be suspended for a certain period of time during which the store would be closed and put up for sale, initially to African American buyers and after thirty days to anyone; (2) that the sale of the store would not include the sale of the liquor license; (3) that African Americans and Koreans would work to establish a dispute resolution center to negotiate disagreements before boycotts erupt; and (4) that the two sides would draft a code of ethics for merchants (Clifford and Stolberg 1991; *KTLA*, October 6, 1991). Many Korean business leaders considered the agreement to be a capitulation to the boycott organizers (*KTLA*, October 6, 1991). They argued that a Korean merchant should not have to give up his store to the African American community because he shot a robber in self-defense, especially when so many Korean merchants had been murdered by Black robbers. Yang Il Kim, president of the Korean-American Grocers' Association of Southern California who signed the agreement, was severely criticized by Korean community leaders for giving up too much to the Black community and getting nothing back (*KTLA*, October 6, 1991).

In early October 1991, an African American church in the neighborhood where John's Liquor Store was located purchased the liquor store for a small amount of money. The store owner, Tae Sam Park, was forced to give up his business, losing his investment of $200,000. He later started another business with a Korean partner, but failed again. After witnessing many other Korean stores in South Central Los Angeles destroyed during the riots, Park decided to return to Korea. In March 1993, at age fifty, he gave up his "American dream" and permanently returned to Korea (*KTLA*, March 14, 1993). In his farewell to his friends at the airport, he said, "I am relieved because I feel as if I am leaving a war zone" (M. Cho 1993).

OTHER INCIDENTS PRIOR TO THE 1992 RIOTS

Even after the boycott of John's Liquor Store ended on October 4, 1991, several incidents that demonstrated hostility toward Koreans occurred in South Central Los Angeles. On October 19, a nine-year-old Korean girl was shot by a Black robber and critically wounded at a Shell gas station mini-market (S. Kim 1991). Because the shooting occurred after the robber had taken $3,000 from the cash register, it was considered unnecessary to the crime and therefore racially motivated. Many African American leaders in Los Angeles, including Danny Bakewell, expressed their outrage at the shooting.

At the end of the month, a Black rap singer, Ice Cube, released an album called *Death Certificate*. The album included a song entitled "Black Korea," which expressed the contempt of African Americans toward Korean merchants. The content of the song and Koreans' responses to it will be discussed in detail in chapter 8. In addition, on November 26, a firebomb exploded in a Korean liquor store in South Central Los Angeles (*SGT*, September 29, 1991). On December 4, a Japanese American woman, apparently mistaken for a Korean, was forced out of her car and beaten with a baseball bat by two African American youths (*KTLA*, December 20, 1991).[5] On December 15, young African Americans smashed the windows of nine cars parked at a Korean Catholic Church in San Diego while the car owners were attending a service inside (*KTLA*, December 18, 1991). Such manifestations of anger against Koreans seemed to be connected with the sentencing of Soon Ja Du, which was seen by many African Americans as unfair, biased, and too lenient for the shooting of an unarmed girl.

In the middle of December 1991, the Brotherhood Crusade organized another boycott of a Korean store in South Central Los Angeles, Don's Market (*KTLA*, December 12, 1991). It began in response to an altercation between a Korean grocery store owner and a thirteen-year-old Black girl who was allegedly running away without paying for some candy. After the girl told police that the store owner severely beat her, he was arrested and charged with assault and battery. However, he denied the accusation, claiming that he was simply trying to stop her from running away with stolen merchandise. Korean community leaders were angry that a television station that reported this story interviewed only the girl, not the store owner as well. The boycott came to an end on the seventh day, after the store owner, as requested by the boycott organizers, sent a letter of apology to the girl's parents (*KTLA*, December 21, 1991).

VICTIMIZATION IN THE 1992 RIOTS

DESTRUCTION OF KOREAN STORES

The most violent expression of African Americans' hostility toward Korean merchants took place during the Los Angeles riots in April 1992. During the three days of rioting, some 2,300 Korean-owned stores in South Central Los Angeles and Koreatown were looted, burned, or both, one Korean was killed; and forty-six Koreans were injured (*KTLA*, May 23, 1992). Korean merchants in Los Angeles sustained approximately $350 million in property damage, 45% of all such damages incurred from the riots (*KTLA*, May 23, 1992). Koreans constituted only 1.6% of the population in Los Angeles County at that time; thus, the losses of the Korean community were far out of proportion to their numbers.

South Central Los Angeles has long been known as a predominantly African American residential area. However, the influx of Mexican and South American immigrants in recent years has markedly altered the ethnic composition of the population. The 1990 census revealed that Hispanics constituted 46% of the residents of South Central Los Angeles whereas African Americans made up only 25% (Navarro 1993). The majority of Koreatown residents are also Hispanic. Post-riot studies have indicated that many Hispanics participated in the violence, as well as fell victim to it. While 51% of those arrested in connection with the riots were Hispanic, 30% of those who died during the riots were also Hispanic (Navarro 1993). Based on these figures, some might argue that the destruction of Korean stores during the riots did not necessarily reflect African Americans' hostility toward Korean merchants. Instead, they might point to the disproportionately large number of Korean stores located in those neighborhoods in South Central Los Angeles where the destruction was the most severe.

Evidence exists, however, that African American rioters selectively targeted Korean-owned stores. Though Koreatown is about four miles away from South Central Los Angeles, rioters attacked 340 stores there (*KTLA*, July 28, 1992). According to an investigation by the FBI, Black gangs, who were responsible for planning the Los Angeles riots, deliberately chose to loot and burn Korean-owned stores (*KTLA,* June 11a, 1992). Given the FBI's traditional suspicion of Black gangs, we should weigh this claim carefully; however, other pieces of evidence strongly suggest such targeting took place. The Anti-Violence Coalition, a Los Angeles–based civil rights organization, monitored programs by KPFK, a radical "listener-supported" radio station in Los Angeles. The coalition reported that the station's announcers urged African Americans to push Korean merchants out of African American neighborhoods and encouraged them to target Korean-owned stores once the riots began (*KTLA,* June 22, 1992). Also, as noted in the previous section, many African Americans attending the hearing held in Los Angeles after the riots indicated that the "unfair" sentence of Soon Ja Du for shooting a Black girl contributed to the *targeting of Korean merchants in the riots.*

Furthermore, African Americans and Hispanics appear to have had different motives for participating in the riots. In South Central Los Angeles, which has the highest percentage of African American residents, Korean stores were more likely to be damaged by arson; a higher percentage of Korean stores in other areas were simply looted (Ong and Hee 1993). Light and his associates (1994) pointed out that this difference was closely related to the difference in motives between African American and Hispanic participants in the riot. While looters basically wish to acquire merchandise, arsonists are motivated by hatred and revenge. Thus, the destruction of Korean stores in South Central Los Angeles during the 1992 riots was partly a reflection of African American residents' longer-standing hostility toward Korean merchants.

CONTROVERSY OVER LIQUOR STORES

Large corporations usually have insurance to cover damages caused by riots and other disasters. However, the majority of Korean small businesses lack such insurance. A post-riot survey conducted by the Korean American Inter-Agency Council showed that only 33% of the Korean stores destroyed during the riots had fire insurance; moreover, the majority of owners with fire insurance received no settlement from their insurance companies (*KTLA,* March 9, 1993). The government supplied minimal financial support for the reconstruction of destroyed businesses, and indeed an ordinance passed by the Los Angeles City Council after the riots actively discouraged the reopening of destroyed liquor stores. As a result, only 28% of the Korean stores destroyed during the riots were reestablished, as of March 1993 (*KTLA,* March 9, 1993).

More than 150 Korean liquor stores in South Central Los Angeles were burned during the riots, and only a very small number of these businesses have been reestablished. According to California state law, one liquor license can be issued for every 2,500 residents in the county. Thus, the law limits the number of liquor stores in each county in proportion to the population, but it does not regulate the location of any specific store. Therefore, once a license is obtained, its holder can open a liquor store in any section of the county. Accordingly, many more liquor stores have been established in South Central Los Angeles than in other areas—up to four times as many, according to one report (*KTLA,* January 9, 1993). After the riots, representatives of African American and Hispanic residents in the area argued that the overabundance of liquor stores encouraged crime; they demanded that those liquor stores destroyed during the riots should therefore be allowed to reopen only upon meeting certain conditions. They stipulated that the store should be approved by the residents at a public hearing,[6] the owner should hire two security guards to lower crime around the store, the store should close before sunset, and the store should have a parking lot for customers. With the strong support of African American residents and council members, the Los Angeles City Council voted to pass this regulation (*KTLA,* June 25, 1992).[7] Most Korean liquor store owners were unable to comply with these strict conditions, and thus few have reestablished stores that were destroyed. Korean community and business leaders agree that the presence of too many liquor stores may contribute to crime in African American neighborhoods in South Central Los Angeles, but they feel it very unfair that those who have paid highly for their businesses—bought largely from Jewish and African American owners—should be prevented from reopening their stores without compensation. Koreans suspect that African American council members who proposed this bill were strongly influenced by the lobby of large chain stores, such as Boys Market, that wished to push Korean merchants out of African American neighborhoods for their own business purposes.

INDIRECT COSTS

The destruction of Korean stores during the Los Angeles riots caused a devastating economic chain reaction in the local Korean community. Nearly 3,200 Korean-owned businesses were located in Los Angeles's Koreatown as of June 1992 (*KTLA*, June 11b, 1992), and the vast majority served Korean customers with distinctively Korean services — restaurants, groceries, and the like. Many of the restaurants and night clubs in Koreatown attracted large numbers of Koreans from all over the Los Angeles area as well as a significant number of tourists from Korea, particularly in the evenings. But after so many stores in the area were destroyed during the riots, many Koreans became reluctant to come to Koreatown, especially at night. The rise in crime, particularly in armed robberies, in recent years also made Koreans afraid to visit Koreatown (Kang 1993). In addition, the number of South Korean tourists has significantly dropped since the riots, for they no longer think of Los Angeles as a safe place to visit (Jameson 1992). Thus, after the riots the Koreatown economy has been very sluggish. Also, the destruction of various Korean businesses has harmed other Korean businesses, such as accounting firms, law firms, and the media, that depended on them.

The destruction of Korean stores caused psychological damage that cannot be quantified numerically. Many Koreans in Los Angeles saw their businesses, built on years of toils and tears, turn into ashes overnight. When they found their stores completely burned or empty, they became hysterical, and many victims continue to experience posttraumatic stress. The Asian and Pacific American Counseling and Prevention Center reported that for the first three and a half months after the riots, some 730 Korean riot victims visited to receive counseling and treatment (*SGT*, September 2, 1992). The victims suffered from symptoms such as insomnia, a sense of inactivity, loss of appetite, and muscle pains. A Korean Ph.D. student compared the mental health of Koreans in Los Angeles who were and were not riot victims. According to this anthropologist, riot victims showed a higher level of stress and had fewer mechanisms for coping with stress than the nonvictims (*KTLA*, April 11, 1993).

REPERCUSSIONS IN OTHER CITIES

Other cities also were affected by the Los Angeles riots, and Korean merchants in other cities were also victimized by African American gangs. Two Korean-owned supermarkets in Las Vegas were looted and set aflame by African American rioters on April 30, 1992 (D. Kim 1992). In New York City, government officials and police tried to prevent racial violence, but when approximately 2,000 African Americans demonstrated in Manhattan on the evening of April 30, some broke the windows of several Korean stores. Almost all Korean stores in New York City were closed for two or three days following the riots, and one of the Koreans who kept his store open on April 30 was shot by one of the demonstrators and paralyzed (*KTNY,* July 6, 1992). Overshadowed by countless Korean merchants victimized in Los Angeles, this New York City victim did not receive much attention even from the Korean media.

In Atlanta, students at Atlanta University, one of the nation's major historically African American institutions, marched from campus into town and caused $300,000 worth of damage to two Korean-owned stores. The owner of one had to flee to the roof of his store to escape the angry students (P. Chung 1993). The repercussions of the Los Angeles riots came to Chicago even later. When the Chicago Bulls clinched the NBA championship on the evening of June 14, African American fans rioted in South Chicago. Approximately forty Korean stores were subjected to destruction, looting, and arson in this so-called Bulls Riot (*SGT,* June 16, 17, 1992).

Beginning in the early 1980s, Korean merchants in Black neighborhoods in New York City experienced multiple instances of boycotting, arson, and physical violence. In contrast, Korean merchants in non-Black neighborhoods in the city did not face such serious hostility. During this time, the Los Angeles Korean business community maintained better relations with African Americans.

However, in the summer of 1990, after the highly publicized Brooklyn boycott of two Korean stores, tensions began to rise in Los Angeles as well. Two separate incidents that occurred in Korean stores in South Central Los Angeles in 1991—the shooting deaths of a young African American girl and an African American robber by Korean store owners—worsened Korean–African American relations. These tensions exploded in the 1992 riots following the Rodney King verdict, during which approximately 2,300 Korean stores were partially or wholly destroyed. Koreans made up less than 2% of the population in Los Angeles County but absorbed more than 40% of the total riot damage. White-Black racial inequality in general and inner-city Black residents' economic problems in particular are fundamental causes of the 1992 riots, and many Korean stores became targets simply because a large number of them were located in South Central Los Angeles, where destruction was most severe. However, it is also true that Korean–African American tensions in Los Angeles markedly increased for the two years before the riots and that to some extent African American gangs selectively targeted Korean stores because of their racial animosity against Korean merchants.

CHAPTER 6

Sources of Hostility toward Korean Merchants

While the preceding chapter was primarily descriptive, this chapter provides a more systematic analysis of why hostility directed against Korean merchants in African American neighborhoods in New York and Los Angeles occurred. After first considering the results of my own survey of how Blacks and Whites in New York City view Koreans, I examine more closely several theoretically derived hypotheses outlined in chapter 2 that explain this hostility.

DEGREE OF REJECTION BY BLACK RESIDENTS

The media's treatment of Korean-Black conflicts generates the impression that the majority of Black residents reject Korean immigrants and, in particular, Korean merchants. It would be unwise, however, to base conclusions about Blacks' attitudes toward Koreans on particular boycotts or on information disseminated by the mass media. The most effective way to determine the extent to which Blacks reject Korean merchants is to conduct a survey; I have done this, and the results are detailed below.

Black and White respondents in predominantly Black neighborhoods in New York City were asked three questions reflecting Blacks' rejection of Korean merchants: (1) "Did you support the 1990–91 Brooklyn boycott?"; (2) "Do you agree that Blacks should not buy from Korean stores?"; and (3) "Do you agree that New York City would be better

TABLE 9.

BLACK AND WHITE RESIDENTS WHO ACCEPTED
STATEMENTS REJECTING KOREAN MERCHANTS,
BY RACE AND EDUCATION

	N	%	Significance
I supported the 1990–91 boycott.			
Black respondents	25/94	26.6	$p < 0.01$
White respondents	4/49	8.2	
Noncollege vs. college graduates for Black respondents			
noncollege	14/62	22.6	$p > 0.1$
college	10/29	34.5	
Blacks should not buy from Korean stores.			
Black respondents	14/97	14.4	$p < 0.005$
White respondents	0/50	0.0	
Noncollege vs. college Graduates for Black respondents			
noncollege	8/65	12.3	$p > 0.1$
college	5/29	17.2	
New York City would be better off without so many Korean immigrants.			
black respondents	21/96	21.9	$p > 0.1$
white respondents	9/50	18.0	
Noncollege vs. college graduates for Black respondents			
noncollege	19/65	29.2	$p < 0.05$
college	2/28	7.1	

Source: The 1992 New York City survey of Black and White residents.

off without so many Koreans?" Many people believe that the fifteen-month boycott of two Korean merchants in Brooklyn marked Blacks' rejection of Korean merchants more generally, and so it was taken here. As shown in table 9, 27% of Black respondents supported the 1990–91 boycott compared to only 8% of White respondents. The results of our survey are very similar to those of the CBS-*Newsday* poll taken in May 1990 during the boycott: 27% of Black respondents and 6% of White respondents supported it (Hartocollis 1990). Though supporters of the boycott were far more likely to be Black than White, we should note that scarcely more than one-fourth of all Black respondents supported it.

To assess more systematically the extent to which Blacks reject Korean merchants, the survey posed two other questions: their responses to these also indicate that only a small proportion of Blacks are hostile. Just 14% of Black respondents agreed that "Blacks should not buy from Korean merchants," and only 22% endorsed the statement that "New York City would be better off without so many Korean immigrants."

The results of the survey indicate that the rejection of Korean merchants is not widespread among Blacks. As will be shown later in this chapter, every Black boycott of a Korean store in New York City was organized by a small number of Black activists and supported by only a very small fraction of Black residents. The mass media—Black, Korean, and mainstream—have sensationalized conflicts between Koreans and Blacks to such a degree that the general public seems to believe that most Blacks are anti-Korean. However, my survey results show that this is a misperception. Indeed, several Black respondents stated that the mass media had exaggerated Korean–African American conflicts.

We should not be at all surprised at the small proportion of Black respondents who supported the 1990 boycott, when we consider the actions of many Blacks in New York City. During long-term boycotts against Korean stores in Harlem and Brooklyn, many Black residents dared to cross picket lines of angry protesters and to shop inside. Numerous clashes between Black picketers and Black shoppers, including physical confrontations, were reported, yet incidents documenting the goodwill of some Blacks were ignored. On May 11, 1990, Bong Jae Jang, the owner of one of the two boycotted stores in Brooklyn, received a letter from an anonymous Black resident containing a one-hundred-dollar bill and asking him not to give up his store (*KCDNY*, September 25, 1990). The same month, Fred McCray, an African American teacher at Erasmus Hill High School, led 450 Black students to shop inside the two boycotted stores (*KCDNY*, May 25 and 30, 1990). McCray and his students also held a peace rally at Prospect Park in Brooklyn, calling for an end to the boycott. Though the *New York Post* and *New York Daily News* praised the teacher for his courage, the *Amsterdam News* and Black nationalists severely criticized him for betraying the Black community. It was reported that he could not sleep at night because of the barrage of hostile phone calls. McCray later lost his job as well as his wife, who divorced him. In June 1992, the Korean Produce Association of New York donated $4,300 to the unemployed teacher in appreciation of the courage he had shown during the Brooklyn boycott (*SGT*, June 8a, 1992).

A survey of Blacks in Los Angeles showed that middle-class Blacks in Inglewood were more likely than lower-class Blacks in South Central Los Angeles to have negative feelings toward Asians (Chang 1990). To determine if the rejection of Korean merchants was influenced by class, we cross-tabulated three independent variables by the education level of the respondent, used here as an indicator of social class. A greater proportion of Black respondents who had graduated from college (34.5%) supported the 1990–91 boycott than those who had not (26.8%). Likewise, a larger proportion of college-educated Black respondents agreed that "Blacks should not buy from Korean stores," though in both cases the differential was statistically insignificant. A larger sample might show that the two subgroups differ significantly in their degree of support for the boycott of Korean stores and the "Buy Black" movement. These findings can be interpreted meaningfully. Support among college-educated Blacks is higher because they are more politically oriented, more conscious of what is regarded as the exploitative nature of Korean business practices in Black neighborhoods, or both.

Table 9 also shows that a substantially smaller proportion of White respondents (8%) than Black respondents (27%) supported the 1990 Brooklyn boycott. Responses to an open-ended question concerning the sources of conflicts between Koreans and African Americans also indicated that White and Black respondents held basically different views. White residents in New York City were far more sympathetic to Korean merchants than to Black boycotters, as evidenced by the strong support they gave to Korean merchants during the 1990–91 boycott. Many White residents from all over the New York metropolitan area made a point of visiting and shopping at the two boycotted Korean stores. One White, Jewish resident sent a letter to then-President George Bush, asking him to take immediate action to end the boycott. Dorothy Walker, a White woman, volunteered to work for the Family Red Apple while it was being boycotted. She was one of the twenty Americans who received awards of appreciation from the Korean Association of New York in 1992 (*SGT,* November 27a, 1992).

THE "SCAPEGOATING" OF KOREAN MERCHANTS

The key task of this chapter is to explain the reasons for Korean–African American conflict, particularly the hostility Korean merchants have encountered in Black neighborhoods. It is a very complicated issue that cannot be fully explained by survey data alone. Thus, I will draw upon newspaper articles, other secondary sources, propositions derived from various theories and survey data, as well as my own observations to explain why Korean merchants have faced hostility in Black neighborhoods. In chapter 2, we reviewed several theories that are useful for this purpose. Let us examine each of the hypotheses derived from the theoretical discussions.

The middleman minority and scapegoating hypothesis suggests that inner-city Blacks, who are frustrated at being unable to improve their economic condition, vent their frustrations and aggression on their nearest, most convenient targets: that is, on local Korean merchants. To evaluate this hypothesis, we first need to consider the historical context. Korean immigrants first established such businesses in African American/Afro-Caribbean neighborhoods in the late 1970s when the economic conditions of inner-city residents were deteriorating. Many indicators, including poverty and unemployment rates, show that after improving substantially in the early 1970s, the economic status of Blacks became increasingly worse (Hacker 1992; W. Wilson 1987). As the spending capacity of inner-city Blacks decreased in the late 1970s and early 1980s, chain stores—grocery and department stores in particular—moved out of low-income minority neighborhoods (Bonacich 1980; Min 1988a). Some White independent store owners also left (I. Kim 1981, 110–11). Korean immigrants rapidly moved to fill the void created by the departure of corporate chains and White-owned small businesses. Given the overlap between the deterioration of economic conditions in inner-city neighborhoods and the Korean merchants' quick entry into these communities, it is easy to understand why Black residents might blame Korean immigrants for their economic problems.

Though the scapegoating hypothesis is logically plausible, it is difficult to find concrete evidence to support it. Black boycott leaders and boycott participants, whatever their motives might be, do not admit to boycotting Korean stores out of their own economic frustrations. Thus, this hypothesis may not be tested by survey data. However, results from a survey of Black and White residents in predominantly Black neighborhoods in New York City do suggest that the scapegoating hypothesis is consistent with the commonsense view of the general public. When asked to identify the major sources of Korean-Black conflicts, 41% of White respondents and 13% of Black respondents indicated that the Koreans' business success was a source of resentment among Blacks. When asked why Black boycotts target Koreans rather than another group, 28% of Whites and 26% of Blacks cited Blacks' jealousy of Koreans' success in business, Koreans as new immigrants being easy targets, or both. These responses are consistent with the scapegoating hypothesis.

Whites, unlike Blacks, are apt to blame Black hostility on resentment of Koreans' business success. Yet, as indicated above, a large proportion of Black respondents also provided responses consistent with the scapegoating hypothesis. During the boycotts in New York City, several articles in Black newspapers highlighted this scapegoating dynamic. For example, in October 1988, during the boycott of a Korean store in Brooklyn, a writer and educator commented in the *Amsterdam News*: "This is not to deny some Korean merchants exhibit anti-Black behavior and attitudes because they are immigrants in a society where 'becoming an American' means learning to put down Black people. But for us to scapegoat them not only smacks of all that we despise in Yonkers and Howard Beach, but shows our own failure to pose alternatives to the system" (Shannon 1988). Such an admission clearly supports the scapegoating hypothesis. However, to evaluate this hypothesis more rigorously, we need evidence that the behavior and statements of Black boycott leaders unconsciously reflected their intent to scapegoat Koreans, despite their explicit denials that this was the case.

One important piece of evidence is found in Blacks' misconceptions about the sources of Koreans' business capital. Many Black boycott leaders argued that the federal government and commercial banks helped Korean immigrants finance businesses in Black neighborhoods (English and Yuh 1990; Lucas 1990). Koreans' opportunity is seen as coming at the expense of Black businesses. For example, during the 1990–91 boycott of the two stores in Brooklyn, Father Lawrence Lucas, who was involved in organizing several boycotts against Korean stores in Harlem and Brooklyn, argued that "Koreans get loans from banks and other financial institutions, insurance, as well as commercial sites from the City and privately owned businesses while the same treatment is systematically denied in general to Africans located in America" (Lucas 1990). In our New York City survey, the majority of Black respondents (52%) also reported that Korean immigrants started their businesses primarily with loans from the federal government or commercial banks. Interestingly, a smaller proportion of White respondents (36%) indicated that loans from the federal government or commercial banks were the major source of Koreans' business capital.

By alleging that government agencies and commercial banks gave preferential treatment to Koreans and discriminated against Blacks, boycott leaders seemed to blame both Koreans and the "White system" for their underrepresentation in small business. However, this reasoning has several flaws. To begin with, the majority of Korean merchants used savings, both earned in the United States and brought from Korea, to finance their initial businesses; only a small proportion depended on

Small Business Administration or commercial loans (K. Kim and Hurh 1985; Min 1988a). My 1992 survey of Korean merchants in Black neighborhoods in New York City showed that savings from U.S. earnings accounted for an average of 47% of their business capital. The money brought from Korea was the second most significant source of their business capital, providing about 22% on average. Only 5 of the 86 respondents (5.8%) reported that they used commercial loans as the main source of their start-up capital. Though Blacks encounter more discrimination than Koreans in commercial loans, new immigrants without any credit also face difficulties in getting commercial bank loans.[1]

Not only African American leaders and residents but also many White Americans seem to misunderstand how Korean immigrants develop business capital. Mainstream newspaper and magazine articles, for example, have often alleged that Korean immigrant businesses are financed by Korean trade associations. Other articles have indicated that the rotating credit association (the *kye,* in Korean) is the main source of Koreans' business capital. The *New York Daily News* even charged that Korean produce retailers were financially supported by the Unification Church (Moritz 1982), an outlandish accusation that prompted more than one hundred Korean produce retailers to stage a demonstration in front of the *Daily News* building (*KTNY,* August 2, 1982). However, as several surveys show, most Korean merchants depend primarily on their own savings for their start-up capital. While relatives and friends are a readier source of loans for Korean immigrants than for American citizens, private loans are not an important source of their business capital. Though many Korean immigrants participate in a *kye,* they intend mainly to accumulate savings and socialize with friends rather than to accumulate business capital.[2] My survey in Atlanta showed that only 4 out of 159 Korean merchants either partly or totally depended on *kye* money for start-up capital (Min 1988a, 80). The 1992 New York City survey yielded a similar result: only 3 of 86 Korean merchants in Black neighborhoods said that they used the *kye* money for business capitalization. Some other surveys show that *kye*s may be more important for Korean immigrants' business capitalization than my studies suggest (K. Kim and Hurh 1985; Light, Kwuon, and Zhong 1990; see Light and Bonacich 1988, 254–59 for an extended discussion),[3] yet none has indicated that they play a major role.

To explain why such a large number of Korean immigrants started businesses in minority neighborhoods, boycott leaders tended to emphasize perceived advantages of Korean immigrants in business capitalization and failed to recognize the disadvantages they faced in the general labor market. To be sure, though Korean immigrants do not receive favorable treatment from either the federal government or commercial banks, they do have advantages over inner-city African Americans. However, it is more important to focus on the difficulties of Korean immigrants in obtaining employment in nonbusiness occupations than on their means of financing small businesses in low-income Black neighborhoods. Though most Korean immigrants are highly educated, they have turned to self-employment in small business because of the language barrier and other problems in finding employment (Min 1984a). Often, college-educated Korean immigrants have virtually no options other than operating small businesses in low-income minority neighborhoods. Few Black college graduates would be willing to establish businesses in these neighborhoods, because they would be able to find better employment in the general labor market.

By emphasizing what they saw as favorable treatment, boycott leaders suggested that the Koreans' business concentration in African American neighborhoods was encouraged by the federal government and mainstream financial institutions, thereby reducing the opportunities for Black businesses and contributing to economic problems facing inner-city Blacks. However, this argument is also problematic, for there is no evidence to support it. Using the 1980 census data for 272 standard metropolitan statistical areas, Light and Sanchez (1987) showed that neither immigrant entrepreneurship in general nor Korean immigrant entrepreneurship in particular has reduced Black entrepreneurship. Using the same data, Boyd (1990) came to a similar conclusion. Though these two studies are not problem free,[4] no study has indicated that entrepreneurship among Korean or Asian immigrant groups has had a negative effect on Black entrepreneurship.

If Korean immigrant entrepreneurship does indeed harm Blacks, we would expect Korean merchants in Black neighborhoods to have frequent conflicts with Black merchants. Yet they rarely have had such conflicts; rather their disagreements have been mainly with residents and community leaders who blamed Korean merchants for the underrepresentation of Blacks in small business. There are some Black-owned businesses in Black neighborhoods, though few compared to non-Black businesses.[5] Black merchants have specialized in service businesses such as barbershops and cosmetics stores, whereas Koreans have concentrated in grocery, liquor, produce, and fish retail stores. Therefore, Korean and Black merchants rarely compete against each other; however, intragroup competition is strong for both groups.

The resource competition theory (Olzak and Nagel 1986) posits that immigrants and the native born compete for the same jobs, businesses, and other resources. However, the preceding discussion clearly indicates that the scapegoating theory is far more useful than the resource competition theory for understanding Korean–African American tensions. Many Korean immigrants are trapped into operating small business in low-income Black neighborhoods whose economies recently have been deteriorating. Because of their middleman economic role, Koreans bear the brunt of Blacks' economic frustrations. Thus such factors as the racial inequality between Blacks and Whites and particularly the poverty within inner-city Black neighborhoods, along with the employment disadvantages faced by Koreans in the general labor market, provide the structural conditions for Korean–African American conflicts.

THE MEDIA AND THE
WHITE CONSPIRACY HYPOTHESIS

Middleman minority theory posits that middleman merchants are hated and scapegoated by the ruling group that controls the economy, as well as by the minority customers they serve. During periods of stress and unrest, the ruling group can use a middleman minority to shield itself from the brunt of the minority customers' hostility. Let us examine the possibility that the "White system" condoned and even encouraged the hostility of Blacks toward Korean merchants in order to reduce Blacks' frustrations over their economic problems. This finds the White system and not Blacks responsible for the hostility that Korean merchants have faced in Black neighborhoods.

This view, blaming the White system, has been popular among Korean Americans since the 1992 Los Angeles riots. The biased and irresponsible media coverage of Korean–African American conflicts, most conspicuous during the riots, caused many Koreans to believe that Whites used Korean merchants as scapegoats onto which the hostility of Blacks was displaced. In the evening of April 29, 1992, when rioting broke out in Los Angeles, ABC-TV repeatedly showed the videotape of Soon Ja Du shooting an African American girl and then the videotape of Rodney King being beaten by the police, thereby effectively equating the two. Also aired, without any sort of background narrative, were scenes of armed Korean men firing toward rioters from the roofs of their buildings. The May 1 ABC *Nightline* featured Korean–African American tensions as its topic of discussion. Ted Koppel, the moderator, invited only African American leaders to appear, in effect encouraging them to criticize Korean merchants without any Koreans being represented. Korean Americans generally believed that the media's irresponsible coverage incited African American rioters to target Korean stores. Many Koreans argued that the mainstream media *deliberately* tried to make scapegoats out of Korean immigrants by focusing on Korean-Black conflicts rather than White-Black conflicts. ABC-TV received many letters and telephone calls from Koreans complaining about its coverage being biased, unbalanced, and sensational. This pressure eventually led ABC to provide subsequent programs showing the damage that the rioters had caused the Korean community and reporting on how Koreans viewed the riots. Many 1.5- and second-generation Korean Americans wrote letters to the editors of major dailies in California criticizing the media's coverage. Youn-Cha Shin Chey, executive director of Korean Center, Inc., commented in her letter to the *San Francisco Chronicle* (Shin Chey 1992):

> We Korean Americans are angered by the wrong message, delivered to the public by the media coverage. The horror we have witnessed during the past few days is not because of animosity between blacks and Koreans. It is not a black vs. Korean issue. It is an American issue. This is a time when every citizen, every resident to America needs to stop and think. . . .
>   The media misled the public as if the tension between blacks and Koreans was a contributing factor. To report only what appears on the surface is a manipulation of facts and doing injustice on another level.

The U.S. Commission on Civil Rights sent an investigative team to visit the Korean and other minority communities in Los Angeles after the riots. In a written report submitted to the Civil Rights Commission, Kapson Yim Lee, an editorial board member of the *Korea Times Los Angeles,* argued that the media's biased coverage was responsible for the victimization of Korean merchants during the riots (Yim Lee 1992):

> I believe the anger of the black motorist and his hostility toward me—all Koreans—is a creation of the mainstream media, which for many years have inflamed the rage and passion of black people toward Koreans through inaccurate, insensitive and unbalanced coverage. Long before the Rodney King and Latasha Harlins incidents, the media have sowed the seed of poison

through biased and inflammatory reporting. Before Korean Americans and African Americans had a chance to get to know each other—to learn each others' culture and history—the media have pitted the two minorities against each other.

The belief that the White system—particularly the mainstream media's exaggerated coverage of Korean–African American conflicts—was to blame for the victimization of Korean merchants during the riots was particularly popular among younger-generation Koreans. In the previous chapter, we noted that younger-generation Koreans in Los Angeles did not agree with Korean immigrant merchants on how to handle the 1991 African American boycott of a Korean store. This generational division over how to deal with Korean–African American conflicts became more serious after the riots. The merchants blamed Black gang members, and a subsequent FBI investigation disclosed that gang members were responsible for targeting Korean stores during the riots. Younger-generation Koreans, in contrast, were careful not to blame African Americans: they charged that the White system was responsible for both the riots and the victimization of Korean merchants.

This generational division on the issue of Korean–African American conflicts clearly surfaces in scholarly interpretations too. In his recently completed doctoral dissertation, Heon Cheol Lee, a Korean immigrant, found Black nationalism and Black nationalists mainly responsible for the 1990–91 Brooklyn boycott of two Korean stores (H. Lee 1993). The dissertation was very critical of Sonny Carson and other Black nationalist boycott leaders for exploiting the boycott to increase their political power within the Black community and to focus on people's attention on Black economic problems. In contrast, John Lie and Nancy Abelmann, a 1.5-generation Korean and his American wife, sounded a theme well-received by younger-generation Koreans in their recently published book, which considered Korean–African American conflicts merely to be a by-product of the media's construction (Abelmann and Lie 1995).

There is no doubt that the media coverage of Korean-Black conflicts before and during the Los Angeles riots was biased and unbalanced, as many Koreans have claimed. However, to examine systematically the relationship between the media's biased coverage and the targeting of Korean stores by African Americans during the riots, we need to answer three separate questions: (1) did the biased coverage contribute to the victimization of Korean stores by Black rioters significantly?; (2) if so, would there have been no targeting of Korean stores without the influence of the media?; and (3) by focusing on Korean–African American conflicts, did the media *intentionally* encourage African Americans to target Korean stores as a means to minimize the damage to "White society"?

I agree that the biased coverage—specifically ABC's repeated airing of the videotape that showed Soon Ja Du shooting Latasha Harlins—encouraged African American rioters to loot and set fire to Korean stores. I believe that even media exposure that is favorable to Koreans can exacerbate Korean–African American tensions, since the media usually frame individual disputes as group conflicts. Interestingly, the mainstream media coverage of Korean-Black conflicts in New York City has been biased against African Americans, whereas the coverage in Los Angeles has been somewhat biased against Koreans. Unfortunately, both types of biased coverage have heightened Korean–African American tensions.

During the two most recent Black boycotts against Korean stores in New York City (1988 and 1990), the major media in the New York area, with the exception of the *Amsterdam News,* were extremely critical of the boycott leaders and highly supportive of Korean merchants. The New York media's bias against the boycott organizers seems to stem from long-standing serious conflicts between the city's Black community and White ethnic groups (Kaufmann 1988; Sleeper 1990) whereas the Black community in Los Angeles has maintained better relations with White ethnic groups. For example, Sonny Carson, the key organizer behind the two most recent boycotts in Brooklyn, has a history of clashes with the White community, particularly New York City's Jewish community, going back to the 1968 battle for community control over schools in the Ocean Hill–Brownsville District in Brooklyn (Ravitch 1974, 317, 368). Carson and other Black nationalists in New York have also had conflicts with Italian Americans, particularly over the Bensonhurst case (Sleeper 1990).[6] Thus the White media in New York may have been predisposed to be critical of Black boycott leaders and sympathetic toward the Korean community.

Korean community leaders in New York generally were satisfied with the mainstream media's treatment of Korean merchants as innocent victims and of Black boycott leaders as political opportunists. In fact, when the second Brooklyn boycott started in January 1990, the Korean Small Business Service Center immediately sent letters clarifying their position to the major media; they considered winning the media's support to be essential to a quick end of the boycott. However, I believe that the media helped prolong the boycott by publicizing it and attacking its leaders. The White media's harsh criticisms may have united Black nationalists and enhanced their determination to continue the boycott rather than give in to the "White system."

We previously concluded that exaggerated and biased coverage, particularly on television, encouraged African Americans to target Korean stores during the Los Angeles riots. The next question is whether or not Korean stores would have been targeted during the riots without the influence of the media. The answer appears to be that they would have been targeted anyway. As discussed in considerable detail in the previous chapter, the relationship between Koreans and African Americans in Los Angeles had already been strained severely prior to the riots, particularly because of the fatal shooting of an unarmed African American girl by a Korean grocery store owner and the lenient sentence later granted to the owner by a White judge. When the Rodney King verdict was delivered four months after the Du decision, many African Americans equated the two. Thus, without the media's influence, fewer but still many Korean stores would probably have been attacked during the riots.

Finally, an important question concerning the relationship between the media's treatment of Korean–African American conflicts and the targeting of Korean stores by Blacks during the riots is whether the White media *intentionally* played up Korean–African American conflicts to make Koreans the scapegoats for African Americans' anger. Though many second-generation Koreans would answer "yes" to this question, I do not. The media sensationalized these conflicts primarily because the media thrive on sensationalism. I agree with the following non-Korean's assessment of the situation (Page 1992):

> Naturally Koreatown is in a justifiable state of fury. But there's another somewhat cooler way of looking at this. Oh, yes, the media did play up the ravaging of Koreatown. But that was done to enhance the drama value of the story beyond simply showing a lot of flames.
> . . . In short what happened was some truth, some media hoopla, in the ways the tabloids, the supermarket papers and TV go for rapes, weird sex and blood. In short, it's American journalism, a bad story is a good story. It used to be called yellow journalism, now it is routine.

To point out negative consequences of irresponsible media coverage is one thing, but to ascribe motive is quite another. The Marxist assumption that all major social agencies and organizations operate to protect the interests of the dominant group may sound theoretically attractive, but, in practice, different social agencies and organizations, including the media, struggle to protect their own self-interests. The media dramatized Korean–African American conflicts during the riots mainly out of such self-interest—primarily, for commercial purposes.

BLACK NATIONALISM AND
FEARS OF ECONOMIC EXPLOITATION

The frustrations of residents with their economic conditions and the vulnerable position of Korean merchants as middlemen contributed to feelings of hostility toward Korean merchants in African American neighborhoods. However, Koreans who act as middlemen in Latino neighborhoods have not encountered boycotts or other forms of violent reactions. Therefore, while economic frustrations may be a necessary condition for organizing such actions against Korean merchants, they are not sufficient. To transform these frustrations into concerted actions, leaders and a politico-economic ideology are needed. Black nationalists have played a leading role in organizing anti-Korean activities, and Black nationalism has provided the needed ideology.

Black nationalists have clearly played an active role in organizing boycotts against Korean stores. Particularly in New York City, with its tradition of Marcus Garvey and Malcolm X, Black nationalism has strongly influenced the politics of the Black community (Kaufman 1988; Sleeper 1990). One of the region's most prominent Black nationalists is Sonny Carson. Chair of the Brooklyn chapter of the Congress of Racial Equality, Carson helped Rhody McCoy lead the battle for community control of schools in the Ocean Hill–Brownsville School District in Brooklyn in 1968 (see Kaufman 1988; Maynard 1970; Ravitch 1974; Sinden 1980). He is currently the chair of the December 12th Movement, a New York–based Black nationalist organization (for the December 12th Movement, see Hornung 1990). Interestingly, he has played a significant role in all five major boycotts against Korean stores in the city's Black neighborhoods and was indeed the central figure in organizing the two most recent, the 1988–89 and 1990–91 boycotts in Brooklyn.

Furthermore, Black nationalists consistently describe Korean merchants as exploiters. Sonny Carson has repeatedly expressed their fears about an invasion of the Black community's economy. For example, in a press interview during the 1990 boycott of two Korean produce retailers in the Flatbush–Church Avenue area, he said: "The Koreans become intruders, upstarts, exploiters. . . . You get a certain ethnic dynamic that can easily become uncontrollable or lead to certain kinds of conflicts. . . . Right now, all these other folks come in, make the money, and take it out before the sun goes down" (English and Yuh 1990, 6). Similar statements were made by George Edward Tait, secretary of the African Nationalist Pioneer Movement and a leader in organizing two major boycotts against Korean stores in Harlem. An ardent supporter of the "Buy Black" campaign, Tait expressed the boycotts' major goal in economic terms: "There is only one uncompromising objective; the removal of non-Black businesses from the Black community; there is only one unequivocal goal, the economic control of the Black community by its Black resident majority" (Jamison 1988; see also Tait 1988).

The involvement of Black nationalists in organizing boycotts against Korean merchants in New York City helps us better understand why Korean merchants in some African American communities have been able to avoid serious conflicts and hostility. For example, Korean immigrants in Atlanta, whose businesses are also heavily Black oriented (Min 1988a), have not experienced any long-term Black boycotts, though there have been some minor incidents of racial tensions between Korean merchants and African American residents and a few brief boycotts. Black nationalists in Atlanta, the home of the Black civil rights movement, seem to have had little influence on the local Black community, which is instead largely dominated by civil rights leaders. In all cases, these leaders intervened to end boycotts at an early stage.

As noted, Black nationalist leaders played a central role in organizing major boycotts against Korean stores in New York City, and the organizers emphasized that their main goal was the economic autonomy of the Black community. Though the boycotts were organized primarily by Black nationalists, many Black residents participated, or at least supported their efforts. This suggests that many residents accepted the Black nationalist ideology that considered commercial activities by non-Blacks in Black neighborhoods to be inherently exploitative.

To examine the extent to which Black residents accepted this ideology, four statements—each describing the business activities of Koreans in Black neighborhoods as an economic invasion—were posed, to which the respondents were asked to agree or disagree. Table 10 shows the percentages of the respondents who agreed with the statements (i.e., those who chose the first two categories, *strongly agree* and *moderately*

TABLE 10.

BLACK AND WHITE RESIDENTS WHO ACCEPTED
STATEMENTS RELATING KOREANS' COMMER-
CIAL ACTIVITIES TO ECONOMIC
EXPLOITATION (PERCENTAGES)

Statements*	Black Respondents (N = 97)	White Respondents (N = 50)	Significance
(1) Exploit	40.2	6.0	p < .000
(2) Reduce opportunity	47.4	16.0	p < .000
(3) Economic invasion	35.1	2.0	p < .000
(4) Drain resources	55.6	20.0	p < .000

Source: The 1992 New York City survey of Black and White residents.
*Respondents were asked whether they agreed with the following four statements:
  1. Korean merchants in black neighborhoods become rich by exploiting black people.
  2. The presence of Korean businesses in black neighborhoods reduces the opportunity for blacks to open their own businesses.
  3. The Korean business development in black neighborhoods is an economic invasion of the black community.
  4. Korean merchants drain black economic resources by taking money out of the black community.

agree) by race. More than one-third of the Black respondents accepted each of the statements. In contrast, few White respondents accepted any of them. This marks a significant difference in how Whites and Blacks perceive the commercial activities of Koreans in Black neighborhoods.

Nearly all Korean merchants in Black neighborhoods are "absentee owners"; that is, they live outside of the neighborhoods where their stores are located. The fact that Korean merchants do not live in the neighborhoods where they operate businesses has helped lead Blacks to perceive Korean merchants as exploiters. Black nationalists argue that absentee owners drain economic resources from Black communities (Harber 1969; Reiss and Aldrich 1971). In my New York City survey, only 7 of the 93 Korean merchants in Black ghettos lived within three miles of their stores. In fact, Korean merchants lived an average of four-teen miles from their stores. At an interracial assembly of Korean and Black pastors in New York City in May 1988, Father Bill Lucas com-plained that the "money earned by Korean merchants remains in the Black neighborhood for no longer than twelve hours." The priest's complaint reflects a common concern among many Blacks about absen-tee-owned businesses in Black communities, whether Korean or White.

The perception that Korean merchants exploit the Black community must be put into historical context. Before Koreans came in large num-bers, Jewish, Italian, and other White store owners had controlled busi-nesses in the Black community. Many Black residents regard Korean immigrants as the latest group of outsiders who are out to exploit the community. Korean merchants, however, have difficulty understanding this perception. When asked whether or not Korean businesses in Black neighborhoods were beneficial to residents, 63% of Korean merchants responded positively. In their view, Korean businesses have benefited the community by offering reasonably priced merchandise and extending business hours until late at night. They have also helped decaying neighborhoods regenerate.

The view of some African Americans that Korean merchants and other outsiders who have controlled businesses in their community are exploiters has been fueled by the rhetoric of Black nationalist leaders and the black media. A representative sample is offered by an article entitled "The Korean Invasion: A New Threat to Black Business," published in *Metro Atlanta,* a black magazine: "The black community is under threat from an outside force that moves in, sucks money and moves on without even as much as a thank you. The small black entrepreneur is constantly being invaded by other groups who seem to have an uncanny knack for moving in and taking over black businesses and making them work" (Pannell 1989). After referring to Jewish and Italian merchants who once dominated businesses in Black neighborhoods, the author continues: "The new forces to move in are the Koreans. They have found a niche that Blacks once controlled—the black hair care market. From Florida to New York, Korean emigrants have opened or bought beauty supply stores that cater to black beauticians and barbers. . . . A new invasion is upon us."

Thus far, we have examined the significant role played by Black nationalists and the Black media in spawning sentiments antagonistic to Korean merchants. However, we also need to note that the primary concern of Black nationalists is maintaining the economic autonomy of the Black community, not eliminating Korean merchants from Black neighborhoods. The Korean and mainstream media as well as scholars usually interpret a boycott of Korean stores in an African American neighborhood mainly as a Korean–African American conflict. However, historically Black intellectuals framed the issue in terms not of ethnic conflict but of community control. They felt that the failure of Black residents to support and patronize Black businesses partly contributed to their dearth in African American neighborhoods, whose businesses were controlled by White merchants. Thus, both the "Double Duty Dollar" doctrine (Drake and Cayton 1945, 430–32) and the "Buy Black" campaign emphasize the obligations of Blacks to patronize Black businesses. Contemporary Black nationalists such as Sonny Carson place more blame for their underrepresentation in small business on outside, middleman merchants than did earlier Black intellectuals. However, one might argue that contemporary Black nationalists and earlier Black intellectuals are similar in that both share a concern with community control.

FURTHER EVIDENCE OF EXPLOITATION

To many Black nationalists, any outsider who opens a business in an African American neighborhood is committing economic exploitation. Black community leaders and residents, however, present more detailed charges against Koreans. In addition to accusations of rudeness, Blacks have complained that Korean merchants do not hire Black employees and that Korean merchants do not contribute money to their neighborhoods (Chang 1990; I. Kim 1981, 257–58; Light and Bonacich 1988, 318–20; Ong, Park, and Tong 1994). It is therefore necessary to examine these two complaints to evaluate the validity of the argument that Korean merchants exploit Blacks.

In several interracial meetings held to end boycotts against Korean stores in New York City, Black representatives demanded that Korean merchants hire more Black employees (*KTNY*, July 30, 1981; January 5, 1985). In the 1980s and in 1992, Black youth demonstrated outside Korean stores and even staged several short-term boycotts in Brooklyn; they demanded that Korean stores employ Black residents (*KTNY*, February 8, 1982; *KTNY*, June 15, 1984; *SGT*, April 15 and 25, 1992). In April 1992, a group known as "the African American Protection Agency" made the lack of Black employees in Korean stores a major issue. "Priest Monk," the apparent leader of the agency, organized three demonstrations outside several Korean stores in the Church Avenue area in April 1992 (*SGT*, April 25, 1992). He targeted Korean stores that had three or more employees, none of them Black.

Considering the extremely high unemployment rate in low-income Black neighborhoods, it is not surprising that Black youths and community leaders are concerned about job opportunities available in Korean stores. Thus we must examine the validity of the claim that Korean merchants do not hire Blacks. In my 1986 Los Angeles survey, Korean respondents with one or more businesses were asked about the ethnicity of their employees. Latinos constituted the largest proportion of total workers (48%) employed by Korean businesses in Los Angeles, though more Korean businesses hired at least one Korean worker (52%) than one Latino worker (41%). Nearly all Latino employees hired by Korean stores in Los Angeles were Mexicans; they outnumbered Korean employees in part because several Korean garment factories hired a large number of them. In contrast, only 7% of Korean businesses in Los Angeles had at least one Black employee, and Blacks made up only 5% of all employees. These findings suggest that Korean businesses usually do not hire Blacks.

A more important issue is whether Korean businesses located in *Black neighborhoods* employ Black residents. To answer this question, Korean merchants in New York City's Black neighborhoods were asked to indicate the ethnic composition of their employees. When Blacks have criticized Korean merchants for not employing Black residents, Koreans have argued that their businesses are usually family oriented and do not have paid employees, a view also endorsed by White residents. New York City data, however, show that this defense is not valid: 90% of Korean stores surveyed in New York City's Black neighborhoods have one or more paid employees. Several Korean merchants who did not have a paid employee refused to respond to the telephone interview, claiming that they had to serve customers. Thus, my survey may have overestimated the proportion of Korean businesses in Black neighborhoods with one or more paid employees. Nonetheless, my surveys conducted in Los Angeles and Atlanta (Min 1988a, 111) also indicate that the vast majority of Korean businesses have at least one paid employee.

Korean businesses in New York City's Black neighborhoods employ more Latinos (42%) than Blacks (31%) or Koreans (23%). However, Black employees outnumber Koreans, which suggests that Korean merchants in Black neighborhoods do not usually avoid hiring Blacks. Yet as long as Korean businesses in Black neighborhoods employ more Latinos than Blacks, they are open to the charge of bias. In the 1986 Los Angeles survey, Korean business owners who hired Latinos but not African Americans were asked why they preferred Latino employees. Most respondents viewed the Mexican workers as cheap, docile, and hardworking, and believed that African American workers exhibit more or less the opposite characteristics. In the 1992 New York City survey, Korean business owners in Black neighborhoods with one or more but no Black employees were asked why they were not hiring Blacks. Most merchants said that Black employees were not responsible or punctual and therefore were not dependable. As one Korean retail owner in Brooklyn who had previously hired Black residents put it: "Black employees are not responsible, not reliable. They often do not come to work without giving any notice. They have no motivation to continue working unless they need money immediately. Two years ago, my Black employee asked for money for lunch. I gave him money, but he did not come back to work after lunch."

It is interesting to note that White employers in Chicago, too, generally evaluated Black workers negatively; but unlike Korean business owners, they also had negative opinions about Mexican workers (Kirschenman and Neckerman 1991). It is not clear what proportion of Mexican workers included in the Chicago study were recent immigrants or illegal residents. Most of the Latino workers employed in Korean-owned stores in Los Angeles were immigrants and illegal residents who, like immigrants in general, are hardworking and generally "docile." In Los Angeles and New York, a large number of Latino workers take low-paying, menial jobs as laborers in Korean garment factories, as cooks and waiters in Korean restaurants, as stockers and laborers in Korean grocery and produce stores, and as sales staff in Korean stores selling handbags, jewelry, and clothing. Many of them have learned some Korean words to communicate with Korean store owners and Korean customers.

The employment of Latino workers in Korean-owned businesses is not limited to Los Angeles and New York; it is a national phenomenon, observable in many cities. When I conducted a survey in Atlanta in 1982, few Korean stores were hiring Latino workers. However, recent discussions with Korean business leaders in Atlanta have revealed that now Latinos are being hired at many Korean stores there, too. New Latino immigrants and illegal aliens, disadvantaged in the general labor market, find needed employment in Korean-owned businesses; they are cheap labor. In this sense, Korean immigrant merchants and Latino immigrant workers help each other. However, approached from another angle, the relationship between Korean merchants and Latino employees is problematic. Korean merchants prefer Latino workers mainly because they are cheap and docile; but for these very reasons Koreans can be charged with exploiting Latino workers.

The strain between Korean business owners and Latino employees is most conspicuous in garment subcontracting, an industry that is notorious for exploiting its workers. Seven hundred Korean garment factories in Los Angeles depend largely on Mexican employees. As Light and Bonacich (1988, 305–8) indicated, Korean garment subcontractors frequently violate labor regulations. My 1986 survey of Korean immigrants in Los Angeles revealed that some Korean women were unwilling to work in Korean-owned garment factories with many Mexican employees because "those garment factories would treat us more like Mexican workers and thus exploit us more."

The ultimate exploiters of Latino workers are not the Korean garment subcontractors but the White manufacturers (Bonacich 1993, 62–65). Because of cutthroat competition among garment subcontractors —mostly Koreans and other immigrants—White garment manufacturers can significantly reduce their production expenses. The subcontracting businesses survive mainly because they rely on family members and new immigrants for cheap labor. Thus White garment manufacturers may profit more than Korean garment subcontractors from the exploitative relationship between subcontractors and employees. However, Korean garment subcontractors, as middlemen, can be subject to the hostility of Latino workers. The Korean-American Garment Industry Association of Los Angeles has made efforts to strengthen ties with Latino employees through such programs as an annual picnic, monthly soccer games, and scholarships for Latino students. In spite of these efforts, the future of the Korean-Hispanic, owner-employee relationship is likely to be tumultuous.[7]

The claim that Korean ghetto merchants economically exploit the African American community is based partly on the perception that Korean merchants do not return any of their earnings to the Black community. African Americans have complained that Korean merchants in their neighborhoods do not participate in community affairs. A popular slogan during the most recent Brooklyn boycotts, "Korean Blood Suckers," reflected the concern of Blacks that Korean merchants earn money from communities without contributing to them. To examine the validity of this complaint, I asked Korean merchants in Black neighborhoods of New York City whether they had donated money or merchandise to the neighborhood in the past year. Thirty-six percent reported that they had directly donated money, merchandise, or both, and another 41% said that they had made donations through Korean merchants' associations: only 16% reported that they had donated nothing. These findings suggest that most Korean merchants in New York City's Black neighborhoods contribute to the community.

However, we must consider a few important facts when interpreting these findings. The Korean merchants who provided data for my survey conducted businesses in the three major Black areas of New York City: Harlem, Jamaica, and the Fulton Street–Church Avenue area. Each of these neighborhoods experienced severe tensions between Blacks and Koreans in the 1980s, and a Korean merchants' association was established in each community to lessen those tensions. Through these associations, Korean merchants have donated money, merchandise, and gifts to local Black organizations (see chapter 7 for an extended discussion). Thus, Korean merchants in the three Black areas where the survey was conducted seem more active in the Black community than those in other Black areas. Nevertheless, as will be shown in the next chapter, other Korean associations in New York have contributed to the Black community with scholarship funds and otherwise. Yet unless Korean ghetto merchants support Black community activities with significant individual donations, the impression that Korean merchants drain resources from the Black community may be ineradicable.

THE IMMIGRANT HYPOTHESIS

According to the immigrant hypothesis, Blacks' rejection of Korean merchants is basically a nativist reaction to foreigners' economic activities. If this hypothesis holds, then immigrant Blacks should more readily accept Korean businesses in Black neighborhoods than do native-born Blacks. Our 1992 survey of Black residents in New York City included an item on place of birth and thus provided data for testing this hypothesis.

As shown in table 11, almost equal proportions of (Afro-Caribbean) immigrant and (African American) native-born respondents supported the 1990–91 Brooklyn boycott. In fact, the two longest Black boycotts of Korean stores in New York, in 1990–91 and 1988–89, occurred in Afro-Caribbean, immigrant neighborhoods. In addition, small proportions of two subsamples endorsed the argument that "Blacks should not buy from Korean stores" (the Buy Black argument). A substantially larger proportion of native-born respondents (27.6%) than immigrant respondents (13.2%) agreed that "New York City would be better off without so many Korean immigrants." However, this statement seems to reflect their nativist rejection of Korean immigrants generally rather than a particular rejection of Korean merchants in Black neighborhoods. It is not surprising that immigrant Blacks were more accepting than native-born Blacks of Korean immigrants.

TABLE 11.

BLACK RESIDENTS WHO ACCEPTED STATE-
MENTS REJECTING KOREAN MERCHANTS, BY
BIRTHPLACE (PERCENTAGES)

	Native Born (N = 58)	Immigrant (N = 39)	Significance
Statements reflecting rejection of Korean merchants[a]			
(1) Support boycott	26.8	26.3	N.S[b]
(2) Not buy	15.5	12.8	N.S.
(3) Better off	27.6	13.2	N.S.
Statements linking Koreans' commercial activities in Black areas to economic exploitation[c]			
(1) Exploit	41.4	38.5	N.S.
(2) Reduce Opportunity	51.7	41.0	N.S.
(3) Economic Invasion	37.9	30.8	N.S.
(4) Drain Resources	62.1	46.2	N.S.

Source: The 1992 New York City Survey of Black and White Residents.
[a] Respondents were asked whether they agreed with the following three statements:
1. I supported the 1990–91 boycott.
2. Blacks should not buy from Korean stores.
3. New York City would be better off without so many Korean immigrants.
[b] Not significant.
[c] See table 10.

More native-born Blacks than immigrant Blacks accepted the four statements linking Koreans' commercial activities in Black neighborhoods to economic exploitation. The percentage differential is not statistically significant for any of the four statements, though with a larger sample a statistically significant difference between the two groups might be found. In any case, these differences in perceptions of Koreans' commercial activities in Black neighborhoods seem practically insignificant, particularly compared to the large difference found between Black and White respondents as shown in table 10. Thus, we can conclude that our New York City survey data do not support the immigrant hypothesis.

As H. Lee (1993) aptly pointed out, Black nationalist leaders who organized boycotts in New York City turned the merchant-customer disputes into racial issues, leading many Caribbean immigrant Blacks to accept their claim that Korean merchants economically exploit Black residents. This suggests that the Black nationalist emphasis on economic autonomy in the Black community contributes more to Blacks' rejection of Korean merchants, particularly as manifested in boycotts, than Black nativism. Though Black nationalism and Black nativism are interrelated, the two do not necessarily occur together. Dating back to Marcus Garvey in the 1920s (Croon 1969), the Afro-Caribbean immigrant community in New York City has a long tradition of Black nationalism. Not only Garvey but also Stokely Carmichael, a leading figure in the U.S. Black nationalist movement in the 1960s, was of Caribbean origin. Though post-1965 Caribbean Black immigrants identify themselves more strongly as West Indian than as Black, they have often made common political cause with African Americans (Foner 1987, 209).

LANGUAGE BARRIERS, CULTURAL DIFFERENCES, AND PREJUDICE

We noted above that Black residents' economic frustrations and Korean merchants' vulnerable position as middlemen in Black neighborhoods contribute to hostility toward Korean merchants, and that Black nationalist leaders and the Black nationalist ideology have transformed those frustrations into concerted anti-Korean actions such as boycotts. Blacks' economic frustrations, Korean immigrants' middleman activities in Black neighborhoods, and Black nationalism result from broad structural forces that have little to do with the sociopsychological factors that affect social interactions between merchants and customers. However, language barriers, cultural differences, and mutual prejudice contribute to conflicts on the individual level that regularly occur in Korean-owned stores in Black neighborhoods. Furthermore, Black boycotts of Korean stores have usually started with disputes between Black customers and Korean merchants or employees. Therefore, examining the sociopsychological factors that affect both parties helps explain Korean-Black conflicts in general and hostility toward Korean merchants in Black neighborhoods in particular.

In our 1992 New York City survey, both Black/White resident and Korean merchant respondents were asked an open-ended question: "What do you think are major sources of conflict between Korean merchants and Black customers?" As noted previously, 35% of Black respondents saw Koreans' lack of respect for Black customers as the major source of conflict. Another 22% blamed cultural differences and communication barriers between Koreans and Blacks. Their responses reflect the complaint of Black customers and community leaders alike that Koreans do not treat Black customers respectfully. Korean merchant respondents pointed to similar factors, with 39% referring to cultural differences and 33% citing mutual prejudice as the major source of Korean-Black conflicts. A significant proportion, 23%, agreed that Korean merchants' rudeness contributed to interracial tensions in Korean stores. In a separate question, the Korean merchant respondents were asked whether they accepted the charge that "Korean merchants are rude to Black customers." Surprisingly, 65% of them reported that they did.

Though the above findings indicate that this claim of rude treatment possesses some elements of truth, it needs to be examined more closely. First, because of frequent shoplifting, many Korean merchants closely watch customers, who naturally resent being treated as shoplifters. Indeed, merchant-customer altercations in Korean stores in Black neighborhoods usually start when a Korean merchant or employee accuses a customer of shoplifting and tries to look inside his or her shopping bag.

Second, language barriers and cultural differences contribute to Korean merchants' alleged rudeness. Many Korean merchants in Black neighborhoods cannot communicate with customers effectively and thus can be easily misinterpreted. For example, when asked about particular items by customers, Korean store owners very often have difficulty answering because of their limited English. Customers tend to take this as a sign of disrespect. Moreover, following their customs, many Korean merchants shy away from direct eye contact and do not smile at customers. Korean customs teach women to avoid physical contact with men, so many Korean female cashiers will drop change on the counter rather than place it in a man's hand. Black customers might interpret these as signs of impoliteness. Native-born store owners who have no language difficulties and who are familiar with American customs, whether Korean or non-Korean, are likely to avoid many of the problems that arise from these cultural differences.

Finally, mutual prejudice, particularly Korean merchants' prejudice against Black customers, partly explains Korean merchants' treatment of Black customers. To examine the extent of Koreans' prejudice against Blacks, Korean merchant respondents were given four statements involving negative stereotypes of Blacks and asked to specify the extent to which they agreed or disagreed with each. Table 12 shows the percentage of Korean merchant respondents who chose either *strongly agree* or *moderately agree* with each statement. Not unexpectedly, a large proportion of the respondents agreed with each statement. In fact, the majority of them accepted three of the four very serious negative stereotypes. Korean merchant respondents were also asked to report their agreement or disagreement with the statement that "a large proportion

TABLE 12.

KOREAN MERCHANTS WHO AC-
CEPTED STATEMENTS STEREOTYP-
ING BLACKS (PERCENTAGES)

Stereotypes	N = 93
(1) Black people are generally less intelligent than white people.	61.3
(2) Black people are generally lazier than white people.	45.2
(3) Black people are generally less honest than white people.	61.3
(4) Black people are generally more criminally oriented than white people.	69.9

Source: The 1992 New York City survey of Korean merchants in Black neighborhoods.

of Black Americans are poor mainly because of racial discrimination." Only 13% of them agreed with this statement, compared to 26% of White and 43% of Black resident respondents. These results support the view that an overwhelming majority of Korean merchants in Black neighborhoods blame Blacks' poverty mainly on their own cultural deficiencies. Though this cultural interpretation is also popular among White Americans, our data suggest that Korean merchants endorse it even more strongly.

The impression that Koreans' prejudice against Blacks may be greater than Blacks' prejudice against Koreans was also partly supported by a survey conducted in Los Angeles by a team from the Political Science Department of the University of Southern California. White, Jewish, Latino, Black, Korean, Chinese, and Japanese groups were listed, and respondents were asked which groups they felt close to. Forty-seven percent of Black respondents reported that they felt close to Koreans, whereas only 22% of Korean respondents said they felt close to Blacks (*KTLA*, April 3, 1993). Of all groups listed, Blacks were ranked last in Korean respondents' rating, but Koreans were ranked above Japanese in Black respondents' ranking.

Some researchers have suggested that Korean immigrants learned negative stereotypes of Blacks prior to immigration through their exposure to the American media (Chang 1990; Cheng and Espiritu 1989; S. Cho 1993; Lim 1982). Though plausible, this explanation, like many other attempts to find the root cause of all racial conflict in White racism, oversimplifies. Prior to immigration, Filipino immigrants were exposed to more of American media and culture than Korean immigrants. Therefore, if Asian immigrants learned anti-Black prejudice mainly through such exposure, Filipino immigrants should show a higher level of prejudice against Blacks than do Korean immigrants. However, there is strong evidence that Filipino immigrants are instead more accepting of Blacks. For example, the Korean population in Queens, New York, in 1990 was 2.2 times as large as the Filipino population. Yet 1,562 Filipinos, in comparison to only 123 Koreans, resided in Queens Community District 12, a predominantly Black residential area (New York City Department of City Planning 1992, 264). This suggests that Filipino immigrants feel more comfortable living in Black neighborhoods and are thus less prejudiced against Blacks than are Korean immigrants.

No doubt, the U.S. media and other forms of U.S. cultural production that are available in Korea have influenced Koreans' attitudes toward Blacks. However, the racial and cultural homogeneity of Korean society seems to be a far more important factor. Korean immigrants come from a society with only one race and one language (Min 1991). Confinement to a homogeneous social environment does not prepare them well for living in a multiethnic society. Unexposed to subcultural differences in their home country, most Korean immigrants have a low level of tolerance for the different values, customs, and lifestyles found in the American social setting. Though many White Americans tend to stereotype Blacks, Korean immigrants seem to stereotype them to a greater extent, partly because of their earlier cultural insulation in Korea. Korean immigrants generally maintain social distance not only from African Americans but also from White Americans.[8]

Like other immigrants, Korean immigrants are a self-selected group. They are more progressive, opportunistic, and economically aggressive than the general Korean population (Min 1988a, 78). This may be a major reason they have chosen to immigrate to the United States. Moreover, leaving a country with a lower standard of living for one with a higher standard of living gives new immigrants the psychological motive to work harder (Light 1984). Many Korean immigrants seem to accept the age-old immigrant view of America as a land of opportunity. This speculation is supported by results of my survey of Korean merchants in Black neighborhoods and of Black and White customers. Forty percent of Korean merchant respondents *strongly agreed* with the statement, "In this country, any one, regardless of race, sex, or national origin, can make it if he/she works hard." By contrast, much lower proportions of White and Black resident respondents—14% and 20%, respectively—*strongly agreed* with that statement. Korean immigrants' positive views of the opportunity structure in American society and their lack of knowledge about the history of Black Americans increase their culturally based prejudices toward Blacks. Many Korean immigrants have a sense of superiority over Blacks, relying on the following comparison: "I have become a successful business owner within five years of immigration. As a native-born American Black, what are you doing now?"

Koreans' prejudice against Blacks also has a class basis. The contact hypothesis proposes that equal status contacts across racial or ethnic lines are more likely than unequal status contacts to reduce prejudice (Deutch and Collins 1951; Ford 1972, 1973; Williams 1964; Zeul and Humphrey 1971). This proposition provides insight into the nature of interracial prejudice between Korean merchants and Black customers. Many Korean immigrants' first encounter with Blacks occurs in their stores in Afro-Caribbean or African American neighborhoods, and these are largely unequal status contacts. Most Korean merchants operating businesses in Black neighborhoods are college-educated, middle-class people, living in intact families, whereas a large proportion of their adult customers are unemployed, often living in nontraditional family settings. Accordingly, Korean store owners and employees tend to stereotype African Americans based on their observations of customers. It is easy for Korean business owners to accept the view that Blacks' cultural deficiencies—a high divorce rate, a large number of children, irrational consuming behavior, and so forth—are mainly responsible for their economic difficulties.

Finally, Korean and African American conflict over economic interests is a source of their mutual prejudice. The contact hypothesis also proposes that the contact situation in which members of two racial or ethnic groups work for common goals is more likely to reduce prejudice than a situation involving conflicting goals and competition (Blake and Mouton 1962; Miracle 1981; Sherif, Harvey, and White 1961; Sherif and Sherif 1953; Yarrow, Campbell, and Yarrow 1958). The nature of the merchant-client relationship is inherently conflictive, and a commercial transaction between members of two different racial groups maximizes that inherent stress. In this connection, it is important to note that economic contacts with Jews as landlords, merchants, and employers greatly contributed to the development of anti-Semitism among African Americans (Marx 1969; Reddick 1942; Tsukashima and

TABLE 13.

BLACK AND WHITE RESIDENTS WHO
ACCEPTED STATEMENTS STEREOTYPING
KOREANS (PERCENTAGES)

Stereotypes	Black Respondents (N = 97)	White Respondents (N = 50)	Significance
(1) Koreans are overly concerned with making money.	45.4	26.0	$p < 0.05$
(2) Koreans do not try to learn English and American customs.	34.4	24.4	$p > 0.1$
(3) Koreans care about only other Koreans.	44.3	30.0	$p < 0.1$
(4) Koreans are in general rude and nasty people.	22.7	8.0	$p < 0.05$

Source: The 1992 New York City survey of Black and White residents.

Montero 1976). Many African Americans and Korean immigrants make their first racial contacts in Korean stores during commercial transactions. Thus, the setting of Korean–African American racial contact facilitates the development of prejudice against each other. This suggests that cultural differences and prejudice may make the initial interracial contacts in Korean stores stressful, and that stressful economic contacts further enhance mutual prejudice.

Given the above discussion, I was curious about the degree of Black residents' prejudice against Koreans. Resident respondents were provided with four items reflecting stereotypes of Koreans and asked to indicate their degree of agreement or disagreement. Table 13 shows the percentages of Black and White respondents who either *strongly agreed* or *moderately agreed* with each statement. As expected, many respondents accepted each negative stereotype; it is not surprising that a significantly greater proportion of Black respondents than White respondents endorsed each statement. Blacks' negative views of Koreans seem to have been largely shaped by the tensions involved in commercial transactions as well as by the cultural and situational differences between them.

There is no necessary causal link between prejudiced attitudes and behavior in the form of discrimination. Depending on the situation, one can be what Merton called a prejudiced nondiscriminator or an unprejudiced discriminator (Merton 1949). As noted above, Korean merchants seem to be more prejudiced against Black customers than Black customers are prejudiced against Korean merchants. However, Korean merchants will try to hide their prejudiced attitudes for the sake of their economic interests, while Black customers will not lose much by displaying their prejudices. Thus, it is true that Black customers are more often impolite and rude to Korean merchants and employees than Korean merchants are to Black customers. Such behaviors include paying less than is owed, tasting and damaging fruits and vegetables, throwing change onto the counter, and asking for refunds or exchanges after using such items as hats, pants, and wigs. In an extreme case, some African American customers pick up merchandise and walk out of the store without paying for it. Korean merchants complain that Black customers would not do the same thing in White-owned stores.

The media exaggeration of Korean–African American conflicts gives the impression that the majority of Blacks reject Korean merchants. But results of a survey of Black residents in New York City reveal that such rejection is not widespread. A larger proportion of Black respondents than White respondents, but still a small proportion overall (approximately one-fourth), rejected Korean merchants.

The middleman minority and scapegoating hypothesis suggests that Korean immigrants' middleman position and poverty in inner-city Black neighborhoods are the major factors contributing to hostility toward Korean merchants. It is difficult to test this hypothesis statistically with survey data, but examination of multiple data sets suggests that this hypothesis is very plausible. Korean merchants began to move into Black neighborhoods in large numbers in the late 1970s when the economic conditions of inner-city Black residents were deteriorating. However, Blacks' economic frustrations provide a necessary but not a sufficient condition for such manifestations of hostility as boycotts and arson. They need a powerful ideology and leaders to transform their dissatisfaction into concerted anti-Korean actions. Black nationalist rhetoric emphasizing the economic autonomy of the Black community has served as an anti-Korean ideology, and Black nationalists have played a key role in organizing boycotts and other forms of anti-Korean activities. Cultural differences, Korean merchants' language difficulties, and mutual prejudice have contributed to individual disputes between Korean merchants or employees and Black customers. But to explain collective forms of Korean–African American conflicts such as boycotts, the active agency of the Black nationalists is necessary.

CHAPTER 7

Koreans' Efforts to Improve Relations with African Americans

Korean immigrants have responded to their business-related conflicts with the African American community in two different ways. On the one hand, they have made efforts to improve relations with the African American community. On the other, they have acted collectively to challenge hostility toward Korean merchants in Afro-Caribbean and African American neighborhoods. The latter response is considered in chapter 8; this chapter focuses on Koreans' efforts to improve relations with Blacks in New York and in Los Angeles, both before and after the 1992 riots.

NEW YORK

Since the early 1980s, Korean merchants in Black neighborhoods in New York have established several local merchants' associations, which have worked to maintain better relations with residents both by listening to their complaints about Korean merchants and by contributing money and gifts to local organizations. The two major Black boycotts of Korean stores in Brooklyn during recent years and the destruction of Korean stores during the Los Angeles riots taught Koreans that maintaining harmony with the Black community is essential to their economic survival. Thus, not only Korean merchants' associations in Black neighborhoods but also specialized Korean business associations, Korean ethnic churches, and Korean community leaders outside business and religion have made efforts to unify the Korean and Black communities.

KOREAN MERCHANTS' ASSOCIATIONS

Korean merchants in Black neighborhoods are more keenly aware of the need to improve their relationship with Blacks than any other Korean group. Because of boycotts and other forms of hostility, Korean merchants' associations in Black neighborhoods were established earlier and have functioned more actively than those in non-Black neighborhoods. In all, there are a dozen Korean local merchants' associations in New York.

There are approximately 180 Korean-owned stores in Jamaica, Queens, a predominantly Black area. Koreans in Jamaica formed a merchants' association in 1981 in their effort to end a boycott of a Korean store. Since its establishment, more than fifty Korean merchants in Jamaica have joined the association. Members meet almost every month and maintain close contacts with elected leaders of the community. They regularly donate money and gifts to local organizations: at the end of 1992, they provided gifts for twenty-three groups. They also periodically make donations in response to special needs, such as Little League baseball teams that need help. In addition, they have maintained close relations with the local police, having regular dinners with police officers (every two months) and giving them annual awards. As a result of building these connections, they have been able to avoid major interracial conflicts since the first boycott in 1981. According to the Jamaica Korean Merchants Association, the police usually respond quickly to Korean merchants when the merchants encounter problems with customers. When Blacks were picketing a Korean store in Brooklyn in December 1988, the boycott leaders attempted to start another boycott in Jamaica but failed, because the residents there did not cooperate (SGT, December 6, 1988).

In the early 1970s, several Korean immigrants peddled in Harlem, selling wigs to African American customers. Beginning in the late 1970s, Koreans began to open stores in Harlem. As of 1994, there are about fifty-five Korean-owned stores along 125th Street, the heart of Harlem. Before Korean immigrants opened businesses, Harlem was still suffering from the effects of the 1964 Harlem riot and many buildings remained dilapidated. Korean immigrants turned Harlem into a thriving business area within a short period of time. Merchants with stores along 125th Street established the Korean Merchants Association of Harlem in 1980 to "maintain a better relationship with Black residents." Since then, Harlem Korean merchants have actively participated in the neighborhood and financially supported a number of local organizations. They have maintained close relations with the residents, especially following the 1984–85 boycott of Korean stores in this area. Association members meet with Harlem community leaders once every two months to hear customers' complaints and assess their needs. When neighborhood organizations in Harlem need money, food, or merchandise, the Korean businesses located along 125th Street, all affiliated with the Harlem Korean Merchants Association, often make donations.

Won-Duk Kim, a store owner in Harlem for fifteen years, has played a central role in creating a bridge between Korean merchants and the African American community. Critical of Korean merchants' "unkind services" to African American customers and their failure to hire African American employees, he treats customers with respect and hires only Black employees. When I visited his clothing store in July 1991, all four employees, including the cashier, were African American. He has frequently donated money and merchandise to several local organizations. In addition, he annually spent around $20,000 to advertise his business in the *Amsterdam News,* a Harlem-based African American daily, mainly to "contribute money" to the newspaper. He was instrumental in establishing the Korean merchants' association in Harlem. As a result, he has become acquainted with many African American pastors and community leaders in Harlem, as well as with the editor of the *Amsterdam News.*

He organized the Korean-African Association for Friendship in 1990 and guided a group of thirty-seven African American pastors (joined by two journalists) on a friendship visit to Korea in October 1991. The New York Korean community offered to raise funds to cover the expenses of their flight to Korea; when the money raised fell short, Kim donated about $14,000 to cover the airfare. The Korean Christian Association covered the expenses of the seven-day stay in Korea (*SGT,* September 29, 1991). On April 30, 1992, the day after the riots started in Los Angeles, most Korean merchants in New York closed their stores early in the afternoon; Kim was the only Korean in Harlem who did not. He had maintained such a good relationship with African American residents that he was not afraid to open his store that evening.

Local business associations can handle issues concerning Korean merchants' relations with residents far more effectively than specialized business associations. Yet specialized associations such as the Korean Produce Association of New York and the Korean Fish Retailers Association have also made efforts to improve intergroup relations. Some Korean trade associations have provided seminars on Black culture and history and on how to serve Black customers effectively. Two trade associations, the Korean-American Grocers Association of New York (KAGRONY) and the Korean Produce Association of New York, have established scholarship funds for Black students, which have annually awarded $1,000 scholarships since 1990. In February 1990, the Korean Produce Association of New York sponsored a Korean–African American cultural exchange program at the Schomberg Center for Research in Black Culture in Harlem, where Korean and African American groups performed their traditional songs and dances for each other (*KCDNY*, February 16, 1990). Since 1989, the Korean Produce Association has annually donated hundreds of turkeys to poor Black people. KAGRONY delivered two hundred Thanksgiving turkeys to a predominantly Black church in Brooklyn in November 1992.

In February 1993, KAGRONY, in coordination with the Coca-Cola Company and the New York City chapter of the NAACP, established a special scholarship program for African American children. This program, named "Share the Dream" in honor of Martin Luther King Jr., annually gives $2,000 awards for the five best essays on "Harmony in a Multiethnic Society: What Does it Mean." The Education Committee of the New York City chapter of the NAACP selected the 1993 winners from about seven hundred essays submitted by Black high school seniors in the New York metropolitan area (*SGT*, May 13, 1993). KAGRONY and the Coca-Cola Company each donate $5,000 every year for this program.[1]

KOREAN CHURCHES AND PASTORS

Both Korean and African American communities are church oriented, and thus Christian churches and pastors play important roles in both. Accordingly, Korean churches and pastors are in a good position to form connections between the two communities. As of August 1994, there are more than four hundred Korean immigrant churches in the New York metropolitan area. But most are mainly concerned with their own growth in membership and with evangelism in other countries. Korean churches have been criticized for paying little attention to social issues affecting the whole Korean community.

However, some Korean pastors and churches, though a small number, have been concerned about conflicts between Koreans and African Americans and have acted, both individually and as a group, to bridge the gap between the two groups. The Korean community has been critical of Koreans' prejudiced attitudes toward African American and other groups. Many Koreans feel that learning about Black culture and history will help Korean immigrants maintain racial harmony through greater understanding. Since the 1990 boycott of Korean stores in Brooklyn, several Korean churches have provided seminars on these subjects, as well as on Korean–African American conflicts. Several Korean churches have made donations to African American churches or individual poor Blacks. Two Korean churches hired African American pastors for youth education—though for less than a year—mainly to improve intergroup relations. These efforts reflect Korean churches' increased concern about interracial issues.

A Korean minister in New York who has done much to unify the Korean and African American communities is the Reverend Joong Sik Ahn. In many talks given to Korean groups, he has emphasized that only interracial dialogue can improve the relationship between the two communities (Ahn 1991). In late 1984, after a boycott of Korean stores in Harlem had started, the Korean Brooklyn Church, which he has served as main pastor, sponsored a pastoral conference between Korean and African American Presbyterians. It also sponsored three other interracial dialogues between Korean and African American pastors between 1989 and 1991. Ahn has been involved in many other social causes, including his leading role in inviting Christian leaders from North Korea to New York for a unification seminar.

The Korean Church and Institute is located in a Manhattan area close to Harlem. Partly because of its tradition and partly because of the liberal ideology of church leaders, it has paid great attention to social issues.[2] The church has organized two seminars on Korean–African American conflicts since 1990: one a panel discussion by church members and the other a lecture by an African American pastor. In November 1992, the church invited church leaders and lay members from four African American churches in Harlem to an interracial Thanksgiving party. Koreans and African Americans ate dinner, sang, and danced together. These activities have greatly contributed to interracial harmony.

The Council of Korean Churches of Greater New York was established in 1976. At the end of 1988, when Black boycott leaders did not show any sign of stopping their picketing against a Korean store in Brooklyn, Korean pastors in New York were under heavy pressure to open a dialogue with African American pastors. The council organized a meeting in the Brooklyn area in early 1989, but only three African American pastors appeared. Though several other small Korean pastoral groups have sponsored such interracial meetings between pastors, they have not produced fruitful results.

In the summer of 1990, when a boycott of two Korean stores in Brooklyn was headline news, a group of Korean pastors in the Brooklyn area contacted Black pastors and held several interracial pastoral meetings. These meetings led to the creation of the Coalition for Racial Harmony in August 1990. Korean and Black pastors in the coalition recommended several measures that would improve intergroup relations, including efforts by Korean merchants to hire more Black workers and the institution of a regular channel of communication between the two communities (*SGT,* September 4, 1990). The coalition helped the Korean Association of Brooklyn organize the Korean-American Friendship Festival at Prospect Park in Brooklyn on September 30, 1990 (*SGT,* October 2, 1990). Unfortunately, the coalition is no longer functioning, and there is currently no other Korean–African American pastoral association that can intervene should major conflicts arise.

As we have noted, Korean pastors have been largely unsuccessful in opening channels with their African American counterparts for dialogues on interracial harmony. They appear to have failed mainly because of major differences between these two groups of religious leaders, both in theological outlook and in degree of social concern. Historically, African American churches and pastors have played a central role in African American political and community activities. As Morris (1984, 4) put it, "The black church functioned as the institutional center of the modern Black civil rights movement." In the tradition of the Reverend Martin Luther King Jr., contemporary African American pastors are deeply involved with social issues.

In contrast, Korean pastors in both the United States and South Korea are generally conservative in their political ideology and theological orientation. Though most African American pastors are seriously concerned with poverty, homelessness, drug abuse, and teen pregnancy, few Korean pastors worry much about these issues, which are not pressing problems in the Korean community. Instead, most Korean pastors are interested in salvation after death and missionary activities in other countries. One of the two Black pastors mentioned above who were hired for youth ministry in Queens was forced to resign within four months because, according to the head pastor of the church, his "teachings and interpretations of the Bible were not acceptable to the parents of young Koreans." Chang (1990) pointed out that Korean and African American religious leaders in Los Angeles could not build mutual respect and feelings of fellowship for the same reasons.

THE REVEREND HENRY HONG

The Reverend Henry Hong has made a significant contribution to bridging the Korean and African American communities in New York and probably in the entire country. After completing the master of divinity program at Alliance Theological Seminary in 1988, he served a Black church in Brooklyn; he currently serves as the main pastor of another Black church, Love Mission Church, in the Bronx. He is the president of the Multiethnic Peace Ministry, which was created in May 1990 in Brooklyn by Korean, African American, and White pastors to achieve racial harmony (*SGT*, May 22, 1990). He has emphasized "love mission" as the principle of his missionary activities, which he characterizes with the phrase "Love Whom You Can't Love." His missionary activities for Blacks in New York City include living in a Black neighborhood and helping Black homeless people. He has given sermons to more than one hundred Black churches in the United States and Jamaica.

In late 1991, the Black rap singer Ice Cube released a new album that included a controversial song "Black Korea." The song scorned, attacked, and threatened Korean merchants (*SGT*, November 20, 1991). In response to Ice Cube's song, Hong created the song "Black Is Beautiful," emphasizing Blacks' cultural strengths and the racial harmony between Blacks and Koreans (*KTLA*, November 27, 1991). His song was first introduced in New York at a multiethnic service held at the Central Presbyterian Church in midtown Manhattan (*KTNY*, January 29, 1992). He collected food from Korean grocery stores, in the name of "Free Food for Those in Need Donated by Korean-American Neighbors," and donated it to the Black and Latino poor in the Bronx and Brooklyn (*SGT*, September 15, 1992). As part of his Korean-Black racial harmony campaign, he also designed a pin declaring "Love One Another—The Best Philosophy to Live By" and distributed it to Korean merchants in Black neighborhoods.

For his efforts to improve the relationship between Koreans and African Americans, the Reverend Hong was given the "Good News Maker"
award by the *New York Christian Times* in 1991. Hong had been involved in missionary activities for poor Blacks even before Korean
and Black communities in New York engaged in bitter conflicts; the
1990–91 boycott of two Korean stores in Brooklyn further strengthened his role and increased his fame as a peace minister as he tried to
heal the wounds in the two communities. By helping poor Blacks, Hong
has greatly contributed to improving Korean-Black relationships. His
efforts in the Korean community have been no less significant in achieving interracial harmony. He has given talks to several Korean church
and secular groups, emphasizing the importance of trying to understand Blacks. He has repeatedly argued that mutual misunderstanding
is the main source of conflict between Koreans and Blacks, but that the
two groups have cultural similarities sufficient to tie them together.[3]

In 1991, Hong played a central role in negotiating with Christian
leaders in Korea to invite African American ministers to Korea and
in organizing the visit, already mentioned, of thirty-seven African
American ministers selected from the New York area (*SGT*, September
29, 1991). In December 1992, he also organized and guided a team of
fifty leading African American pastors from New York, Los Angeles,
Chicago, Washington, and Atlanta on a ten-day visit to Korea. During
their stay in Seoul, African American pastors each gave sermons in two
or three Korean churches. They also met with many high-ranking government officials, including President Roh Tae Woo. Particularly since
the Los Angeles riots, the Korean government has been greatly concerned with improving the relationship between Korean and African
American communities in the United States. Korean communities in the
pastors' home cities made donations to cover part of the expenses for
their air travel, and ASIANA, a newly established Korean airline, provided a free flight back to all participants on its first flight from Seoul
to New York. The Korean Christian Association in South Korea paid
for lodging, food, and transportation in Korea.

THE KOREAN ASSOCIATION OF NEW YORK

As an umbrella organization representing the entire Korean community, the Korean Association of New York (KANY) has intervened in
all major Black boycotts of Korean stores that have occurred since
1981. KANY has also made efforts to reduce Korean–African Ameri-

can conflict by bringing the two communities closer and by maintaining better relations with African American organizations. Between 1988 and 1993, KANY had three presidents, each serving a two-year term. All three presidents tried to improve relations with the African American community.

In December 1988 KANY, under the leadership of Moon Sung Lee, attended a dinner party for racial harmony organized by the *New York Voice,* a major African American daily in New York. At the party, Koreans and Blacks performed their traditional music and dances, and KANY donated $5,000 to the newspaper (*KCDNY,* December 16, 1988). At that time, the Korean community was struggling to end a four-month-long boycott of a Korean store in Brooklyn. Whereas the *Amsterdam News* generally supported the radical position of Black boycott organizers, the *New York Voice* published articles encouraging racial harmony and criticizing the 1988 Brooklyn boycott for "going too far" (*KTNY,* December 12, 1988). KANY also had several meetings with African American community leaders to facilitate mutual understanding (*KCDNY,* April 15, 1989).

In the spring of 1990, when two rival candidates running for the president of KANY engaged in bitter election campaigns, a Black boycott of Korean stores in Brooklyn was receiving media attention. Each candidate promised that, once elected, he would take effective measures to improve intergroup relations, particularly Korean–African American relations (*SGT,* March 26, 1990). When elected president in April 1990, Jong Duk Byun took quick action. Under his leadership, KANY organized a twenty-five-member interracial team for a ten-day visit to Korea in June, called "A Good Will Mission." The mission consisted of ten Koreans and fifteen African American, Latino, Jewish, and Italian American religious, educational, and political leaders. The ten New York Korean community and business leaders who accompanied the non-Korean leaders covered their own expenses as well as the non-Korean participants' airfare. Kyung Hee University in Korea covered the travel expenses incurred in Korea. The main goal of the mission was to help visitors understand Korean culture. The non-Korean visitors attended lectures on Korean history and culture given at Kyung Hee University. The lecture on Confucianism reportedly helped the visitors understand why Korean merchants do not usually say hello to customers or make direct eye contact with them, both behaviors taken by American customers as signs of disrespect.

In July 1990, after the community leaders returned from visiting Korea, KANY turned the interracial team into the Ethnic Committee for Racial Harmony and Outreach (ECHO). It was created to provide a permanent forum for contributing to interracial harmony. The president of the board of KANY and the president of the Brooklyn chapter of the NAACP became its cochairs. In early 1992, the interracial committee, along with KANY, selected seven Black students for graduate study in Korea. In March 1993, three of the selected students went to Korea to study at Kyung Hee University with full financial support from the host university. They were talented students who had graduated from major American universities, including New York University and Cornell University. Depending on the results of this first group, similar numbers of Black students may continue to be sent to Korea under this program.

Beginning in the summer of 1991, KANY, under the leadership of Jong Duk Byun, initiated a campaign to encourage Korean merchants in Black and Latino neighborhoods to make friends with residents. Encouraged by KANY, the New York City Human Rights Commission, and the local police, Korean merchants in areas of Harlem, Jamaica, Soho, Brooklyn, and the Bronx gave "block parties" for their residents, serving them Korean traditional food such as *boolgogi* and entertaining them with performances of tae kwon do (*SGT,* September 4, 16, 1991). Also in 1991, KANY began a program of donating turkeys to poor and homeless Blacks. That year alone, they gave approximately three thousand turkeys to Black church shelters and to City Harvest, a nonprofit charity. In 1992, they donated seven hundred turkeys (*SGT,* November 25, 1992).

LOS ANGELES BEFORE THE RIOTS

THE BLACK-KOREAN ALLIANCE

Well before the 1992 riots, the Los Angeles Korean community made multifaceted efforts to reduce tensions with the African American community. Most important in this connection was the formation of the Black-Korean Alliance.[4] In the wake of the successive murders of four Korean merchants in African American neighborhoods in April 1986, the Black-Korean Community Relations Commission convened in May 1986; it later was renamed the Black-Korean Alliance (BKA). Religious, business, civic, police, and community-based organizations of both the Korean and African American communities participated in the BKA. Its main goals were to facilitate mutual understanding and seek peaceful resolutions to Korean–African American conflicts. To achieve the intended goals, it initially established five subcommittees: employment, community education and cultural exchange, fund-raising, religious leadership, and economic development (Chang 1990).

Because of lack of financial resources, misunderstandings between Korean and African American members, and nonparticipation by Korean merchants in African American neighborhoods, the organization did not achieve two of its specific objectives: increasing employment of African American residents by Korean merchants and undertaking Korean–African American joint economic projects. It was ultimately abolished in 1992, after the Los Angeles riots. Nevertheless, it did contribute to reducing tensions and increasing understanding between the two communities. For two years prior to the 1992 riots, Korean–African American tensions heightened, with the shootings and subsequent deaths of two African Americans in Korean stores. During this critical period, the BKA served as an important channel for interracial communication and dialogue. Though the Los Angeles County Human Relations Commission was instrumental in forming and maintaining the biracial organization, the Korean-American Grocers Association of Southern California and several other Korean community and business associations supported it and participated, at least in its early stages of development.

KOREAN CHURCHES

Korean churches in Los Angeles have made greater efforts to reduce intergroup tensions and facilitate communication with the African American community than those in New York. Their efforts include cultural exchanges, joint religious services, and scholarship programs with African American churches on both the individual and group level.

Beginning in 1984, the Oriental Mission Church, the largest Korean congregation in the United States with over 6,000 members, held several joint services with African American church members and choirs. Also since that time, it has delivered scholarships amounting to $5,000 annually to African American students. Several other Korean churches have made contributions to African American residents and church members by donating Korean food, turkeys, and other charitable items. For example, Hebron Presbyterian Church, located in an African American neighborhood, has given residents a Thanksgiving party with Korean food, traditional Korean songs, and traditional dances every year since 1988. More than 1,000 African American residents attended the party in 1990 (*KCDNY,* November 14, 1990). In September 1991, Grace Korean Church started a program in which thirty low-income African American children met with Korean children monthly for sight-seeing and Bible study (*KTLA,* September 18, 1991). At about the same time, Young Nak Presbyterian Church of Los Angeles, the second largest Korean church in Los Angeles, started a scholarship program for African American children with awards of $3,000 per year; it also donated a large quantity of food and clothing to homeless and poor Blacks. The church spent approximately $20,000 on such charities in 1991 alone.

In February 1985, Korean and African American church leaders initiated a sister-church program in which about twenty Korean churches would maintain close relationships with a similar number of African American churches through choir exchanges, joint services, and cultural exchanges (Dart 1985). On April 7, 1985, some 130 Korean and African American churches participated in a joint Easter Sunday service held at McArthur Park, near Koreatown in Los Angeles (Chang 1990). In addition to joint services, this program contributed to organizing a ten-day friendship visit of seven African American pastors to Seoul in 1985, much earlier than Koreans in New York arranged such a visit. Korean Catholic churches in Los Angeles, too, participated in Korean–African American Christian fellowship activities. Korean and African American Catholic churches in Southern California established a friendship committee in December 1991 and have held regular meetings to discuss common interests and enhance their mutual understanding (*KTLA,* December 15, 1991; March 3, 1992). Korean Catholics donated $10,000 to the African American community in 1991. The Korean–African American Catholic friendship was greatly facilitated by Los Angeles Catholic Cardinal Roger Mahony. The Korean-Black Catholic Friendship Committee planned to hold a Korean-Black Harmony Cultural Festival in July 1992, but the event did not materialize because of the riots.

In October 1991, following the agreement to end the boycott of John's Liquor Market, Korean and African American church leaders established the African/Korean-American Christian Alliance to improve the relationship between the two communities. The formation of this biracial Christian alliance was strongly supported by Mayor Tom Bradley, who was anxious to bring Koreans and African Americans together through a variety of biracial organizations (*KTLA,* October 25,

1991). The organization's major achievement was arranging a mass meeting for interracial harmony. The meeting was held in front of City Hall the day before Thanksgiving 1991. Approximately three thousand Korean and African American Christians talked, hugged, danced, and sang together, hand in hand (*KTLA*, November 28, 1991). At the meeting, Koreans provided lunch and 14,000 items of clothing to homeless people.

KOREAN MERCHANTS' ASSOCIATIONS

The Korean Chamber of Commerce of Los Angeles and the Korean-American Grocers Association of Southern California are considered the two major trade associations in the Korean community in Los Angeles, and they have done much to reduce tensions with the African American community. The Korean Chamber of Commerce of Los Angeles represents all Korean merchants. I interviewed the secretary of the association in person in August 1990, and again by telephone in December 1992. As these interviews and as newspaper articles indicate, the association did a number of things to promote interracial harmony. In 1986, it awarded some $2,000 in scholarship funds to African Americans. Since 1989, it has arranged frequent Korean–African American merchants' forums. It has given humanitarian awards to eminent African American leaders every year since 1990. In April 1991, it arranged a seven-day visit to Korea for Mayor Tom Bradley and seven leaders of the Black Business Association, and it also covered part of their travel expenses (*KTLA*, April 11a, 1991). Korean and Black chambers of commerce also planned a long-term joint project to build an apartment complex in a low-income African American area. The project, actively supported by Mayor Bradley, involved an investment of $2 million by the Korean Chamber of Commerce. The 1992 riots broke out before they were able to find a suitable site for apartment construction, delaying its construction indefinitely (*SGT*, April 28b, 1992).

Another Korean trade association that made efforts to improve relations with the African American community prior to the riots was the Korean-American Grocers Association of Southern California (KAGROSC). Because of the large number of Korean grocery and liquor stores located in South Central Los Angeles, it was quite natural that this association made great efforts to ameliorate relationships with the African American community. In 1986 when four Korean merchants in South Central Los Angeles were murdered, KAGROSC offered $10,000 for the arrest of the murderer. After the arrest was made by a Los Angeles police officer, whom departmental policy prevented from accepting the reward, KAGROSC allotted the money to a scholarship fund for African American and Mexican students.

In November 1991, KAGROSC, African American leaders, and the Los Angeles City mayor's office developed a program to promote the employment of African American youngsters by Korean merchants (*KTLA*, November 16, 1991; *SGT*, November 20, 1991). African American organizations were to select one hundred Black youngsters in low-income neighborhoods for job training by the city government and employment in Korean businesses. After the selected youths completed a two-month education and training program, KAGROSC would recommend them for employment in Korean stores in African American neighborhoods. The program was designed by KAGROSC with strong support from Mayor Bradley, who tried to tie Korean and African American communities together through economic projects. However, as this program got underway, the riots hit South Central Los Angeles and especially the Los Angeles Korean community. As a result, this program, like the Korean-Black apartment program, never materialized.

LOS ANGELES AND OTHER CITIES AFTER THE RIOTS

THE VALUE OF ECONOMIC PROGRAMS

The Los Angeles riots taught Korean Americans that they cannot live in isolation from other groups. A review of Korean ethnic newspaper articles indicates that since the riots, Korean community and business leaders in various cities have more consciously worked at avoiding isolation. However, Korean merchants' willingness to invest money in the African American community through donations and other economic programs intended to lessen Korean–African American tensions has been significantly reduced by the riot experience, at least in Los Angeles. Instead, Koreans there have focused on using various social and cultural programs to increase mutual understanding. The financial and psychological damage Koreans in Los Angeles suffered taught Koreans in other cities a lesson; other Korean communities are now making more positive efforts to improve relations with the African American community.

Koreans' efforts to reduce Korean–African American tensions in Los

Angeles culminated during the six-month period before the 1992 riots; many Korean business and nonbusiness organizations spent much time, energy, and money establishing communication channels with the African American community. Before the riots, Korean merchants in Los Angeles tried to join the Korean and African American communities through economic programs, hoping to protect their business activities in African American neighborhoods. The *Korea Times Los Angeles* estimated that the donations made to the African American community by various Korean ethnic organizations in Los Angeles in 1991 alone amounted to more than $100,000 (*KTLA*, January 7, 1992). However, the riots have convinced the Korean merchants that such economic efforts will not protect them from victimization.

A visit to Los Angeles in August 1992, approximately four months after the riots, provided me with the opportunity to interview several Korean business leaders. I also interviewed by telephone a dozen Korean business leaders in Los Angeles at the end of 1992 and in early 1993. These interviews revealed that Korean merchants in Los Angeles reject the earlier assumption that Koreans' monetary investments in the African American community would help prevent more radical forms of hostility such as boycotts, looting, and arson. They generally agree that as long as a large number of Koreans own businesses in poor African American neighborhoods they will be targets of hostility, regardless of their efforts to improve relations. Many Korean business leaders in Los Angeles now believe that Korean merchants must either leave African American neighborhoods or make individual efforts to improve relations with their customers. Before the riots, Mayor Bradley was anxious to tie the Korean and African American communities together more or less permanently through joint economic programs, and Korean business leaders responded positively to his efforts. However, after the riots, the business leaders questioned the worth of such programs that involved Koreans' economic aid to the African American community.[5]

Korean merchants' decreased commitment to joint economic programs in African American neighborhoods was reflected in their reactions to meetings between representatives of the Korean-American Grocers Association of Southern California and Black gang leaders. Through the Reverend James Stern, who counseled the gang members, two Black gangs, the Bloods and the Crips, proposed a meeting with KAGROSC approximately one month after the riots, and KAGROSC accepted. Representatives of the gangs and KAGROSC first met on May 25 at the Wilshire Sheraton Hotel (*KTLA*, May 26, 1992). Though they had agreed to have a closed meeting, Black gang leaders invited the major media to the meeting and thus it became widely publicized. The gang leaders proposed seven points, which included the employment of Black youths by Korean stores, the establishment of a Korean bank in African American neighborhoods, and Korean-Black joint projects. The media reported that Korean and Black representatives reached an agreement on the seven points proposed by Black gang leaders. However, the Korean representatives argued that they had only promised to consider them. Four days later, they had a second meeting at which gang leaders asked Korean merchants to establish a vocational school in African American neighborhoods and to help them get a commercial loan from a Korean bank for start-up capital (*KTLA*, May 31, 1992).

These meetings came a few days after the news that Black gang members had selectively targeted Korean stores during the riots. According to my interviews, representatives of the Korean grocers' association, Yang Il Kim and David Kim, agreed to meetings with Black gang leaders out of their concern that Korean grocery and liquor store owners in South Central Los Angeles could not be protected until they opened a communication channel with the gangs. However, other Korean business leaders and those in the community severely criticized the leaders of KAGROSC for meeting with those who they believed were responsible for attacking Korean stores during the riots. They argued that the Korean community should not sit down for talks with Black gang members until the latter made a formal apology for their acts of looting and arson. Furthermore, they maintained that any proposal involving agreements between Korean and African American groups would not be effective in protecting Korean merchants in African American neighborhoods. Thus, the seven points proposed by Black gang leaders were never given serious consideration by Korean business leaders.

CULTURAL AND SOCIAL PROGRAMS

Whereas Korean trade associations in Los Angeles no longer have any motive to make monetary contributions to the African American community, nonbusiness organizations have made greater efforts than before to improve long-term mutual understanding through social and cultural programs. Korean churches, second-generation organizations, and even organizations in Korea have played key roles in social and cultural programs for interracial harmony.

For one month between September and October 1992, the Korean

Cultural Center displayed the works of six famous African American artists to a Korean audience (*KTLA*, October 8, 1992). The general purpose of this branch of the Korean Information Ministry is to introduce and advocate Korean culture to American citizens. Before the riots, the Los Angeles office of the cultural service had never in its eleven-year history displayed works by African American artists. In November 1992 there was further interaction between the races, as Korean and African American community leaders had the opportunity to play golf together (*KTLA*, October 28, 1992). With Mayor Bradley and Sammy Lee, a Korean American Olympic gold medalist in diving, serving as honorary copresidents of the preparation committee, the first Korean-Black golf classic served as a channel for communication and dialogue between the leaders of the two communities. The money donated by the participants was used to start a scholarship fund for Korean and African American college students in Southern California. They plan to continue the biracial golf tournament as an annual event to help bridge the two communities.

The Korean community in Los Angeles prepared several Korean–African American cultural exchange programs in 1993. In February, the Korean Association of Southern California organized a Korean–African American friendship concert in which a chorus from South Korea (the Korean Mothers' Chorus), a chorus from the Los Angeles Korean community (the Los Angeles Seoul Choral), and an African American chorus (the Hallman Chorus) performed hymns, popular music, and national songs for the audience of about 450 (*KTLA*, February 22, 1993). Under a program started in March, Korean and African American elementary school children exchanged visits and studied each other's culture and history (*KTLA*, March 3, 1993). This program was sponsored by the Los Angeles Unified School District.

On April 17, 1993, when the jury announced a guilty verdict in the second Rodney King beating trial,[6] Korean and Black directors of two libraries, one in Koreatown (Pico Koreatown Library) and the other in an African American neighborhood (Washington Irving Library), organized a Korean-Black dance festival, "Seoul to Soul: Dance"; it was held at Exposition Library, in an African American neighborhood (*KTLA*, April 22, 1993). Over one hundred Koreans and African Americans enjoyed participating in traditional Korean and African American dances. In December 1991, the two libraries had initiated a Korean-Black cultural exchange program, displaying works by Korean and African American artists at both libraries, which was disrupted in 1992 when the riots broke out (*SGT,* December 7, 1991). A similar effort was made by the Watts Foundation, a nonprofit organization serving low-income African American residents in South Central Los Angeles. As part of its 1993 summer counseling and educational programs, it arranged for African American children to learn Korean wrestling, tae kwon do, and Korean dances from Korean instructors (*KTLA,* July 21, 1993).

We noted in the previous two chapters that the views of younger-generation Koreans about Korean–African American conflicts differ from those of Korean immigrants, views that include blaming the "White system" rather than African Americans for Korean–African American interracial tensions. This suggests that 1.5- and second-generation Koreans can reach out to African Americans more effectively than Korean immigrants. Since the 1992 riots, younger-generation Korean organizations in Los Angeles and other cities have played an increasingly important role in Korean Americans' efforts to improve their relationship with the African American community. For example, in January 1993 the Korean Youth and Community Center, a major second-generation service organization in Los Angeles, prepared a Korean–African American interracial recreational program in which Korean and Black adolescents went fishing and watched basketball games together (*KTLA,* January 1, 1993). The Coalition of Korean-American Voters, a major second-generation Korean political organization in New York, coordinated with several non-Korean intergroup conflict resolution centers in undertaking the Black-Korean Mediation Project between 1993 and 1994. The project gave nine Korean and ten Black young volunteers a six-month training in conflict resolution (*KCDNY,* April 25, 1994). The Korean American Alliance, a major second-generation Korean organization in Washington, D.C., coordinated with two Black organizations in organizing a Korean-Black ten kilometer race in October 1993 (*KTLA,* October 4b, 1993).

GOODWILL TRIPS TO KOREA

Even before the Los Angeles riots, Korean community leaders in New York and Los Angeles arranged Black ministers' goodwill visits to Korea as part of an attempt to improve relations with the African American community. Such visits have become a more popular technique of promoting interracial harmony since the riots. Not only African American ministers but also African American high school and college students have been recently invited to Korea. Korean Christian leaders and organizations have been sponsors, and the Korean government has played an important role recently in inviting these African American community leaders and students to Korea.

Two African American groups in Los Angeles made separate visits to Korea in October 1992. Twenty-two African American leaders were invited by the Korean Press Center in Korea, and ten African American high school and college students visited as well. The students' trip was sponsored by the Korean Association of Full Gospel Churches in Korea and Young Nak Presbyterian Church of Los Angeles (*KTLA*, October 25, 1992; November 10, 1992). During their visit, the students had the opportunity to tour Korean cultural sites and talk with Korean students. In the summer of 1993, the Korea Society initiated a program, "Kids to Korea," that enabled sixteen Black students, eight from Los Angeles and eight from New York, to visit Korea for ten days to increase their understanding of Korean society and Korean culture (*KTLA*, August 7, 1993). In 1994, the Korean government, too, started a similar summer visiting program for Black students. That summer, forty-seven Black students selected from the high schools and colleges in the Los Angeles area made a three-week visit to Korea (*KTLA*, August 11, 1994). This is part of the Korean government's broader efforts to help lessen Korean–African American tensions since the riots. The Philadelphia and San Francisco Korean communities arranged similar summer visiting programs for African American students.

In the New York Korean community, Korean trade and local merchants' associations, Korean Christian churches and pastors, and the Korean Association of New York have all worked to improve relations with the Black community. Two Korean local merchants' associations—the Jamaican Korean Merchants Association and the Harlem Korean Merchants Association—have had particular success in maintaining close relations with Black neighborhoods by donating money and merchandise to local organizations and by regularly meeting with Black community leaders and the local police. Unfortunately, with rare exceptions, such as the Reverend Henry Hong, Korean and African American religious leaders have not been able to move beyond their differences in theological outlook and social concerns to create a dialogue that would build on their shared church-oriented values.

Whereas the Black population in New York City is widely scattered in different areas, Blacks in Los Angeles concentrate in South Central

Los Angeles. Partly because of this difference in settlement patterns, Korean local merchants' associations in Los Angeles have not been active in promoting close relations with African American neighborhoods. Instead, two trade associations—the Korean-American Grocers Association of Southern California and the Korean Chamber of Commerce of Los Angeles—have more aggressively promoted intergroup relations. The Korean-Black joint economic projects that they were developing immediately before the riots, when Korean–African American tensions had already heightened, have been halted. However, Korean Christian leaders and churches in Los Angeles, both individually and collectively, have made greater efforts to moderate Korean–African American tensions and promote interracial harmony than their counterparts in New York. Their efforts include cultural exchanges, joint church services, and scholarship programs for African American students.

The victimization of many Korean merchants during the riots has led Koreans to be more conscious of their need to improve Korean–African American relations. Thus Koreans in Los Angeles and other communities have made greater efforts to improve these relations. It is important to note the shift in focus from economic programs before the riots to cultural and social programs after the riots. It is also important to note that younger-generation Koreans, who can better understand the African American community than can Korean immigrants, have played a particularly significant role since the riots in bridging the two communities.

CHAPTER 8

Korean–African American Conflicts

Positive Effects

Members of an ethnic group tend to join ranks in internal solidarity when they encounter threats from the outside world. Several groups have posed threats to Korean merchants, the most serious undoubtedly being the danger of physical violence, murder, arson, boycott, and looting in Black neighborhoods. Therefore, Korean–African American conflicts have more strongly fostered Korean internal solidarity than have any other type of business-related intergroup conflict. Korean merchants in Black neighborhoods have established local business associations to try collectively to solve problems with Black customers and residents. Black boycotts of Korean stores in New York and other cities and the destruction of Korean stores during the Los Angeles riots have threatened Korean immigrants' economic survival itself. Thus, these hostile actions have led not only Korean ghetto merchants but also other Korean immigrants to be concerned about their common fate and marginal status in this country. This chapter focuses on how Koreans' ethnic solidarity has been affected by the 1990–91 Brooklyn boycott of two Korean stores and the victimization of Korean merchants during the riots. In addition, it will examine Koreans' responses to Ice Cube's "Black Korea."

ICE CUBE'S "BLACK KOREA" AND KOREANS' RESPONSES

At the end of October 1991, Ice Cube, a Los Angeles–based Black rap singer, released a new album entitled *Death Certificate*. "Black Korea," a controversial song included in this album, reflects African Americans' hostility toward and violence against Koreans in such phrases as "they make a nigger mad enough to cause a little ruckus" and "pay respect to the black fist or we'll burn / your store right down to your crisp." In his interview with the *Los Angeles Times,* Ice Cube stated that the song reflected African Americans' and Koreans' mutual hatred rather than his own contempt for Koreans (Hunt 1991).

Naturally, Koreans were seriously concerned about the negative impact of this song on Koreans' image and Korean–African American relations. Since the song included many incendiary phrases, they worried it would encourage Black youngsters to use violence and arson against Korean merchants. As soon as the album was released, Korean community leaders in Los Angeles and New York had a series of meetings to discuss what measures to take to protest it. Both the Korean Embassy in Washington and the Korean Consulate General in Los Angeles were gravely concerned about its possible negative impact (*KCDNY,* November 9, 1991). Interestingly, the album also included a song, "No Vaseline," that encouraged the murder of Jerry Heller, Ice Cube's Jewish former manager. For this reason, the Simon Wiesenthal Center, a Jewish human rights organization, called on four national record chains to stop selling *Death Certificate* (Philips 1991).

Korean community leaders in Los Angeles, led by the Korean Consulate General, tried with no success to stop the distribution of the album by pressuring the record company, Priority Records. The St. Ice Beer Company, which used Ice Cube in their commercials, partly depended on Korean grocery and liquor retailers to distribute their merchandise. The Korean-American Grocers Association of Southern California threatened to boycott the company if it did not stop using Ice Cube as a model (*KTLA,* November 20, 1991). When there was no positive response, KAGROSC began a boycott. The boycott prompted the company to run an advertisement in Korean dailies in Los Angeles, emphasizing their difficulty in influencing Ice Cube and asking Korean grocers to stop the boycott. However, the National Korean-American Grocers Association, which has its office in Orange County, influenced other local KAGROs, including KAGRO New York, to increase the pressure on the St. Ice Beer Company, using the boycott as a lever for negotiation (*SGT,* November 14, 1991).

The grocers' boycott inflicted severe monetary damages on the beer company; the former president of KAGROLA told me that the company lost approximately $7 million from seven days of Koreans' boycotts.

On the seventh day, the company acceded, firing Ice Cube as a model. They also asked him to make a formal apology to the Korean community. Under pressure from the St. Ice Beer Company, Ice Cube apologized to Korean merchant leaders in Los Angeles for his inflammatory lyrics in April 1992, just prior to the eruption of the Los Angeles riots (S. Kim 1992a). Ice Cube arranged meetings with the president of the National Korean-American Grocers Association (Yang Il Kim) and the president of KAGROLA (David Kim), in which he told them, "I respect Korean Americans. It was directed at a few stores where I and my friends have had actual problems" (S. Kim 1992a). He later sent copies of a letter of apology to the Korean community and to members of the media. Though Korean merchants failed to stop the sale of the album, by pressuring their supplier they at least succeeded in making the singer formally apologize.

EFFECTS OF THE 1990 BROOKLYN BOYCOTT

The positive effects of business-related conflicts with the Black community on Korean solidarity were well exemplified in Koreans' reactions to a Black boycott against two Korean produce stores in Brooklyn in 1990–91. It started approximately one year after another Black boycott, led by the same activists, had successfully forced a Korean store in Brooklyn to close. Korean business and community leaders agreed that if the two boycotted stores were allowed to be coerced into closing, another Korean store would soon be targeted. Therefore, they made all efforts to support the two produce stores financially until the boycotters retreated.

In the early stage of the boycott, the Korean Produce Association of New York and the Flatbush Korean Merchants Association raised funds, mostly from their members, to help their fellow store owners. The Korean Association of New York and other business associations quickly followed them. Later, the Korean ethnic media joined the fundraising and buy-merchandise campaigns, using inflammatory advertisements and articles. For example, the *Sae Gae Times,* a New York–based Korean daily, aggressively campaigned to help the two Korean stores in an editorial (*SGT,* May 25, 1990): "To counteract the increasingly violent picketers effectively, we Koreans should visit the two victimized stores in long lines and buy fruits and vegetables. The two Church Avenue Korean stores have now become shrines where we Koreans should visit to learn about the sufferings of racial prejudice. We should offer sympathy to our compatriots by participating in the buy-merchandise campaign. All Korean ethnic organizations and individuals should share the sufferings and agony by participating in the buy-merchandise campaign." Many Korean ethnic churches, too, raised funds from their members for the two stores. Moreover, Koreans in other communities, both individually and as a group, contributed money to these merchants, who were seen as victims of Black racism against Koreans. Approximately $150,000 was raised during the first year of the boycott, providing each boycotted store owner with about $7,000 per month. Though the sales volume of each store was reduced to almost nothing during that year, each was able to stay open, mainly because of the community contributions.

The two store owners received not only financial but also strong moral support from Koreans all over the country throughout the boycott period. They confessed to me that they wanted to close their stores to end the "ordeal" as quickly as possible, but that they could not because of community pressure and support. One of the two boycotted stores was closed for two weeks in August 1990 for repair work. The Korean Association of New York, the Korean Produce Association of New York, and many other Korean community and business leaders pressured the owner to reopen (*KCDNY*, August 1, 1990). The two store owners received many letters from Koreans, including second-generation Korean elementary school children, encouraging them not to give up their stores. They were interviewed by the ethnic media numerous times and invited to give talks at many important ethnic meetings. Even the Korean Lions Club in Los Angeles invited one of the store owners for an interview (*SGT*, August 17, 1990). In an interview with the Korean ethnic media in Los Angeles, Bong Jae Jang promised that he would never close his store. Suddenly, the two store owners became heroes in the Korean community. A number of Korean churches demonstrated their support by taking their church members to shop at the stores on Sundays. Several Korean greengrocers in Brooklyn took turns working at the stores at night to encourage the dejected store owners, who faced defiant picketers for many days. One Korean lawyer volunteered to provide free legal services for them for a $6 million lawsuit against the picketer who beat the wife of Man Ho Park, one of the boycotted store owners (*SGT*, May 24, 1990).[1]

Koreans also tried to use political means to terminate the boycott. Thus the boycott heightened Koreans' political consciousness and helped to improve their political skills. Korean community and business leaders visited the Brooklyn borough president, the New York City mayor, the New York state legislature, and even the U.S. president and pressured them to take effective measures to break the boycott. In particular, Korean community leaders asked Mayor David Dinkins to enforce the court order that picketers stay fifty feet away from the stores. Under heavy pressure by politicians and the media to act quickly to end the boycott, Mayor Dinkins gave a special televised address on May 12, 1990.[2] In his speech, he vowed to do anything needed to halt the "racial bigotry" and promised to help stop the fifteen-week-old boycott (Murphy 1990). Yet, emphasizing "delicate diplomacy," he did not actively intervene. Much to the disappointment of the Korean community, he did not enforce the court order.

At the end of July, with no end in sight to the six-month boycott, the Korean Association of New York, in the hands of the newly established Korean-American Civil Rights Committee, planned to hold a mass demonstration in front of the City Hall in September to show Koreans' dissatisfaction with Mayor Dinkins's "lukewarm effort" to stop the boycott (KCDNY, August 3, 1990; KTNY, August 6, 1990). Many Korean community leaders were initially opposed, arguing that a demonstration would only exacerbate the already strained relationship with the Black community. However, when the owner of one of the boycotted store was beaten by picketers at the end of August (KCDNY, August 24, 1990), support from the community for the proposal to hold a rally became overwhelming. Moreover, many White politicians and leaders of other Asian communities encouraged Koreans to take political action, suggesting that they had waited long enough. The media criticisms of Dinkins for not personally intervening in the boycott spurred Korean community leaders to target him in the rally.[3]

As a member of the Korean-American Civil Rights Committee, I was involved in organizing the rally, made a prerally survey of Korean households to predict the number of participants, and actually participated in it. Therefore, I can provide many inside stories concerning the planning and progress of the rally. The Korean community leaders who organized the rally decided to focus their attack on Mayor Dinkins rather than on African American boycott leaders. So as not to worsen Korean-Black tensions, they also decided to emphasize racial harmony and avoid any anti-Black slogans. They intended to achieve two objectives through the rally: to make Mayor Dinkins take quick actions to end the boycott, and to show American society that Korean Americans will not silently accept any injustice done to them.

Though Korean community leaders attempted last-minute negoti-ations with the New York City government to terminate the boycott, using the planned rally as leverage, they failed to get any positive re-sponse. Therefore, the demonstration was held as planned on Septem-ber 18, 1990, in front of City Hall, urging the mayor to enforce the court order requiring the picketers to stay fifty feet away from the two stores. About seven thousand Koreans, approximately 15% of the adult Koreans in New York City, participated (*SGT,* September 19, 1990). In order to bring as many Koreans to the rally as possible, most Korean taxicab companies in New York City provided free transportation via more than a hundred taxis. Several Korean local and specialized busi-ness associations asked their members to close their stores on Septem-ber 18 so that they and their Korean employees could participate in the rally. Many White, Black, and Chinese politicians invited to the rally as guest speakers condemned African American boycott leaders and Mayor Dinkins's inadequate handling of the boycott.[4]

Many Koreans other than merchants participated in the rally, includ-ing younger-generation Koreans. Only a small number of Korean busi-nesses were actually closed on the day of the rally, but Korean mer-chants encouraged Korean employees to take the day off so that they could attend. Thus, employees of Korean businesses made up a large proportion of the participants. The Korean-American Senior Citizens Center mobilized its members, many of whom came in traditional Ko-rean dresses. The Council of Korean Churches of Greater New York encouraged all Korean churches to mobilize as many members as possi-ble, and many church members came to the rally in church vans. Korean community leaders from New Jersey, Philadelphia, Connecticut, and Georgia traveled to New York City to give their support for the rally. Initially, many younger-generation Koreans were concerned about pos-sible negative effects of such a rally on Korean-Black relations, and one radical second-generation Korean pastor expressed his opposition in pamphlets distributed in the Korean community. But younger-genera-tion Koreans generally supported the final plan of the rally, which em-phasized racial harmony and eliminated anti-Black slogans. A few 1.5-generation Korean lawyers were involved in organizing the rally as members of the Korean-American Civil Rights Committee.

As a participant-observer, I vividly remember how Korean speakers and participants in the rally expressed their anger and frustrations about the Brooklyn boycott and Mayor Dinkins's inadequate handling of it. When Dinkins came forward to speak to the crowd, many angry

Koreans booed him, delaying his speech for ten minutes. Some Korean speakers and many Korean participants in the rally equated Black boy-cotts of Korean stores with the Japanese colonization of Korea. For them, the two historical events were similar because both reflected Ko-reans' suffering from discriminatory practices by other races. "Just as we Koreans resisted the Japanese colonization," they argued, "we should challenge unjustifiable Black boycotts of Korean stores." At the end of the two-hour rally, the participants sang a traditional Korean song, "Arirang," hand in hand. I saw many Koreans shedding tears when they were singing.

Koreans achieved their objectives through the rally. They told the media, politicians, and the public that they would not keep quiet if they were treated unfairly. The rally was covered by all major U.S. media and many foreign media. Moreover, the rally finally prompted the mayor to act. The next day, he enforced the court order to keep picketing fifty feet from the stores. As a result, many Black picketers were arrested by the police, thereby weakening the boycott. On September 21, Dinkins also made a symbolic gesture by visiting the boycotted stores and pur-chasing some merchandise, thus encouraging Black residents to shop at the targeted stores (Purdum 1990). The news that he would visit the stores stimulated many Afro-Caribbean residents, weary of the long du-ration of the boycott, to swarm into the two stores even before he arrived.

As they strove to utilize political resources to end the Black boycott, Korean community leaders realized their lack of political power, par-ticularly in comparison to the African American community. Whereas many high-ranking officials, including the mayor, in the New York City government were Black, the assistant commissioner of the Manpower Department was the highest Korean officer in the city government at that time. The only elected Korean representative in New York City in 1990 was a school board member representing the 25th School District (Flushing). Korean immigrants often complained that Black govern-ment officials and police officers discriminated against them. Korean community leaders even complained that they had difficulty getting permission to hold the 1990 City Hall rally from Black city government officials. Koreans in other cities, including Los Angeles, also com-plained that they were subjected to discriminatory treatment by Black government officials and police officers. These complaints reached their highest level in Los Angeles in March 1991 when Black police officers arrested two Koreans instead of the Black security truck driver who had threatened them with a pistol and beaten them (*KTLA*, March 31, 1991).

This realization sensitized Koreans to the long-term need for Korean political power and political participation. As a result, two semipolitical organizations were created in the New York Korean community in the aftermath of the 1990 boycott. One such organization was the Korean-American Civil Rights Committee, established under the Korean Association of New York. The long and bitter strife between the Korean and Black communities spurred Korean community leaders to create a special committee to handle intergroup relations and to protect Korean Americans' human rights. The committee consisted of well-known Korean community leaders in the New York metropolitan area—lawyers, professors, journalists, pastors, social workers, and businesspeople. This committee was responsible for organizing the 1990 September rally held in front of City Hall.[5]

The other political organization is the Coalition of Korean-American Voters, which consists of 1.5- and second-generation Koreans and has two major organizational goals: to help Koreans with voter registration and to develop young Korean politicians. As the only effective political organization in New York City run by younger-generation Koreans, it has been involved in organizing Koreans' voter registration drives, supporting Korean political candidates, presenting Korean community issues to non-Korean political candidates, and surveying Koreans' political attitudes.

It is also noteworthy that in 1992 Koreans in New York elected Jae Taek Kim, a college professor, as president of the Korean Association of New York, breaking the long tradition of electing a successful businessman to that position. In the wake of the 1990–91 boycott and the Los Angeles riots, Korean community leaders were keenly aware that they needed a president who could protect Koreans' interests through effective communication with government agencies and other ethnic groups. This is the main reason they preferred an academic to a prosperous merchant candidate.

The 1990–91 boycott of Korean stores also strengthened pan-Asian solidarity in New York City. In spring 1990, when Black picketers in Brooklyn were receiving wide media attention, members of several Chinatown-based Chinese ethnic organizations took bus tours to the boycotted Korean stores to show support and to shop (KCDNY, May 22, 1990). The leaders of the Asian American Legal Defense Fund and the Committee on Anti-Asian Violence publicly expressed their concern about the victimization of Korean merchants by Black boycotters (Liu 1988). In May 1990, three Vietnamese young men who lived in a neighborhood close to the boycott site were attacked by Black gang members, who mistook them for Koreans; one of the Vietnamese men was seriously injured (McFadden 1990). This incident enhanced pan-Asian solidarity. The next morning, Korean community leaders went to visit the hospitalized Vietnamese victim. After the incident, Virgo Lee, director of Asian Affairs at the Mayor's Office, organized a meeting for Asian American community leaders at City Hall to discuss matters of common concern (*KCDNY*, May 19, 1990). Asian American staff members of the U.S. Commission on Civil Rights, too, closely watched the 1990–91 Brooklyn boycott and severely criticized Mayor Dinkins for his inadequate response (U.S. Commission on Civil Rights 1992, 34–40).

EFFECTS OF THE LOS ANGELES RIOTS

The Los Angeles riots marked a turning point in history for Korean Americans, much as the internment experience did for Japanese Americans. The riots brought about significant changes in the Korean community in Los Angeles. The material and nonmaterial damages inflicted by the riots have enhanced community solidarity to a far greater extent than any other major case of business-related intergroup conflict that Korean immigrants have experienced. The victimization of many innocent Korean merchants during the riots increased Korean's political consciousness and political development. Finally, the riots heightened second-generation Koreans' sense of ethnic identity and increased their influence and power in the Los Angeles Korean community.

OVERALL COMMUNITY SOLIDARITY

Threats from the outside world generally increase internal unity, and thus the riots, as major external threats, strengthened internal solidarity in the Korean community in Los Angeles. Koreans were angry about the large-scale destruction that the Korean community suffered during the riots, and they were even more outraged by what they believed to be the White conspiracy behind the destruction than by the destruction itself. As noted in chapter 6, many Koreans believed that the U.S. media intentionally focused on Korean-Black conflicts to direct Blacks' frustration toward Korean merchants. Angry about the biased media coverage, a number of Koreans sent letters of protest to the American media and to the *Korea Times Los Angeles* (see the English section of the *Korea Times Los Angeles,* May 11, 1992). On May 3, about one thousand

Korean students rallied at the local ABC-TV affiliate to protest the station's biased coverage (Hwangbo 1992).

Many Koreans also considered the failure of the police to respond to Koreans' desperate calls for help to protect Koreatown part of the White conspiracy to use Koreans as scapegoats. There was widespread speculation in the Korean community during the riots that the police allowed Koreatown to be burned and destroyed to protect Beverly Hills, a wealthy White community. After hearing the radio report that Koreatown was being attacked without defense, many Korean former marines and young men volunteered to defend Koreatown. One of the volunteers, eighteen-year-old Edward Lee, died and two others were injured during cross fire on the second night of the riots. The Korean self-defense team guarded Koreatown for several weeks after the riots.

In February 1993, Korean former marines and other war veterans who helped protect Koreatown during the riots created Tae Kuk Bang Bum Dae, a crime prevention patrol (*KTLA*, February 12, 1993). The team, consisting of nine men, patrols the heart of Koreatown in two cars between noon and 8 P.M. to protect Koreatown businesses and residents from crimes. Few areas in Los Angeles have as high a rate of crime as Koreatown. Though a police box is located in Koreatown, the department lacks the resources to combat panhandling, robberies of businesses, and other crimes there. The president of the Korean Veterans Association donated $200,000 to establish Tae Kuk Bang Bum Dae (*KTLA*, January 4, 1993), which was also intended to protect Koreatown from a similar riot occurring again. In fact, the rumor about another riot in Los Angeles following the second verdict in the Rodney King case led to the creation of the patrol team in a hurry.

Koreans in Los Angeles held a solidarity and peace rally at Ardmore Park in Koreatown on May 2, just one day after the riots ended. About 30,000 Koreans from all over the Los Angeles area participated, the largest Korean meeting ever held in the United States (Sunoo 1992). Though the rally was hurriedly organized and not well publicized, many Koreans came to protest the unfair treatment of Korean Americans by the media and the police during the riots and to show Koreans' solidarity. Marching through the ravaged portions of Koreatown and wearing white headbands, the demonstrators called for peace, requested justice for Rodney King, and vowed to rebuild Koreatown and the destroyed Korean stores. A large number of second-generation Koreans participated in the rally, sharing the grief and agony of first-generation immigrants.

Throughout the month of May 1992, a number of well-known American and Korean politicians visited Koreatown, held meetings with Korean community leaders, and listened to their grievances. These leaders included President Bush, Bill Clinton, Jesse Jackson, a delegation from the U.S. Civil Rights Commission, and Dae Joong Kim, a long-time opposition party leader in South Korea. Their visits provided Korean community leaders with the opportunity to express their views concerning the injustice done to Korean Americans by the media, the police, politicians, and rioters. In additions, the meetings with top-level politicians helped Korean community leaders learn political skills and heightened their political consciousness.

In the wake of the Los Angeles riots, Koreans showed solidarity in their efforts to help riot victims. Korean Americans all over the country participated in fund-raising campaigns. As a result, more than $5 million was collected from the Korean American community, and another $4.5 million was donated from South Korea (KTLA, July 23 and 29, 1992; April 30, 1993). Though large Korean corporations were responsible for much of the funds raised in Korea and the United States, many Korean immigrants individually donated money. Even Mindan, a pro–South Korean Korean-Japanese organization, contributed $200,000 to help fellow Koreans in Los Angeles (SGT, May 12, 1992).

Though Koreans in both the United States and Korea showed solidarity by generously donating money to help riot victims, these large sums also created problems. There were several sources of conflict over the donated money. First, because the donations were collected by a dozen ethnic organizations—primarily the ethnic media—the Korean Riot Victims' Association (KRVA) had difficulty in subsequently getting all the funds forwarded from these various organizations. Leaders of the KRVA complained that some organizations did not release all the donations they had received. Responding to their complaints, the Korean C.P.A. Association of Southern California audited the ethnic organizations involved. Furthermore, the Korean Consulate General in Los Angeles, which handled the donations from Korea, was reluctant to transfer the money to the KRVA. Though the consulate finally did so, KRVA leaders accused the consul general and some others of taking some of the donated money for personal use (KTLA, August 14, 1992; SGT, October 27, 1992). Riot victims demonstrated in front of the Korean Consulate General building several times.

Second, riot victims could not agree on who should be eligible to receive the donated money, since some victims lost their entire businesses whereas the stores of others suffered only minor damage. Some of the self-identified riot victims, who were eliminated from the list of "victims eligible for receiving the distribution of the donations," sought redress in the Los Angeles Municipal Court. In November 1992, accepting their claim as justified, the court ordered the KRVA to pay all who had been eliminated from eligibility (approximately two hundred merchants) the amount of $2,500, which the other victims had received as the first distribution of the donations (*KTLA*, November 7, 1992).

Third, Korean community leaders and riot victims in Los Angeles did not agree on how to use the donated money. Whereas riot victims argued that all the donated money should be distributed to them, Korean community leaders representing professional associations (the Korean-American Bar Association of Los Angeles and the Korean C.P.A. Association of Southern California) maintained that part of the donated money should be used for long-term community programs (*KTLA*, July 15, 1992). As of April 1993, they still had $1.8 million from the donations, which will most likely be used for the construction of a community center (*KTLA*, April 30, 1993). In July 1994, the Korean-American Relief Fund Foundation that managed the unused fund opened an escrow to buy a $2 million building located in Koreatown to be used as a Korean community center (*KTLA*, July 30, 1994). In September 1993, the South Korean government provided financial support with $1.25 million to be used for reconstruction of the Los Angeles Korean community. The Korean Consulate General at Los Angeles turned it over to the Korean American Scholarship Foundation, established in memory of the victimization of Koreans during the Los Angeles riots (*KTLA*, October 4a, 1993).

Before these riots, Korean immigrants did not generally use protest as a means of achieving their goals.[6] However, having lived through the outrage and pain over the unprecedented destruction and looting of their businesses, they now readily accept this technique as a means of getting their messages across to government officials. When President Bush met with Korean community leaders at Radio Korea Los Angeles in Koreatown, approximately five hundred Koreans rallied outside the building, chanting slogans such as "We Need Compensation" and "Where Is My Tax?" In the middle of June 1992, Korean riot victims started a rally at the Los Angeles City Hall (*KTLA*, June 17, 1992). For the next month, an average of two hundred victims participated daily in the rally. The president of the KRVA even went on a hunger strike for a few days.

In order to make their demands in a more concerted manner, Korean riot victims established the Korean 4.29 Riot Victims Association. In their meetings with Mayor Bradley, other city and state government officials, and lawmakers, its representatives demanded (1) that the Los Angeles City government apologize to victims for what happened, (2) that victims be compensated for their losses, (3) that the association send a representative to the Los Angeles City Reconstruction Committee, (4) that the bylaw requiring Korean liquor stores in Black neighborhoods to get a permission from the residents for reopening be abolished, (5) that SBA loan application procedures be simplified, and (6) that the Los Angeles City government expand loan programs for riot victims (*SGT,* July 7, 1992). In mid-July, when Mayor Bradley promised to accept some of their demands, they stopped the month-old rally (*KTLA,* July 12, 1992).

KOREANS' POLITICAL CONSCIOUSNESS

Many Koreans in Los Angeles and other cities felt that their lack of political power was mainly responsible for Koreans' becoming innocent victims of the Black-White racial conflict during the riots. Thus, the Los Angeles riots have heightened Korean Americans' political consciousness. Koreans in Los Angeles, in particular, have made efforts to exercise political influence to make the government compensate Koreans for their losses during the riots and to protect Koreans' overall interests. The Korean-American Bar Association of Los Angeles held several meetings to discuss the possibility of suing the government for neglecting to protect Koreatown during the riots (*KTLA,* June 15, 1992). In July 1992, a group of Korean lawyers in Los Angeles also organized the Korean American Legal Advocacy Foundation, a nonprofit organization, to protect Koreans' human rights against assaults by the government and other groups. With their central office in Los Angeles and local chapters in several other Korean communities, this organization plans to play a role in the Korean community similar to the role that the Anti-Defamation League and the Mexican American Legal Defense and Education Fund play in other ethnic communities (*KTLA,* July 25, 1992).

The post-riot political consciousness among Korean Americans is not limited to specific Korean ethnic organizations. Before the riots, Korean immigrants were preoccupied with politics in South Korea. However, there is evidence that after the riots Korean immigrants in general and those in Los Angeles in particular became more keenly aware of their need to improve their political position in this country.[7] A survey in New York City indicates that the number of Koreans who took the citizenship test dramatically increased from March to June 1992 (*KTNY*, June 17, 1992). According to the Korean Federation of L.A. as well, the number of the Korean immigrants who inquired about the citizenship test noticeably increased after the riots (*SGT*, September 29, 1992). Before the riots, the ability to bring over their family members was Korean immigrants' main motive for gaining citizenship. However, in the wake of the riots more and more Korean immigrants seem to have applied for citizenship to be able to exercise their right to vote. Paralleling this increase in acquiring citizenship, Koreans' voter registration increased significantly in 1992. For example, a study based on county voter registration records estimates that 2,400 Koreans in Orange County registered to vote in 1992 alone, accounting for 30% of the Koreans who had registered since 1983 (*KTLA*, October 31, 1992).

During the 1992 presidential election year, Jay Kim (whose Korean name is Kim Chang Joon) was elected to the House of Representatives from the 41st District in California, becoming the first Korean congressional member in American history. In 1992, three other Koreans became members of the Washington, Oregon, and Hawaii state legislatures (*KTLA*, November 5, 1992). Kim and the Washington and Oregon state representatives were elected mainly because, as members of the Republican Party, they received support from conservative White voters. However, Koreans' support, not only as voters but also as helpers in election campaigns, contributed to their success. In particular, Jay Kim received enthusiastic support from Korean Americans in the first post-riot election (*KTLA*, November 15, 1992). Even a large number of Koreans in New York responded generously to a fund-raising party for Kim, for in the aftermath of the riots they were keenly aware of Koreans' lack of political power.

YOUNGER-GENERATION KOREANS' ETHNIC CONSCIOUSNESS

Korean immigrants feel a sense of brotherhood with co-ethnics partly because of their commonalities in culture—the Korean language, customs, and Confucian values. They also feel connected to one another because they share common historical experiences. Their memories of major historical events that occurred in twentieth-century Korea, such as Japanese colonization, the Korean War, and the subsequent division of Korea into two halves, have strengthened their ethnic ties. However, until the tragedy of the Los Angeles riots, younger-generation Koreans in the United States had not lived through major historical experiences together as Korean Americans. The Los Angeles riots were the first major event that provided 1.5- and second-generation Koreans with an opportunity to think about their common fate as Korean Americans. They witnessed their parents being targeted by rioters simply because they were Koreans. They realized that they, too, could be targets of attack by another group simply because they were Korean Americans. Edward Lee, the only Korean who died in cross fire during the riots, was an eighteen-year-old second-generation Korean who had volunteered to protect Koreatown businesses from attack by rioters. His funeral drew a large number of Korean mourners.

Young Koreans suspected that the police did not care about protecting Koreatown from attacks by rioters, primarily because Korean Americans were a powerless minority group. Thus, the Los Angeles riots heightened younger-generation Koreans' ethnic consciousness and identity. In an essay written almost two years after the riots, Julie Lee, a 1.5-generation Korean American, described how experiencing the riots wakened her ethnic identity (J. Lee 1994):

> My Korean-American heritage was something I took for granted until the 1992 riots forced me to re-evaluate my identity. 'Wasn't I an American?' I asked myself when witnessing the destruction of so many stores and businesses belonging to other Korean-Americans. Why have we been singled out? I kept wondering, thinking that we were no different than any other ethnic groups that came to this nation to work, endure and find our place in American history. . . .
>
> I didn't know—until the riots. Watching the flames rise from Korean-American businesses, listening to frightened friends and relatives, then hearing the voices of the angry rioters, accusing Korean-Americans of exploiting them in the lower-income neighborhoods that were being destroyed, I sensed that I was Korean and I was an American.

Young Koreans quickly responded to the riots by writing articles in major English dailies in California; they attacked the media bias and the police failure to protect Koreatown and defended the position of the Korean community. For example, Thomas Chung, a political science major at UCLA, responded to an interview by a *Korea Times* reporter (Ha 1992):

Korean Americans felt abandoned by the police and the whole justice system. It is really hard for me to watch the news because this is where I grew up and it was on fire everywhere. The culmination of the whole thing is just anger.

Before I felt alienated because I wanted to support the African American community, but the Korean American was targeted purposely, and I felt like we were being used as scapegoats to channel their anger. On Saturday, when I went to the Koreatown rally, I was so glad I was there. After that, I realized that we all have to pitch in.

A large number of 1.5- and second-generation Koreans participated in a solidarity rally held at Ardmore Park, Koreatown, on May 2, making it a truly multigenerational event. On May 3, about a thousand Korean American students rallied at the local ABC-TV station to protest the station's unfair coverage of Korean Americans. On May 6, over three hundred UCLA Korean American students on campus voiced their anger and concern about losses the Korean American community had suffered during the riots (S. Chung 1992). Also, many young Koreans volunteered at relief centers to help Korean riot victims. Second-generation Koreans in Los Angeles, in other cities, and on college campuses have held a number of seminars on the causes of the riots and on the Korean community in general. They agreed that the riots exposed the political weakness of first-generation Koreans and that it was their obligation to protect their parents' interests (*KTNY*, May 16, 1992; *SGT*, May 15, 1992). In July 1993, Los Angeles's Korean American Coalition, the Coalition of Korean-American Voters in New York, and several other 1.5- and second-generation Korean American organizations in other cities established a national coalition organization, similar to the Japanese American Citizens League. The national coalition plans to coordinate local Korean associations in campaigning for voter registration and bilingual voting, aiding Koreans' political development, lobbying lawmakers for Korean interests, and resolving interracial conflicts (*SGT*, November 27b, 1992; *KTLA,* July 28, 1993).[8]

We noted in earlier chapters that younger-generation Koreans held views about Korean–African American conflicts different from those of Korean immigrants, particularly Korean immigrant merchants. This generational difference emerged clearly when various groups explained the riots and the victimization of Korean merchants during them. Korean merchants and even many Korean pastors emphasized the criminality of the riot participants in general and Black gang members in particular. In contrast, as is clear from many interviews and letters cited in this chapter and in chapter 6, younger-generation Koreans directed their attack toward the mainstream media and the police, who they believed allowed and even encouraged the rioters to target Korean stores. Younger-generation Korean community leaders were careful not to criticize African Americans for victimizing Korean merchants,[9] and some second-generation Koreans emphasized the need for a Korean–African American alliance to fight against the White system. However, it is significant for the central thesis of this book that the victimization of Korean merchants during the riots stimulated younger-generation Koreans' ethnic consciousness as much as it increased the solidarity of Korean immigrants. Younger-generation Koreans realized that their parents were scapegoated and victimized by the White system mainly because of lack of power and that as a powerless minority group they, too, are vulnerable to victimization in the future.

As mentioned in chapter 2, a number of scholars have indicated that major historical events such as the Holocaust and the internment of Japanese Americans during World War II have played an important role in the persistence of ethnicity. The victimization of innocent Korean merchants during the riots is another such event, and it will have an impact on the ethnic identity of Korean Americans for many years to come. Young Koreans are already talking about the 4.29 movies, 4.29 arts, and 4.29 literature. These artistic works, focusing on the theme of the victimization of Korean merchants during the riots, will serve as a symbol for Korean ethnic identity in the future. In 1992, artistic works reflecting the experiences of Japanese Americans in relocation camps during World War II were displayed at the UCLA campus to celebrate the fiftieth anniversary of the Japanese Americans' internment. In the year 2042, similar artistic works may be displayed at the same campus in commemoration of the fiftieth anniversary of the victimization of Korean merchants during the riots, and they will enhance third- and fourth-generation Koreans' ethnic identity.

A POWER TRANSFER FROM FIRST- TO YOUNGER-GENERATION KOREANS

The growing involvement of younger-generation Koreans in the Korean American community since the riots shows that they are taking on a greater share of obligations to the community. However, it also indicates their growing power and influence in the Korean community, relative to first-generation Koreans. The internment of Japanese Americans during World War II brought about a transfer of power from first- to second-generation Japanese Americans. The Los Angeles riots brought about a similar significant change in the structure of the Los Angeles Korean community.

Even before the riots, younger-generation Koreans and their organizations played a more important role in community politics and services in the Korean community in Los Angeles than in New York or Chicago. Therefore, it would be inaccurate to say that younger-generation Koreans have emerged suddenly in Los Angeles. Yet it is true that younger-generation Koreans' authority increased markedly there after the riots. Before the riots, various trade associations, particularly the Korean-American Grocers Association of Southern California and the Korean Chamber of Commerce of Los Angeles, played a central role in community activities in the Korean community in Los Angeles. However, since the riots, three 1.5- and second-generation Korean organizations—the Korean American Coalition, the Korean Youth and Community Center, and the Korean Health, Education, Information, and Referral Center—together with the Korean American Bar Association of Southern California, which consists largely of American-educated young Koreans, have played an increasingly important role in the Korean community in Los Angeles. These groups have been central providers of various services for Korean riot victims. The Korean American Coalition was established in 1983 by 1.5- and second-generation Koreans to increase Koreans' political power and to protect the interests of the Korean community from threats by the American media, governmental bodies, and outside interest groups. Since the riots, the KAC has been increasingly recognized as the primary organization representing the Korean community in Los Angeles; it has received more than $500,000 in donations from New York Life Insurance and other American corporations to reconstruct the Korean community. The Korean Youth and Community Center was founded in 1975 as a nonprofit community-based organization mainly to serve "recent immigrant, low-income, and high-risk youths and their families who are experiencing significant coping and adjustment difficulties because of language and cultural barriers" (Korean Youth and Community Center 1990). With an annual budget of nearly $2 million and a number of youth, family, and community programs, it has emerged as the most important social service agency in the Korean community in Los Angeles. Since the 1992 riots, it has established several programs to help the Korean riot victims with government funds. Though it has served mainly immigrant children and immigrant families, its staff has undergone a gradual generational shift from immigrants to 1.5- and second-generation Koreans. As of June 1994, Bong Hwan Kim, executive director of the center, and most of the seventy employees are younger-generation Koreans.

Even major Korean trade associations and other social service agencies in Los Angeles controlled by Korean immigrants have increasingly hired 1.5-generation Koreans as secretaries and other key staff members since the riots. For example, the Korean-American Grocers Association of Southern California hired two 1.5-generation Koreans in 1993, one as the executive secretary and the other as a public relations director (*KTLA*, August 21, 1993). When I called the Korean Chamber of Commerce of Los Angeles for an interview in October 1993, I found that the former executive secretary, a first-generation Korean whom I had interviewed twice, was replaced by a second-generation Korean. This generational change reflects the growing realization by first-generation Koreans after the riots that maintaining successful public relations with the mainstream media, government agencies, and other American organizations is important for protecting their group interests.

Many Korean immigrants feel grateful to the active role that these younger-generation Korean organizations play in providing services for Korean riot victims and other members of the Korean community. However, many others are concerned about the effectiveness of their programs. For example, the Korean Youth and Community Center has established several programs, including one in business counseling, for riot victims. Yet many Korean riot victims are reluctant to visit the center to get advice from Americanized young staff members. Connie Kang, a *Los Angeles Times* staff reporter, observed this friction caused by generational and cultural gaps: "It is difficult for Koreans, to whom age and status mean a great deal, to seek advice from young staff members. One Korean American grocer who sought counseling at the center said she was taken aback. 'I thought to myself, how can I possibly get help from people my children's age?' she said. 'I came home thinking I should be helping those kids, not the other way around' " (Kang 1994). Some Korean immigrants believe that the riot victims aid centers run by younger-generation Koreans "are more interested in counting the numbers of the victims served by the centers so that they can get more funds from government agencies than really helping them" (*KTLA*, November 22, 1992).

Before the riots, power and influence in the Korean community in Los Angeles lay with successful Korean businessmen with leadership positions in trade associations. Many young Korean activists complained that their opinions were not respected by first-generation Korean leaders and that they were eliminated from decision making on important community issues. Since the riots, however, an increasing number of young Koreans have emerged as influential figures. As will be discussed in detail in chapter 10, in their efforts to resolve business-related intergroup conflicts, Korean trade associations and Korean businessmen have increased their power and influence in the Korean community in New York. Before the 1992 riots, this was true in Los Angeles as well. But the crippling impact of the riots on that community exposed the limitations of first-generation Koreans in handling intergroup conflicts. When the American media provided biased coverage of Korean–African American conflicts just before and during the riots, Koreans needed to defend themselves by making the American public aware of that bias. However, the vast majority of Korean business leaders had been educated in Korea and thus had difficulty communicating the position of the Korean community either orally or in writing. Thus, it was 1.5- and second-generation Koreans who protested the biased media coverage through their letters to American newspapers during the several weeks following the riots.

Facing strong protest from the Korean community after airing a *Nightline* in which only Black representatives were invited to discuss Korean–African American conflicts, ABC-TV invited both Korean and African American leaders for another *Nightline* program on May 4, 1992. This gave Angela Oh, a second-generation Korean lawyer, an opportunity to argue persuasively for the Korean community, using fluent English. Since her appearance on *Nightline*, Oh, president of the Korean-American Bar Association of Los Angeles, has been considered by the outside world as the spokesperson for the Korean community in Los Angeles. She has been invited to speak by a number of American and second-generation Korean organizations. She was even invited to the 1994 annual meeting of the American Sociological Association, held in Los Angeles, as one of the three panelists in a plenary session entitled "Reflections on the 1992 Los Angeles Rebellion: Views of Community Leaders." Public Counsel, a nonprofit public lawyers' association, gave her an individual achievement award for the year 1992 (*KTLA*, March 28, 1993).

Jerry Yu, executive director of the Korean American Coalition, Bong

Hwan Kim, executive director of the Korean Youth and Community Center, and Tong Soo Chung, a 1.5-generation lawyer who made an unsuccessful bid for a California state senate seat in 1991, have played an increasingly important role in the Korean community since the riots. These younger-generation Korean community leaders have recently received more coverage by the mainstream media than have Korean business leaders. On May 24, 1992, three weeks after the riots, the *Los Angeles Times* carried a full-page interview with Tong Soo Chung, a 1.5-generation Korean who is a Harvard graduate, with his picture (Proffitt 1992). Responding to the interviewer, he made sophisticated comments on many issues facing the Korean community, speaking more effectively than any immigrant community leader could have. Before this, probably no Korean had ever received a full page of coverage from the *Los Angeles Times*. The 1992 riots brought recognition to younger-generation Koreans as community leaders in Los Angeles.

This change has also altered Korean Americans' dependence on the Republican Party in their political dealings. The Republican Party's slogans, which emphasize a work ethic, family values, and free enterprise, are generally consistent with Korean immigrants' Confucian values. Moreover, such conservative catchwords resonate with the values on which Korean immigrants operate small businesses. For these reasons, Korean immigrants have leaned heavily toward Republican political ideology (Hwangbo 1991). A recent survey conducted by Gallup found that 36% of adult Koreans were affiliated with the Republican Party versus 21% with the Democratic Party (*KTLA*, July 2, 1992). Almost all first-generation Koreans who have run for seats in state and federal legislatures have been Republicans.

However, after the 1992 riots, many Koreans realized that the Republican Party, as a representative of the White system, cannot protect the interests of Korean Americans as a minority group. Thus, Koreans' efforts, particularly young Koreans' efforts, to connect the Korean community with the Democrats increased dramatically during the first year after the riot. The Korean American Democratic Committee was established in September 1992 by young Koreans in Southern California (*KTLA*, October 2, 1992). A similar group supporting the Democratic Party was established in the Korean community in New York in November 1992. Second- and third-generation Japanese and Chinese Americans have moved into politics mainly as Democrats. In the future, the Democratic Party is likely to play an increasingly important role

in promoting Korean American politicians, particularly second-generation Korean politicians, though even many second-generation Korean
Americans currently support the Republican Party.

Korean merchants in Black neighborhoods have encountered different
forms of hostility: boycotts, arson, looting, and destruction of their
stores. Hostility toward Korean merchants in its turn has strengthened
Korean ethnic solidarity more than any other type of Korean immigrants' business-related intergroup conflicts. The two most salient cases
of hostility toward Korean merchants in Black neighborhoods—the
1990–91 Brooklyn boycott of two Korean stores and the destruction of
many Korean stores during the 1992 Los Angeles riots—clearly led to
strengthened Korean ethnic solidarity.

Koreans in New York used a number of collective actions to challenge the 1990 Brooklyn boycott against two Korean stores. Their approach included fund-raising campaigns to help the owners of the boycotted stores, group tours to the boycotted stores for shopping and for
moral support, concerted lobbying of administrators and politicians to
end the boycott, and a large-scale rally in front of City Hall condemning Mayor Dinkins. The community donations helped the boycotted
stores stay open until the picketers withdrew, and the City Hall rally
forced Dinkins to take action. Korean immigrants' long struggle to end
the boycott taught them political skills and awakened their political
consciousness. In the wake of the Brooklyn boycott, two major political
organizations were created in the Korean community in New York.

Korean immigrants' victimization due to their middleman economic
role climaxed in the 1992 Los Angeles riots during which 2,300 Korean
stores were partially or entirely destroyed. As the most significant historical event in Korean American history, it has most greatly strengthened Korean ethnic solidarity. Immediately after the riots, Koreans
in Los Angeles held a large peace and solidarity rally in Koreatown,
mounted fund-raising campaigns in the Korean American community
and South Korea to help Korean riot victims, picketed in front of City
Hall for a month, and created a self-defense and crime prevention
patrol in Koreatown. The victimization of Korean merchants during
the riots also sensitized Koreans to their need for political power, thus
heightening their political consciousness. After the riots, several local
and national political organizations were created to protect Korean
Americans' civil rights.

Most significantly, the Los Angeles riots awakened younger-generation Koreans' ethnic identity and political consciousness. The victimization of Korean merchants during the riots forced 1.5- and second-
generation Koreans to think about their common fate as Korean
Americans. Though younger-generation Koreans interpreted the riots and
the victimization of Korean merchants differently from Korean immigrants, the riots enhanced their ethnic identity as much as it unified first-
generation Korean immigrants. Moreover, the riots contributed to a
transfer of power from first- to younger-generation Koreans, at least in
the Korean community in Los Angeles. While earlier intergroup conflicts had helped increase Korean merchants' influence and power in the
Korean community in Los Angeles as well as in other Korean communities, the crippling impact of the riots exposed the merchants' limitations. The riots gave younger-generation Koreans the opportunity to
defend the Korean community against the mainstream media, whose
coverage of Korean–African American conflicts was biased, and against
the police, who took no action to protect Korean merchants during
the riots.

The Union Street Korean Business District in Flushing, Queens, has many stores with Korean language signs. Photo by the author.

One of the four hundred or so Korean wholesale stores that sell manufactured goods imported from Korea and other Asian countries, located in the Broadway Korean business district in Manhattan. Photo by Yoshiko Chujo.

Many stores in the Broadway Korean business district in Manhattan cater mainly to Korean wholesalers. This is one of the two Korean bookstores located in the district. Photo by Yoshiko Chujo.

Many Korean stores in New York City combine grocery and flower retail operations. This grocery and flower shop located in Manhattan serves customers of different ethnic backgrounds. Photo by Yoshiko Chujo.

Korean retail stores that sell Asian-imported manufactured goods are heavily concentrated in low-income Black and Latino neighborhoods. This is one of these stores in Jamaica, Queens. Photo by the author.

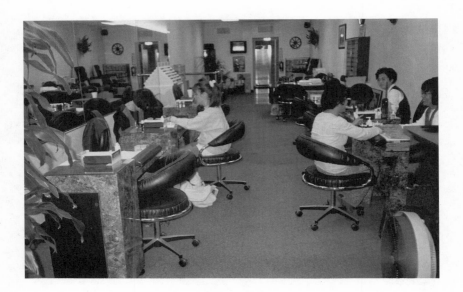

Many nail salons in New York City are run by Korean women. This salon is located in Bayside, Queens, a predominantly White, middle-class neighborhood. Photo by the author.

Seoul Plaza in Los Angeles's Koreatown has all kinds of businesses that serve Korean customers. Photo by Steve Gold.

Los Angeles's Koreatown has several mini shopping plazas, such as this one. Photo by Steve Gold.

Grocery/beer/wine retail shops, such as the one at top, are the most popular Korean businesses in Los Angeles. Photo by Steve Gold.

Several hundred Korean-owned garment factories, such as the one at bottom, are located in downtown Los Angeles. Photo by Steve Gold.

(Top left) Buildings in South Central Los Angeles that were burned during the 1992 riots. Photo by Steve Gold.

(Bottom left) Koreans in Los Angeles created Koreatown, a territorial community, which has several shopping malls. Photo by Steve Gold.

(Above) Many Korean stores are located in Black neighborhoods. This is a Korean grocery and produce store located in Jamaica, a predominantly Black neighborhood in New York City. Photo by the author.

Approximately 2,300 Korean stores in South Central Los Angeles and Koreatown were burned and looted during the 1992 Los Angeles riots. Photo by Steve Gold.

CHAPTER 9

Korean Merchants' Collective Responses to Suppliers, Landlords, and Government Agencies

Korean merchants do not have conflicts with African American custom-ers alone. Chapter 8 examined how hostility toward Korean merchants in African American neighborhoods has increased the solidarity of the Korean community. This chapter examines how Korean merchants have acted together to protect their economic interests against suppliers, landlords, and government agencies, focusing only on the context of New York. There, the White suppliers and landlords on whom Korean merchants depend are largely Jewish. Thus, the conflicts in Koreans' commercial activities involve issues of Korean-Jewish relations, a topic that is very important but neglected by researchers.

COLLECTIVE RESPONSES TO SUPPLIERS

Korean business owners who sell merchandise, such as wigs, handbags, costume jewelry, and toys, imported from South Korea and other Asian countries depend on co-ethnic suppliers (see table 8 in chapter 4). The favorable treatment they receive gives them a number of advantages. For example, they can buy merchandise from Korean suppliers on a credit basis and can thus start and operate businesses with a relatively small amount of capital (I. Kim 1981, 142–44; the Korean Businessmen's Association of New York 1987, 78–79; Min 1988a, 47).When entering their businesses, Koreans have easy access to information through Ko-rean suppliers. When operating their businesses, they receive preferential treatment in item selection, price, speed of delivery, and credit (Min 1988a, 147).

However, Koreans in other business specialties usually depend on White suppliers. New York Korean produce retailers, grocers, and fish retailers depend particularly on Jewish and Italian wholesalers for the supply of their merchandise. Approximately 350 Korean jewelry retailers in New York depend almost entirely on Jewish suppliers. Korean dry cleaners and nail salon owners, who provide services rather than merchandise, are not as vulnerable as Korean retailers to exploitation by White suppliers. But they do purchase chemicals, cosmetics, equipment, and other goods from White suppliers, many of whom are Jewish. Korean merchants have encountered discrimination by White wholesalers in terms of prices, quality of merchandise, item selection, speed of delivery, parking allocations, and overall service. In response, the merchants have used collective strategies to protect their economic interests. They have negotiated prices with White wholesalers, boycotting several to make them provide better services.

Korean produce retailers and produce delivery truck drivers buy fruit and vegetables at Hunts Point Market, the largest produce wholesale market in New York. According to the Korean Produce Association of New York, most wholesalers at Hunts Point Market are either Jewish or Italian, while only five of them are members of racial minorities (as of March 1993). Korean produce retailers go to the market early in the morning carrying cash and are easy targets of robbery. Because so many Korean merchants have been robbed, security at the market has been an important issue to them.

Korean merchants visiting Hunts Point Market have also had altercations with employees of wholesalers; some Korean merchants have been severely beaten. These disputes have been caused primarily by White owners' and employees' prejudice against and stereotyping of Koreans, though Korean merchants' language problems and cultural differences have played a role. Korean produce retailers have also been discriminated against by wholesalers in business transactions. Many times they have not been allowed to exchange merchandise; they have often received rotten fruit; they have been forced to buy items they did not want; they have had to wait longer than White retailers to get their purchases loaded in their cars.

In 1974, Korean produce retailers established the Korean Produce Association of New York (KPANY). Its main goal is to protect their common interests by making possible a collective response to White wholesalers at Hunts Point Market. The KPANY's office is at Hunts Point Market itself. Whenever a Korean produce retailer is treated unfairly by a wholesaler, he or she is supposed to report the incident to the KPANY, which immediately sends a troubleshooter to the scene to resolve conflicts. The organization also has funds ready for legal actions against wholesalers. Since most wholesalers at the market largely depend on Korean customers, boycotting is effective for Korean merchants. Since the late 1970s, the KPANY has organized five demonstrations, four against suppliers and one against the *New York Daily News,* as well as five boycotts against wholesalers (see figure 6 in chapter 10). In every action taken, Korean produce retailers have been successful in making the targeted wholesaler accept their demands.

At the end of February 1980, KPANY leaders decided to boycott a White supplier, Wishnatzki and Nathel Produce, for racist attitudes toward Korean merchants. Not one specific incident but rather the Koreans' long-standing perception that they were being discriminated against led to the decision to boycott the wholesale store. In particular, Korean merchants were unhappy about White employees' attitude toward the Korean custom of putting saliva on the fingers to separate bills effectively: employees of Wishnatzki would not take money that had been treated this way. They started a boycott to make the wholesaler improve services to Korean merchants. They requested that the wholesaler stop discriminating against Korean merchants, give receipts to Korean merchants whenever a business transaction was completed, allow Korean merchants to exchange items or get cash refunded when they were not satisfied with the purchased items, load merchandise in order of purchase, and not sell items that Korean merchants did not want (*SGT,* September 14, 1988).

The KPANY warned the supplier that Korean merchants would continue boycotting until their demands were met. On March 5, representatives of Wishnatzki and Nathel and the Produce Wholesalers Association at Hunts Point Market met with KPANY leaders. Whenever there is a dispute between a supplier at Hunts Point Market and a retail customer, the Produce Wholesalers Association intervenes. At the meeting held at the KPANY office, Chang Ill Kim, president of that association, insisted out of ethnic pride and for his convenience that he speak Korean and that an interpreter translate into English; the wholesaler's representatives accepted that condition. In Korean, Kim severely criticized the wholesaler for not respecting Korean cultural traditions and for being rude to Korean merchants. One Korean who attended the meeting told me that Wishnatzki, the president of the wholesale store, was defensive throughout the meeting and that he accepted most of the demands and offered a sincere apology. This was the first major Korean boycott of a White wholesaler that demonstrated the power of Korean produce retailers.

In May 1985, 250 Korean merchants participated in a demonstration, organized by Korean produce retailers, against another White wholesaler (D. Loi). The wholesaler's employees falsely accused two Korean merchants of stealing merchandise; the merchants' truck was searched and they were detained for two hours until they found their receipts. Furious about the abuse and humiliation that they had suffered, Korean produce retailers decided to retaliate against the store with a demonstration and a boycott. They started with a rally and then began a boycott of the wholesaler that lasted one week (*KTNY*, June 2, 1985). Severely damaged by the loss of business, the wholesaler arranged a meeting with the KPANY's leaders to negotiate a settlement. At the meeting, Korean representatives demanded that the wholesale company formally apologize to Korean merchants for the incident, that employees of the company be more polite to Korean customers in the future, that the company educate its employees on how to serve Korean customers more politely, and that the company compensate the Korean produce retailer for the monetary loss and psychological damage caused by the two-hour detention. The company accepted the first three of the four demands and made a formal apology in front of sixty Korean merchants.

Wholesalers at Hunts Point Market are now well aware that they will be the targets of boycotts if they do not treat Korean merchants properly. Therefore, they try to satisfy Korean retailers. The secretary of the KPANY told me that they no longer need to use boycotts because wholesalers respond quickly to their complaints and requests. The simple threat of boycotting is effective because Korean immigrants in New York monopolize the produce retail business. Since Korean merchants make up the majority of customers for most wholesalers at Hunts Point Market, their boycotts can seriously hurt wholesale stores.[1]

Korean grocers in New York have also taken collective actions to protect their common interests from suppliers. Unlike the retailers who visit wholesale stores at Hunts Point Market, many Korean grocers purchase grocery items delivered to their store by wholesale trucks. Therefore, Korean grocers have not experienced frequent confrontations with employees of wholesalers, and the Korean-American Grocers Association of New York (KAGRONY) usually does not need to resort to boycotts. Instead, KAGRONY has used price bargaining and collective purchasing to protect its members' interests against suppliers and manufacturers. The president and staff members of KAGRONY regularly visit vendors and manufacturers, present them with data on Korean grocers in the New York metropolitan area, and explain how important Korean grocers are to them as customers. They then ask manufacturers and wholesalers to lower prices of major grocery items for Korean retailers, threatening to endorse other competing companies if they do not comply. KAGRONY has successfully negotiated with many wholesale companies for price reductions for Korean grocers.

Leaders of KAGRONY have also induced vendors and manufacturers to participate in a KAGRONY/supplier joint program in which suppliers provide financial support and KAGRONY advertises the suppliers to Korean grocery retailers. Aware of the power of Korean grocery retailers in New York, many companies have participated in the program. For example, Anheuser-Busch Distributors of New York sponsored the KAGRONY/Anheuser-Busch Cup Golf Tournament in May 1992; its 140 participants were Korean grocery retailers and staff members of several grocery manufacturing companies. KAGRONY used the funds raised by the golf tournament for Korean riot victims in Los Angeles. In June 1992, the association reached an agreement with R. J. Reynolds, a major cigarette manufacturer, that Korean grocery stores that displayed the company's cigarettes would be awarded $2,520 per year (*SGT,* June 20, 1992).

KAGRONY has encouraged vendors and manufacturers to advertise in its monthly newsletter, *New York KAGRO's Advocate,* which is delivered to all identified Korean grocery retailers in the New York metropolitan area. Each issue carries dozens of advertisements with special discount offers from vendors and manufacturers. Even major dailies in the New York metropolitan area are affected when Korean grocers, at the urging of KAGRONY, do not carry the newspapers in their stores. Thus KAGRONY induced the *New York Times* and *New York Daily News* to advertise in its newsletter, along with many other manufacturers and distributors. The advertisements have been an important source of revenue for the trade association, and the discounts have helped Korean grocers save money. KAGRONY has also organized annual grocery shows at which manufacturers and wholesalers pay large sums of money to advertise their grocery items. At the 1993 show held at the New York Marriott Marquis Hotel in Manhattan, 121 major American manufacturers displayed their grocery items. KAGRONY persuaded some eight thousand Koreans to attend this show to demonstrate the power of New York Korean grocers (*SGT,* February 23, 1993). President Clinton, Governor Cuomo, and Mayor Dinkins sent greetings to the show.

Other interesting collective strategies employed by Korean grocers in New York are their promotion of group purchases and their plan to establish a cooperative wholesale company. KAGRONY has helped Korean grocers save money by purchasing items such as milk, cigarettes, and candy in bulk, and the organization is currently in the process of establishing a Korean grocery cooperative (the KAGRO New York Cooperative). This wholesale store will be modeled after a grocery cooperative established by the Ontario Korean Grocers Association in 1983 in Canada (*KCDNY,* November 6, 1991, and January 9, 1992; *SGT,* May 28, 1993). KAGRONY began planning a Korean grocery cooperative at the end of 1991, and, after two years of research and preparation, the group began looking for a location to construct a warehouse. This cooperative will buy key grocery items from manufacturers and distribute them to Korean retailers in the New York metropolitan area.

To accumulate the capital for constructing this cooperative, KAGRONY has already collected more than $1 million through the sale of stock to its members. The Korean Trade and Distribution Center, an American-based Korean company that advertises and distributes Korean processed agricultural and fishery products to American customers, will cover the expenses (approximately $400,000) for building the warehouse. In return, it will get the benefit of distributing Korean agricultural products to Korean produce retailers through the KAGRO New York Cooperative. The Korean Trade and Distribution Center already displayed a dozen Korean agricultural products at the 1993 food show organized by KAGRONY.

Korean immigrants in other cities are also heavily concentrated in the grocery retail business, especially in Los Angeles, Seattle, Atlanta, Washington, and Philadelphia. Korean grocers' associations in North America established a national association in 1989 (*SGT,* June 6, 1989). All local Korean grocers' associations belong to this national organization and use the same name, KAGRO (the Korean-American Grocers Association), to show grocery manufacturers and vendors the unity and purchasing power of Korean grocers. Leaders of local Korean grocers' associations regularly visit other local associations and exchange business information, particularly information about which vendors or distributors are offering the best wholesale prices on specific items. The National Korean-American Grocers Association, whose central office is in Orange County, California, has held several grocery shows, in which Coca-Cola, Pepsi-Cola, and other large manufacturers participated. KAGRO's monthly newsletter, published in both Korean and English, is delivered to tens of thousands of Korean grocery retailers and manufacturers in North America. The Korean version carries a number of advertisements by manufacturers and wholesalers.

Korean seafood retailers go to the Fulton Fish Market in Manhattan, the largest fish wholesale market in New York, early in the morning to purchase merchandise. Like Korean produce retailers who visit Hunts Point Market, they often get robbed, and they are frequently involved in disputes with employees of fish wholesale stores during business transactions. Korean seafood retailers had long complained about White wholesalers' rude treatment, unreasonable prices, and cheating in weighing, yet they only recently began to take collective actions against suppliers. The Korean Seafood Retailers Association of New York was established in 1977. In its first ten years, the association functioned mainly as an organization for friendship and mutual help, not as a powerful interest group to protect Korean seafood retailers against White suppliers and government agencies, partly because there were not enough members to exercise any power.

When their number reached 500 in 1988, Korean fish retailers realized that they could use their collective power to make wholesalers improve their services. In July 1988, approximately 250 Korean fish retailers demonstrated in front of a large fish wholesaler, Slavins and Sons, for "selling rotten fish, cheating in weighing, and treating Koreans rudely" (SGT, July 29, 1988). After the demonstration, they began a boycott of the wholesaler that lasted nearly four months. Severely damaged by the boycott, the wholesaler sent a letter of apology to the Korean Seafood Retailers' Association and promised to serve Korean customers better and cooperate with the association, to which it also promised donations (SGT, December 2b, 1988). The letter of apology was published in major Korean dailies. The demonstration and boycott convinced other White fish wholesalers that Korean fish retailers were not passively going to accept unreasonable treatment. The association has since sent formal complaints to several other wholesalers, each of whom has responded favorably.

Korean fish retailers frequently complained that the wholesalers at Fulton Fish Market cheated when weighing. They often found a box of fish with a 125-pound label weighing only 100 pounds and a 65-pound box weighing only 55 pounds. Though fish wholesalers blamed their suppliers for this problem, Korean fish retailers strongly believed that wholesalers intentionally changed weight labels to exploit them. In early January 1994, the Korean Seafood Retailers Association sent a letter to all fifty-seven fish wholesalers at Fulton Fish Market, warning them that any wholesaler who commits "this crime of cheating in weights will meet with collective action from Korean fish retailers" (*SGT,* January 8, 1994). The Korean Seafood Retailers Association has reportedly received fewer complaints from its members about this practice since it sent the warning. Since Korean retailers make up approximately 40% of the customers at Fulton Fish Market, the fish wholesalers naturally pay special attention to warnings by the Korean trade association.

According to my interviews with the Korean Apparel Contractors Association of New York (KACA), 95% of Korean garment manufacturers subcontract work from large garment manufacturers. Russian Jewish immigrants initially entered the garment manufacturing business in New York City at the turn of the twentieth century (Morokvasic, Waldinger, and Phizacklea 1990). Jewish Americans now control garment manufacturing corporations in the city and supply 80% of the Korean garment subcontractors. Staff members of the KGSANY said that they also subcontract work from Italian American manufacturers.

My interviews show that Korean garment subcontractors, unlike produce, grocery, and fish retailers, have been unable to effectively use collective actions to protect their interests against White garment manufacturers, mainly because they are in excessive competition with both co-ethnic and non-Korean immigrant garment subcontractors. Whereas in grocery, produce, and fish retail businesses manufacturers and suppliers are in mild competition to get Korean retail customers, in the garment business the competition is cutthroat. Since Korean garment subcontractors approach White manufacturers individually and offer low prices to get work, the Korean Apparel Contractors Association of New York can do little collectively to protect the interests of its members. The president of the KACA told me that even if Korean garment subcontractors were to take concerted actions they would have to compete with other immigrants (mostly Chinese and Hispanic in New York City) who are willing to do anything to get work from manufacturers. Many garment manufacturers in New York have also established factories in South American countries (particularly Guatemala), where they pay full-time workers only $100 a month. Therefore, large manufacturers have the upper hand in setting prices for Korean and other immigrant subcontractors.

COLLECTIVE RESPONSES TO LANDLORDS

Telephone interviews with 93 randomly selected Korean merchants in Black neighborhoods in New York City indicated that 19% used their own buildings for business operations, whereas the other 81% leased store buildings. It is easier for Korean merchants to buy buildings in Black neighborhoods, where real estate values are substantially lower, than in predominantly White areas. Few Korean merchants in Manhattan, where real estate values are highest in New York City, run businesses in their own buildings. The Korean Small Business Service Center (KSBSC) estimated that less than 10% of Korean merchants in New York City own the buildings where their businesses operate; the others usually depend on White landlords, who are mostly Jewish (*SGT,* July 8, 1988).

Since they first began opening businesses in large numbers in the early 1970s, Korean immigrants in New York City have experienced several severe rent hikes. As Korean-owned businesses have become more successful, some landlords have doubled or tripled rents within a short period. Many Korean produce owners in New York have had to keep their stores open twenty-four hours a day to cover this escalating cost. Some White landlords have also made the Korean business owners responsible for property taxes and other types of building maintenance expenses.[2] Furthermore, it is not uncommon for Korean merchants to be forced to pay substantial amounts of "key money" to landlords when they buy ongoing businesses. Thus, Korean merchants in New York, as elsewhere, feel greatly exploited by White landlords. Many Korean merchants agreed that the money earned by their hard work goes more to White landlords than to themselves.

Korean merchants cannot change their landlords as easily as they can change their suppliers, a dependence that makes them more vulnerable to exploitation. Nevertheless, they have also collectively responded to protect themselves from landlords. About four hundred Korean-owned wholesale and trading companies specializing in merchandise imported from Korea and other Asian countries are located in the Broadway Korean Business District in Manhattan. These Broadway-based Korean importers and wholesalers were hit especially hard by severe rent hikes. As a solution, in the early 1980s the Broadway Korean Businessmen's Association planned to establish a commercial complex to house all Broadway-based Korean wholesalers and importers (*SGT,* July 8, 1988). They failed to achieve this goal, partly because they could not collect enough money for a down payment on the building and partly because some Korean merchants who used their own buildings for commercial activities were unwilling to move (Korean Association of New York 1985, 201).

Beginning in 1983, several Korean trade associations started a campaign for enacting a law regulating commercial rents. In its early stage, they tried to politicize the issue in the Korean community by collecting petitions from Korean merchants and urging them to write letters to New York City Council members and to the mayor (*KTNY,* May 19 and 24, 1983). In 1985, major Korean business associations, in close cooperation with non-Korean small business associations, began lobbying the Manhattan borough president, Mayor Koch, and city council members to propose a law regulating commercial rents (*KTNY,* May 14 and July 24, 1985). Korean business leaders played an important role in organizing three major demonstrations in which hundreds of Korean, Chinese, White, and Latino merchants participated, asking for such legislation (*KTNY,* May 8, 1986).

In February 1986, several small business organizations in New York City, including the Korean Small Business Service Center, created a multiethnic small business coalition to lobby for the regulation of commercial rents effectively: the Coalition for Fair Rents. Sung Soo Kim, director of the KSBSC, was elected as one of the two copresidents of the organization. A proposal for regulating commercial rents (Intro 914) was submitted to the New York City Council in 1988, but it was narrowly defeated. Korean business leaders felt that Mayor Ed Koch, under the strong influence of Jewish landlords, did not show much sympathy to the Korean merchants' campaign. In the 1989 mayoral election, they rejected Koch and supported David Dinkins, a Black candidate, who promised to take some measures to regulate rent (*SGT,* August 22, 1989).

Though Dinkins was elected mayor of New York City in 1989, he did not take action to regulate commercial rents. In 1991, another proposal for rent regulation (Intro 262) was submitted to the New York City Council but was again narrowly defeated. Rent regulation has recently become even more important for small business owners in New

York City, especially because of the recession. Unable to get a law passed by the city council, Korean business owners have recently utilized a collective bargaining technique to lower or freeze rents. The Broadway Korean Businessmen's Association and the Korean Apparel Contractors Association of New York have sent letters to members' landlords, warning them that a rent hike would be met with a legal challenge by each Korean trade association. Several Korean merchants who lease buildings from the same landlord have negotiated as a group, threatening that all of them would move out if rents were not lowered (*KCDNY*, June 16, 1990; *SGT*, February 25, 1991). This technique has proven successful. For example, in early 1991, about forty Korean merchants with stores in the same indoor flea market in Flushing negotiated with the building owner for two months (*SGT*, February 25, 1991). Finally, after the merchants had closed their stores for nineteen days, the landlord agreed to reduce rents by 25%. A few Korean business associations have held seminars on how to negotiate with landlords.

As noted above, Korean merchants in New York have made a class alliance with merchants of other ethnic groups for commercial rent control. Though their interethnic class alliance put pressure on landlords and policy makers, it did not result in concrete actions to protect Korean merchants' economic interests against landlords. Instead, intraethnic collective strategies such as collective bargaining over rents were found to be more successful. This suggests that ethnic boundaries are so rigid and impermeable that an interethnic merchants' coalition cannot be an effective organization, or at least not effective enough to protect Korean merchants' economic interests.

MIXED FEELINGS TOWARD JEWS

With approximately 1.5 million Jews, the New York metropolitan area has the largest Jewish community in the country. Many buildings in New York City, particularly in Manhattan, are owned by Jews. Korean small business owners often lease buildings from Jewish landlords, which provides the context for intergroup conflicts. Korean ethnic newspapers are replete with stories of Korean merchants' conflicts with Jewish landlords, including several court cases (*KTLA*, September 7, 1991).

As already noted, Korean produce and fish retailers rely heavily on Jewish suppliers, and Korean garment subcontractors get contracts mainly from Jewish garment manufacturers. Because more than in any other city Korean merchants in New York are dependent in their com-

mercial activities on Jewish Americans—as suppliers, landlords, or garment manufacturers who give them contracts—these merchants tend to
overgeneralize about Jews, seeing them as a homogeneous group of powerful capitalists. Though Korean merchants in New York City depend
on many non-Jewish White landlords, I have heard many speak as if all
Korean merchants' landlords were Jewish. Conflicts with Jewish suppliers, garment manufacturers, and landlords over economic interests have
caused Korean merchants to stereotype Jews as "moneymongers" or
"misers." Korean garment subcontractors in particular depend heavily
on both Jewish landlords and Jewish manufacturers. Therefore, Korean
garment factory owners as a group view Jews more negatively than
other Korean merchants. I asked a Korean garment subcontractor in
Queens how he thought about Jewish landlords and suppliers. His comment reflects many Korean merchants' stereotypical attitudes:

> Jewish landlords have no tears, no blood; they will do anything to exploit
> renters. If you are not careful as a renter, they will exploit you in a hundred
> different ways. They will cheat you through contracts. So, if you don't read
> the lease contract carefully, they will make you pay for many other types of
> expenses. Of course, they will raise your rent if your business goes well. If
> you cannot pay your rent, they will use a lawyer and kick you out quickly.
> They are quick to use their lawyers to give you a legal trouble. Jewish land-
> lords are tough about money.
>
> Oh, being tough about money is not limited to Jewish landlords. Jewish
> wholesalers, Jewish manufacturers, and all other Jewish merchants are tough
> about money. That's why Jews are so successful in business.

I have heard several Korean merchants say that Jewish wholesalers have
prevented Korean merchants from entering the wholesale business in
produce, grocery, jewelry, stationery, and other specialties, though they
have not specified how.

But some Korean merchants do not agree with these negative stereotypes. They point out that Korean merchants can learn much from Jewish landlords and wholesalers who conduct business according to rules
and laws. Mr. Lee, who owns a jewelry retail booth alongside many
Jewish jewelers on 47th Street ("Jewelry Street") in Manhattan, commented:

> Korean merchants keep saying Jewish landlords and Jewish suppliers are too
> harsh and too cruel. I do not agree. On the contrary, Koreans can learn much
> from Jews about business know-how. Jews run businesses rationally; they are
> cool but fair in business transactions. Jews know how to protect their busi-

ness interests without breaking laws. Korean merchants are not rational in business transactions and are too emotional. That's why they are often involved in arguments and fighting. Korean merchants easily break laws and get into trouble, because they come from a society with no strict rules.

If a renter fails to pay rent for a few months, a Jewish landlord tries to solve the problem legally by using a lawyer. A Korean landlord usually tries to solve the problem by arguing with and cursing the renter. And he easily gets into legal trouble with no protection of his business interest. But some Korean landlords have learned rational business techniques from Jewish landlords and are doing very well.

In spite of conflicts with Jewish suppliers and landlords over economic interests, Jewish Americans and Korean immigrants have commonalities in culture and historical experiences. Jews in the 1960s, like Koreans in the 1980s and 1990s, operated businesses in African American neighborhoods where they, too, experienced hostility in the forms of boycotts, arson, and looting. Because they too have been middleman merchants, Jewish Americans have been very sympathetic to Korean merchants in conflict with the African American community.[3] Jewish Americans' sympathy for Korean merchants and critical attitudes toward Black boycott organizers were typified by an editorial in the *New York Post,* a daily owned by a Jewish American, during the 1990–91 Black boycott of two Korean stores: it compared the boycott to the Nazis' persecution of the Jews ("Race-Baiting in Flatbush" 1990).

Aware of Jewish Americans' experience as middleman merchants, Korean community and business leaders have sought advice from Jewish community leaders. For example, Korean community leaders in Los Angeles and other cities invited Jewish speakers to seminars on intergroup conflicts that focused on Korean–African American conflicts. During the 1990–91 Brooklyn boycott, Korean business leaders turned to Jewish lawyers for advice on ending it. Attorney Richard Izzo, who represented the owners of the two boycotted stores in Brooklyn, was also Jewish. Izzo was not only legally but also emotionally involved in the case; in many press conferences with Korean and mainstream reporters, he severely criticized African American boycott leaders and Mayor Dinkins and staunchly supported the position of Korean merchants. His effort earned him the respect and affection of many Korean immigrants in New York City in 1990. Koreans showed their admiration for Izzo at the Korean rally in front of City Hall, where his speech received more applause than any other non-Korean speaker's.

Moreover, impressed by what they believe are values that emphasize children's education and strong group ties, many Korean immigrants have favorable attitudes toward Jewish Americans.[4] The following account by a Korean pastor in New York who is familiar with the Jewish community typifies Korean immigrants' positive views about "Jewish values":

> We can learn a lot from Jews. First of all, they are best in children's education. Many Korean parents, too, emphasize children's education, but as far as child socialization is concerned, Koreans do not compare to Jews. While Korean parents emphasize children's good grades in school, they do not do much at home for child socialization. In contrast, Jewish parents spend lots of time and energy at home to teach children good manners and habits.
>
> The Jewish community is solidly unified and this is another thing we should learn from Jews. They know how to help their own people, I understand the Jewish community has all kinds of social service agencies to provide services for co-ethnic members. And Jews, unlike Korean immigrants, do not compete in the same business.

Korean merchants are most impressed by what they perceive to be the Jewish style of collective approach to business. When Korean trade associations discuss how to moderate intragroup competition in business, they often emphasize Jewish merchants' ethnic coordination as a model to adopt. Most Korean merchants have heard that when a Jewish store owner does not have what a particular customer is looking for, he or she usually sends the customer to the closest Jewish store. In contrast, though Korean immigrants monopolized the wig wholesale business, because of their strong intragroup competition wig wholesale prices have significantly dropped since the mid-1970s. I have heard several Korean wig wholesalers say that if Jews had monopolized the wig wholesale business they would have been able to keep the prices high for a long time.

As we have noted thus far, many Korean immigrants have both positive and negative feelings about Jewish Americans. They have positive attitudes toward Jews partly because of cultural characteristics that are perceived as similar to their own and partly because of their knowledge of Jewish Americans' historical experiences as middleman merchants in African American neighborhoods. Their negative attitudes toward Jews stem mainly from their conflicts as small business owners over economic interests with Jewish suppliers or landlords. Obviously, these Jewish businesspeople do not have as much power as Coca-Cola and other large American corporations. Yet they have much more power than Korean small business owners. Ironically, Jewish Americans, who once played a vulnerable middleman role similar to that of Korean immigrants, have become the suppliers, manufacturers, and landlords on whom Korean merchants depend to operate their businesses. The transformation of Jewish Americans from middleman merchants into "orthodox capitalists" and Korean immigrants' replacement of Jews as middleman merchants are indications of ethnic mobility and ethnic succession in business (Aldrich and Reiss 1976; Chang 1993b; Elazer and Friedman 1976). In thirty years or so, Korean Americans may move into wholesale and manufacturing sectors, as they in turn achieve ethnic mobility in business.

COLLECTIVE RESPONSES
TO GOVERNMENT AGENCIES

Korean merchants in New York also have responded collectively to government regulations on small business activities. First of all, New York City has many laws and administrative orders pertaining to business licensing, commercial parking, commercial leases, disposal of commercial wastes, sidewalk obstruction, sanitary conditions of stores, and other aspects of operating a business. To increase dwindling revenues, the city recently raised business license and registration fees and imposed heftier fines for rule violations (Breznick 1991). Regulations have not been made specifically to hurt Korean merchants; they have negative effects on all small business owners in New York City. However, since a majority of Korean immigrants engage in small business, they have responded together to protect their economic interests.

The Korean Small Business Service Center, established in 1986, serves as the representative for all Korean trade associations in dealing with government agencies. Two of the major functions of the KSBSC are negotiating with city and other government officials to help Korean merchants who have violated business regulations and lobbying lawmakers and government agencies to make business regulations less strict. Staff members of the KSBSC visit City Hall at least three times per week, meeting with city government officials to protect Korean merchants both individually and collectively.

For example, at the end of 1990, the New York City Environment Control Department increased the fine for violating the sidewalk litter law (which requires a store owner to clean the store area) from $25 for a regular violation and $50 for a repeat violation (thirteen times or more) to $125 and $250 respectively. In 1991, when the increased rates went into effect, Korean produce owners charged with violations found themselves owing large amounts of money, with about thirty Koreans receiving tickets amounting to $10,000 or more (*SGT,* February 9, 1991). Staff members of the KSBSC have helped many Korean merchants reduce fines significantly by negotiating with city government officials.

The KSBSC has also actively lobbied officials and politicians to change regulations. For example, the center successfully lobbied the New York City Consumer Affairs Department to make the Trade Waste Association lower the commercial waste disposal fee by 7.5%, helping nearly 10,000 Korean merchants save considerable amounts of money (*KCDNY,* July 29, 1991). Another instance involved the regulation of sidewalk stands. New York City had stipulated that stores located on streets sixteen feet wide or wider could have stands displayed on the sidewalk up to four feet wide and ten feet long. Many Korean producer retailers extended their sidewalk stands beyond these limits and thus paid heavy penalties for violations. Sung Soo Kim, director of the KSBSC, lobbied city government administrators and the city council relentlessly, arguing that such a strict rule made it difficult for small produce and flower retailers to survive in New York City. In April 1993, the city council passed a bill effective as of July 1993 that increased the allowable width from four feet to five feet (*SGT,* April 28, 1993). Kim's lobbying activities were instrumental in the bill's passage. He estimated that the extension of sidewalk stands would result in a $25 million increase in annual sales for New York City Korean-owned businesses.

As part of its lobbying activities, the KSBSC has invited city government officials, including the mayor and members of the city council, to its annual dinner party, where community service awards were presented. Approximately seven hundred people participated in 1992, including two hundred lawmakers, city government administrators, and other non-Korean community leaders. At the dinner, Mayor Dinkins declared a "Korean Small Business Day" to "recognize Korean small business owners' contribution to the New York City economy" (*SGT,* December 1, 1992). Seven lawmakers and New York City administrators, including Mayor Dinkins, were given awards recognizing their services to the Korean business community.

New York City has a large number of street peddlers, some licensed and others unlicensed, who sell food and fruits. Though the presence of street food vendors may be convenient for people who live and work in the city, it has negative effects on small business owners, especially on Korean grocery and produce store owners. Korean business associations have pressured the city government to take actions to regulate these vendors. Two Korean business associations in particular, the Korean Small Business Service Center and the Korean-American Grocers Association of New York, have been actively lobbying city government administrators and lawmakers. In 1992 and 1993, leaders of KAGRONY visited the New York City Health Department and the Consumer Affairs Department, city council members, and state senate members, emphasizing the negative effects of street food vendors on consumers and small business owners and asking them to take measures to restrict street vending (*KCDNY*, June 25, 1992; *SGT*, January 4, 1993). KAGRONY conducted research and made a videotape on street food vendors in New York City for an effective presentation to administrators and lawmakers. The organization also sent a memorandum to the New York City Council and the New York City Health Department, which read in part:

> The Korean-American Grocers Association of New York (KAGRO) strongly urges the city to change its policies on mobile food vendors. Currently legislation permits vendors to locate 20 feet from any entrance of a business. This policy has proven harmful to small food businesses, many of which are run by more than 2,500 KAGRO members. Our research has shown that besides 5,000 licensed food vendors in the city, thousands of illegal ones also compete for unregulated space on the sidewalks in front of our stores. Many of these vendors are run by corporations and have anywhere from two to four people working on just one mobile cart. This kind of corporation-run set-up placed in front of small family-owned businesses dispels the myth that mobile push carts allow needy people to earn a living. Current policies instead allow established big businesses to irresponsibly make greater profits while driving down the morale and business of local delis and grocery stores. Many of the mobile food vendors also disregard city health and sanitation regulations.

Harlem probably has more street peddlers than any other area in New York City. Koreans merchants in the Harlem area estimated that there were some 350 street peddlers, as of December 1992, selling not only food and fruit but also clothing and other manufactured goods. Most peddlers in Harlem are new immigrants from African or South American countries. Korean merchants in Harlem have complained that they cannot compete with peddlers who do not pay license fees, taxes, and rents. In 1992, in response to these complaints, the Korean Small

Business Service Center strongly urged the New York City police to crack down on illegal peddlers and to regulate licensed peddlers in Harlem more strictly. In the summer and fall of 1992, the police raided the Harlem peddlers several times, arresting many illegal vendors (*SGT,* December 22, 1992). Suspecting that Korean merchants asked for the police intervention, the peddlers threatened to boycott Korean stores in Harlem.

Throughout the summer and fall of 1993, the Korean Dry Cleaners Association of New York was active in lobbying members of the New York State Legislature in connection with Proposal NYCRR 2-32. The proposal aimed to tighten regulations on the ventilation, exhaust, and emission of perc, a nonflammable fluid used for dry cleaning, in response to the finding that perc fumes can cause cancer, particularly in the elderly and babies. If the proposal had passed without revision, many dry cleaning owners would have had to spend large amounts of money to install new equipment and renovate their facilities. Leaders of the Korean Dry Cleaners Association, along with leaders of the Neighborhoods Cleaners Association, the major dry cleaners' association in the Northeast, lobbied lawmakers to propose a compromise bill whose regulations are less strict. In the summer of 1993, the New York State Health Department created the Dry Cleaning Regulations Negotiating Committee, consisting of lawmakers, administrators, scholars, lawyers, and representatives of dry cleaners. A staff member of the Korean Dry Cleaners Association was selected as one of the four committee members representing the dry cleaners in New York State. Although the four committee members representing dry cleaners were forced to accept a proposal at the end of 1994 that required dry cleaners to replace older equipment, they succeeded in extending the deadline for compliance until 1997. However, in 1995 the newly elected governor, Geroge Pataki, nullified the proposal before it was passed by the state legislature. Pataki plans to open hearings in the spring of 1996 to develop another proposal that will probably be more favorable to dry cleaners.

In March 1992, the national Consumers Union reported, based on their own investigation, that the fish sold in markets are generally contaminated by pollution. This report was nationally televised by the major networks. As a result of this negative publicity, Korean fish retailers in New York City experienced a significant reduction in sales. In response, leaders of the Korean Seafood Retailers Association and Sung Soo Kim, director of the Korean Small Business Service Center, argued that the Consumers Union's findings derived from "a scientifically inadequate and biased investigation" (*KTNY*, March 26, 1992). To counteract the negative publicity, they lobbied staff members of the New York City Business Development and Sanitation Departments to issue a statement that Consumers Union's findings were invalid. City officials initially refused, but they were finally persuaded to hold a joint press conference with Korean business leaders at a Korean fish retail store. In the press conference, which was covered by the local ABC-TV news, Korean business leaders argued that Consumers Union's conclusion concerning the pollution of fish on sale in markets was unfounded and that in fact the fish sold in Korean fish retail stores were usually fresher than those sold in supermarkets.

The Consumers Union's report must have had negative effects on all fish retailers, including many supermarkets that carried fish. However, it is interesting to note that only Korean fish retailers in New York City immediately responded to this report, acting together to improve the image of fish sold in markets. Koreans acted quickly because the negative publicity threatened their economic survival, and their large numbers made collective action effective. The publicity might have harmed large supermarkets that carried fish, but it certainly did not threaten their business survival. The economic survival of other non-Korean independent fish retailers was certainly threatened, but unlike Korean fish retailers, they did not have the ethnic resources for collective action. Fish retailers in New York or other cities could have made a multiethnic business alliance to fight the negative publicity. But, once again, ethnic boundaries are so impervious that any kind of panethnic small business alliance could not effectively act in concert.

Approximately 350 Koreans engage in garment manufacturing, and 95% of them subcontract from White manufacturers. Korean garment subcontractors, like other immigrant garment subcontractors, are able to survive mainly because they have access to cheap labor. Cheap labor is made possible by violating labor regulations, which puts Korean garment subcontractors in conflict with the New York State and federal Departments of Labor. Korean garment subcontractors in New York have been subject to numerous investigations by the New York State Department of Labor, and many have been found in violation of labor laws (*KTNY*, May 4, 1991; *SGT*, June 29, 1991). Most recently, in 1992 the U.S. Department of Labor raided Korean garment factories in New York and levied penalties ranging from $60,000 to $100,000 on about ten factories. The three most common violations are paying employees below minimum wage, not paying overtime, and not keeping records of employees and payment of wages. My interview with the Korean Apparel Contractors Association revealed that many Korean owners of garment factories in New York do not pay employees overtime and often pay their employees off the books. Korean garment subcontractors' conflicts with the Department of Labor are more widely publicized in Los Angeles (see Light and Bonacich 1988, 304–8) than in New York.

The Korean Apparel Contractors Association (KACA) has responded to the government's sanctioning of Korean garment subcontractors for violations of labor standards in two different ways. First, it has provided regular seminars to educate members on how not to violate labor laws. Second, it has actively lobbied the state Department of Labor, the New York State legislature, and the U.S. Department of Labor to moderate regulations and to relax enforcement of labor laws (*SGT*, July 5, 1990; March 11, 1992). KACA's lobbying activities have included explaining to lawmakers and government officials the economic difficulties that force its members to violate labor laws for survival, promising to teach Korean garment owners how to obey labor laws, and inviting staff members of the state Department of Labor to seminars to speak on labor laws. Because the Department of Labor, like other government agencies, is understaffed, it is not feasible for its inspectors to investigate immigrant garment factories regularly. Therefore, they are willing to listen to representatives of the KACA when the Korean representatives promise to educate their members on labor laws.

Korean garment subcontractors are also often in conflict with the Immigration and Naturalization Service (INS). Korean owners of garment businesses, like other immigrant owners, hire many illegal residents to save labor costs. A large proportion of workers employed in Korean garment factories in New York and Los Angeles are illegal Latino residents. One of the two major components of the 1986 Immigration Reform and Control Act is the sanctioning of employers who knowingly hire illegal aliens. INS officials have recently raided immigrant garment factories in New York City, arresting many illegal workers and fining their employers (*SGT*, May 4, 1991, and January 8, 1993). In the January 1993 investigation, INS officials found violations in thirty Korean garment factories in New York City. The KGCA has also actively lobbied the INS to ease the enforcement of employer sanctions by promising to educate Korean owners of garment factories on employer sanctions, inviting INS staff members to lecture on the regulation to KGCA members, and complaining about its unfairness.[5] In the

1992 election year, they made donations to the political campaigns of former President Bush and Senator Alphonse D'Amato (R-N.Y.), hoping that they might influence the Immigration and Naturalization Service to cut back on employer sanctions.

In 1991, the New York State legislature proposed a bill that would require anyone operating or working in a nail care salon to have a nail care specialty license and would levy heavy penalties on those who violated sanitary regulations. According to the original bill, the nail care specialty license would have required six hundred hours of education followed by a qualification examination (*SGT,* January 29, 1991). The Korean Nail Salon Association of New York (KNSANY) actively lobbied New York State government officials and members of the state legislature to get their alternative bill accepted. Leaders of KNSANY recommended that those with one or more years of nail care experience in New York State be given a license without any mandatory instruction or examination. Though the Association of Nail Schools strongly opposed this recommendation, the final bill contained a grandfather clause to accommodate KNSANY's request. This helped many Koreans save thousands of dollars. Furthermore, in enforcing the law, the New York State Division of Licensing Services initially stipulated that only official documents such as Social Security cards, work permits, and W-2 or tax return forms would be accepted as evidence of job experience. KNSANY successfully negotiated with the Division of Licensing Services to eliminate this requirement, thus enabling many Korean women with no work permits, such as students' wives, to keep their jobs in Korean nail salons. Though a regulation requiring a nail care specialty license would affect most nail care professionals, Koreans were the only group to actively lobby government officials and politicians.

In September 1993, the Korean Small Business Service Center, representing Korean small business owners in New York City, drafted the Korean Bill of Rights, which centered around twenty-four major demands on the New York City government. These demands were intended to protect the rights of Korean small business owners from unreasonable city government regulations and to increase the city government's financial support for small business owners (*SGT,* September 10, 1993). The KSBSC based the bill on requests received from various Korean trade associations. It included the demands that the government issue legislation regulating commercial rents, select Korean merchants to receive city government contracts assigned to minorities, and oppose the entrance of large chain stores into New York City minority neighborhoods.

The KSBSC declared the Korean Bill of Rights just two months before the November mayoral election to pressure David Dinkins and Rudy Giuliani, the two main mayoral candidates, to support Korean small business interests: both were asked to respond to the demands in writing. Depending on those responses, the KSBSC planned to influence Korean voters to support one or the other candidate. Then, after the election, the Korean business leaders would pressure the mayor to honor the promises he had made to them. To their disappointment, however, while both candidates said they supported the Korean Bill of Rights in principle, they avoided responding to specific points (*SGT*, October 4, 1993). Thus, this technique did not achieve the intended objective. Yet it put enough pressure on both candidates to compel them to take Korean small business interests seriously.

To lobby city government administrators and lawmakers effectively to protect Korean small business owners' economic interests, the KSBSC needed to form a coalition with small business associations of other ethnic groups. Sung Soo Kim, director of the center, succeeded in organizing such a multiethnic coalition. In August 1991, sixteen multiethnic small business associations joined together to form the Congress of Small Business.[6] Serving as one of three cochairs, Kim was central to the creation of this multiethnic coalition of small business owners in New York City. At the inaugural ceremony in August 1991, the Congress of Small Business declared the Bill of Small Business Rights, pertaining to fourteen major issues concerning small business owners' interests (*KTNY*, July 26, 1991; *SGT*, August 15, 1991). Kim and other leaders of the Congress of Small Business pressured the city government to relax various regulations that they claimed were driving small business owners out of New York City.

Mayor Dinkins made sweeping changes in his small business policy in February 1993, accepting most of the fourteen demands made in the Bill of Small Business Rights two year earlier (*SGT*, February 18, 1993). In response to one recommendation by the Congress of Small Business, Dinkins established the Small Business Advisory Board at the city government and appointed Sung Soo Kim one of two cochairs. After this appointment, Kim had even more influence on the New York City government's small business policy than before. Many people believed that Mayor Dinkins acted mainly to satisfy small business owners and win their votes for his reelection. However, it is also true that Sung Soo Kim's lobbying activities contributed to Dinkins' changes in his small business policy.

Korean grocery, liquor, produce, fish, and jewelry retailers depend largely on White corporations to supply their merchandise. These Korean retailers are subject to various forms of unfair treatment from White suppliers. However, by establishing trade associations Korean merchants in each business specialty have used collective strategies to protect their economic interests. Collective strategies used by Korean merchants in New York included demonstrations, boycotts, group purchases, and price bargaining. These approaches have been very effective, in part because Korean merchants are heavily concentrated in several business specialties, thus accounting for a large proportion of total city businesses in each. They have also been effective in part because "monopoly" corporations (White suppliers) are, in fact, in mild competition. In contrast, Korean garment subcontractors in New York have been unsuccessful in acting together to protect their economic interests from exploitation by garment manufacturers because there is overcompetition among Korean and other immigrant garment subcontractors to get work from these manufacturers.

Korean merchants also depend on non-Korean landlords for their commercial buildings, and in these dealings they are even more vulnerable to exploitation. However, Korean merchants have also fashioned collective responses to landlords in economic self-defense, though less effectively than in their dealings with White suppliers. Korean business leaders have been more active than any other small business group in New York City in lobbying politicians for a law regulating commercial rents, leading several multiethnic small business owners' demonstrations in support of the legislation. After the New York City Council several times failed to pass such a law, Korean merchants began to use the technique of group bargaining to lower their commercial rents.

Korean merchants are also in conflict with the city, state, and federal governments, which regulate their small business activities with a number of laws and administrative orders. Korean merchants also have collectively responded to governmental agencies to protect their economic interests from what they see as unreasonable regulations. Various Korean trade associations in New York have individually lobbied politicians and administrators to moderate regulations that affect them. The Korean Small Business Service Center, representing all Korean trade associations and Korean merchants in New York City, has engaged in numerous administrative and political lobbying efforts to protect Koreans' business interests. Through these activities, Korean immigrants have learned political skills. Though the Korean population in New York City is much smaller than the Chinese population and substantially smaller than the Indian population, they seem to have been more active in political lobbies than either of the other two Asian groups.

CHAPTER 10

Collective Actions and Power in the Korean Community

In the previous two chapters, we examined major cases of collective actions taken by Korean merchants in New York in dealing with conflicts with African Americans, White suppliers and landlords, and governmental regulation of small business activities. The descriptions indicate a high correlation between Korean immigrants' business-related intergroup conflicts and their ethnic collective actions. This chapter analyzes the correlation further by assessing the extent to which Koreans' business-related intergroup conflicts have contributed to all ethnic collective actions taken by Korean immigrants in New York. In their efforts to resolve such conflicts, major Korean business associations and business leaders have gained influence and power in the Korean community. This chapter also makes clear that in New York the influence of Korean trade associations has far exceeded that of Korean professional associations.

AN ANALYSIS OF KOREANS' COLLECTIVE ACTIONS

BUSINESS-RELATED INTERGROUP CONFLICTS AND ETHNIC COLLECTIVE ACTIONS

Looking at particular cases of ethnic collective action taken against outside groups is helpful to understanding the economic basis of Korean ethnic solidarity. However, it is also important to determine what proportion of all these actions taken by Koreans in New York were intended to protect Koreans' commercial interests. To this end, all cases of collective actions taken by Koreans against other groups between 1970 and 1994 in the New York metropolitan area in the forms of *demonstrations* and *boycotts* have been identified from Korean ethnic newspapers and content-analyzed. Interviews with leaders of Korean trade associations have provided further information about those organized by the trade associations. I decided to include only demonstrations and boycotts in the analysis because these are the most radical forms of collective action. The others, such as meetings with government officials and African American leaders, are too numerous to count.

As shown in table 14, Koreans in New York held thirteen demonstrations against non-Korean groups or government officers between 1970 and 1994. As expected, Koreans' business-related conflicts largely contributed to these mass demonstrations: nine (69%) of them, mostly organized by Korean trade associations, were staged to protect Koreans' business interests. In most cases, suppliers, landlords, or city officials were the targets of the demonstrations. The last column of the table gives the duration of boycotts that Koreans in New York held against outside interest groups. Korean business associations organized all seven boycotts, and White suppliers were their targets in each case; all but one were directed at produce wholesalers (the exception targeted a fish wholesaler).

The summary information presented in table 14 suggests two major points concerning the relationship between Koreans' concentration in small business and their collective actions in the form of demonstrations and boycotts. First, in New York Koreans' commercial activities and business-related intergroup conflicts are mainly responsible for these radical forms of ethnic collective actions. Of course, Korean merchants' conflicts with external interest groups and government agencies have contributed to many other forms of collective action already discussed and not presented in this table—fund-raising campaigns, community hearings, and meetings with other interest groups. For example, even during the relatively brief (four months long) and unpublicized Black boycott of a Korean store in Brooklyn in 1988, Korean community leaders held seven rounds of meetings with African American leaders on ending the boycott.

TYPES OF BUSINESS

Second and more important, the summary information in table 14 suggests that certain types of business involve more intergroup conflicts and

TABLE 14.

DEMONSTRATIONS AND BOYCOTTS BY KOREANS IN NEW YORK AGAINST
NON-KOREAN INDIVIDUALS AND GROUPS (1970–94)

Date	Issue and/or Immediate Cause	Korean Ethnic Organization Involved	Form of Collective Action	
			Demonstration-Number of Participants	Boycott-Duration
6/13/1977	Labeling of Korean produce retailers as "Moonies" by a White wholesale employee	Korean Produce Association of New York	Yes—100	No
2/28–3/6/1980	Discrimination against a Korean produce retailer in services by a White wholesale employee	Korean Produce Association of New York	No	Yes—1 week
8/4–8/11/1981	A Korean produce retailer beaten by employees of a White wholesaler	Korean Produce Association of New York	Yes—250	Yes—1 week
8/6/1982	*Daily News* article charged Korean produce retailers owners with being financially supported by the Unification Church	Korean Produce Association of New York	Yes—500	No
4/21/1985	A Korean beaten and indicted by the police in Queens	Ad hoc committee	Yes—300	No

TABLE 14. (*continued*)

Date	Issue and/or Immediate Cause	Korean Ethnic Organization Involved	Form of Collective Action	
			Demonstration-Number of Participants	Boycott-Duration
5/26–6/2/1985	A Korean produce retailer falsely accused of stealing by a wholesaler	Korean Produce Association of New York	Yes—60	Yes—1 week
3/12–19/1986	A Korean produce retailer beaten by employees of a wholesaler	Korean Produce Association of New York	Yes—200	Yes—1 week
5/8/1986	Need for a commercial rent regulation law	Uptown Korean Business Association	Yes—100	No
6/8/1986	A Korean baby fell to death from 17th-story window with no protection rail	Ad hoc committee	Yes—200	No
7/8/1986	Need for a commercial rent regulation law	Rent Regulation Committee for Korean Small Business Owners	Yes—20	No
10/18/1987	A Korean student beaten by the police in Manhattan	Ad hoc committee	Yes—400	No

TABLE 14. (*continued*)

7/14–11/9/1988	A fish wholesaler selling rotten fish and cheating in weights	Korean Fish Retailers Association	Yes—250	Yes—4 months
10/28,29,11/10/1988	A Korean customer beaten by an employee of a car dealer in New Jersey	Ad hoc committee	Yes—200 (3 days)	No
9/18/1990	Boycott of two Korean green grocery stores in Brooklyn by Blacks for 8 months and the New York City mayor's failure to act to stop the boycott	Korean Association of New York	Yes—8,000	No
7/4–8/20/1991	A Korean produce retailer beaten by a White wholesaler's employee	Korean Produce Association of New York	No	Yes—7 weeks
7/25–8/3/1991	A Korean grocer at Bronx Terminal beaten by a White wholesaler's employee	Bronx Korean Merchants Association	No	Yes—1 week

Sources: Articles in the *Korea Times New York* (1970–94), the *Korean Central Daily New York* (1988–94), and the *Sae Gae Times* (1988–94); interviews with Korean trade associations and the Korean Small Business Service Center.

thereby more often contribute to ethnic collective actions than others. Based on information included in table 14 and on descriptive information in the two previous chapters, I have made a typology of Korean businesses in New York by levels of intergroup conflicts encountered and collective actions used (see table 15). Korean produce, grocery, and fish retail businesses in New York are typical middleman businesses that connect White manufacturers or suppliers and minority customers. Merchants engaged in these businesses have experienced more intergroup conflicts than other merchants and have therefore used more collective actions. In particular, Korean produce and fish retailers purchase their merchandise at Hunts Point Market or Fulton Fish Market, where they have frequent confrontations, sometimes including physical violence, with employees of wholesalers. That is why these two trade associations have also been involved in more conflicts with White suppliers and have used supplier-oriented collective actions more frequently than other trade associations.

Korean service businesses such as nail care and dry cleaning depend heavily neither on minority customers nor on White manufacturers, and thus generally avoid intergroup conflicts. Accordingly, Korean merchants who engage in these non-middleman occupations have not had frequent recourse to collective actions. Korean retailers dealing in manufactured goods imported from Korea and other Asian countries heavily rely on minority customers; conversely, Korean garment subcontractors depend on White manufacturers for subcontracting. Koreans in these semi-middleman businesses fall between the other two groups in their levels of intergroup conflicts and use of collective actions. But all Korean merchant groups, including nail salon owners and dry cleaners, have used collective strategies to protect their economic interests against White landlords and against government agencies.

The above discussion indicates that Koreans' business-related intergroup conflicts—rather than their concentration in small business itself—generate ethnic solidarity. Thus typical middleman businesses such as produce and grocery retail that involve more intergroup conflicts generate stronger ethnic solidarity than other types of businesses in New York. From this, we can make inferences about other minority and immigrant groups active in small business. For example, Chinese immigrants in New York are heavily concentrated in Chinese restaurants and garment subcontracting (Kwong 1987; Zhou and Logan 1989). The Chinese restaurant business is not heavily dependent on either minority customers or White suppliers. So we can infer that Chinese res-

TABLE 15.

TYPOLOGY OF KOREAN BUSINESSES IN NEW YORK, BY LEVELS OF
INTERGROUP CONFLICT AND ETHNIC COLLECTIVE ACTION

Type of Businesses	External Groups with Whom Conflict Is Likely				Levels of Intergroup Conflict and Ethnic Collective Actions
	minority customers	White suppliers	White landlords	government agencies	
Typical middleman businesses (grocery, produce, and fish retail)	yes	yes	yes	yes	high
Semi-middleman (retail of manufactured goods imported from Asian countries)	yes	no	yes	yes	medium
Semi-middleman businesses (garment subcontracting)	no	yes	yes	yes	medium
Non-middleman businesses (nail care and dry cleaning services)	no	no	yes	yes	low

taurant owners in New York have encountered far fewer business-related intergroup conflicts and have therefore used ethnic collective actions far less frequently than Korean produce or fish retailers. As we
noted in chapter 9, Korean garment contractors are so dependent on
White manufacturers for subcontracting that they have done little to
bargain with the manufacturers to protect their economic interests. For
the same reason, Chinese-owned garment subcontractors are unlikely
to have acted together against White manufacturers.

Iranian immigrants in Los Angeles are highly entrepreneurial too.
In fact, a study of them conducted in 1987–88 (Bozorgmehr 1992; Bozorgmehr, Sabagh, and Der-Martirosian 1993; Bozorgmehr, Sabagh, and
Der-Martirosian 1996; Light, Sabagh, Bozorgmehr, and Der-Martirosian 1994), one year after my survey of Koreans in Los Angeles was
conducted, showed that Iranians had a higher self-employment rate
(57%) than Koreans (45%). However, Iranian immigrant businesses in
Los Angeles, unlike those of their Korean counterparts, have not attracted much publicity; many Americans outside of Los Angeles may
not even know about the high self-employment rate of Iranian immigrants. Because Iranian immigrants engage in non-middleman businesses, they have not frequently had business-related intergroup conflicts or resorted to ethnic collective actions. Iranians in Los Angeles are
more widely dispersed than Koreans in different types of businesses
(Bozorgmehr 1992; Bozorgmehr, Sabagh, and Der-Martirosian 1993;
Bozorgmehr, Der-Martirosian, and Sabagh 1996); moreover, they include a larger proportion of professional businesses such as real estate
and medical services. Thus, they do not encounter much conflict with
White suppliers. In addition, few Iranian immigrants run businesses in
South Central Los Angeles and thus they do not have conflicts with African American customers either.

Cuban immigrants in Miami have developed a high level of ethnic business (Portes and Bach 1985). But their businesses (Portes and
Manning 1986) differ significantly from those of Koreans in the ethnic
composition of customers and suppliers. Cuban-owned businesses
mainly serve co-ethnic customers in the Cuban enclave. They also depend on Cuban-owned manufacturers and wholesalers; Wilson and
Martin (1982) emphasized the economic advantages of linkages of
businesses from Cuban manufacturers or wholesalers to retailers. This
pattern—a non-middleman business in an enclave economy—enhances
Cuban immigrants' *ethnic attachment* by increasing intragroup social

interactions. However, since their business operation does not involve a high level of intergroup conflict, it does not increase their *ethnic solidarity*. We therefore expect Cuban merchants in Miami to have utilized ethnic collective actions far less frequently than Korean merchants in New York.

Though not all Korean business owners play a middleman role between suppliers and minorities, a larger proportion of Korean merchants engage in typical middleman and semi-middleman businesses than any other minority or immigrant group active in small business in the United States. In fact, Korean immigrants control grocery, produce, and fish retail stores—prototypical middleman businesses—in many Black neighborhoods in New York. Koreans in Los Angeles monopolize grocery and liquor retail businesses in many neighborhoods in South Central Los Angeles.

The high correlation between the type of Korean business and the level of intergroup conflict also helps explain why the Korean communities in New York and Los Angeles have used collective actions to different degrees. Many Korean grocery or liquor and swap meet stores in Los Angeles are located in African American neighborhoods in South Central Los Angeles. Thus, as previously noted, Korean merchants in Los Angeles have had conflicts with the African American community, which has in turn led to great solidarity in the Korean community. However, service businesses, such as dry cleaning, maintenance, house painting, and fast-food restaurants, constitute a much larger proportion of Korean businesses in Los Angeles than in New York. Because Korean merchants in service businesses rarely need to use collective actions against White suppliers, they have acted together far less often than Korean retailers in New York.

According to my interviews with Korean business leaders in Los Angeles, the Korean-American Grocers Association's boycott of a beer wholesaler to force it to stop using Ice Cube to endorse their product was the only boycott or demonstration taken by Korean merchants in Los Angeles against White suppliers (see chapter 8). Again, the types of Korean businesses in Los Angeles make it clear why Korean merchants have not needed to use these more radical forms of collective actions. Only Korean produce and fish retailers in New York have boycotted and demonstrated against White suppliers, since Korean produce and fish retailers frequently clash with employees of wholesalers at Hunts Point Market and Fulton Fish Market. As neither produce nor fish retail is one of the main Korean businesses in Los Angeles, merchants there have not experienced the serious conflicts with suppliers that would have forced them to use boycotts or demonstrations in self-defense.

Garment subcontracting, fast-food franchises, and gas stations account for a significant proportion of Korean businesses in Los Angeles. By the typology of Korean businesses given in table 15, these are semi-middleman businesses in that they depend on White corporations but not on minority customers. However, as discussed in chapter 9, the dependence of Korean garment factories in New York on White corporations for subcontracting is so extreme that they have done little to counteract their exploitation by those corporations. In Los Angeles, not only Korean garment factories but also fast-food franchises and gas stations are almost entirely dependent on big corporations. Therefore, they have not done much to negotiate with corporations. In fact, in neither business have Koreans established a trade association. Korean garment manufacturers in Los Angeles established their association, the Korean-American Garment Industry Association, in 1979. Its main objectives, however, are to lobby government agencies (the state and federal Departments of Labor and the Immigration and Naturalization Service) and to handle labor disputes with Mexican employees. In view of this, Bonacich's interpretation of Korean businesses in Los Angeles as almost entirely controlled by corporations makes much sense. Their concentration in businesses entirely dependent on White corporations is another reason that Korean merchants in Los Angeles have used collective actions against White suppliers and manufacturers far less than Korean merchants in New York.

TRADE ASSOCIATIONS' INCREASED POWER AND INFLUENCE

Korean merchants established specialized trade associations or local business associations to protect their interests against outside groups. In the process of collectively resolving intergroup conflicts, several business associations have emerged as powerful organizations in the Korean community in New York. Perhaps the easiest way to assess their power and influence is by comparing them to nonbusiness, professional Korean associations, as table 16 does (based on interviews with the leaders of these associations).

The first column shows the number of members who paid annual dues to each association. There are many other Korean trade associa-

TABLE 16.
KOREAN BUSINESS AND PROFESSIONAL
ASSOCIATIONS IN NEW YORK (1991)

	Membership Size[a]	Office	Number of Paid Employees	1991 Budget
Business Associations				
Korean Produce Association	1,100 (1,800)	Yes	3	$650,000
Broadway Korean Businessmen's Association	120 (500)	Yes	2	$420,000
Korean-American Grocers Association of New York	600 (1,850)	Yes	2	$235,000
Korean Apparel Contractors Association of New York	420 (500)	Yes	3	$350,000
Korean Nail Salon Association of New York	450 (1,200)	Yes	1	$70,000
Korean Fish Retailers Association	200 (720)	Yes	0	$185,000
Korean Dry Cleaners Association of New York	100 (1,500)	No	0	$70,000
Professional Associations				
New York Metropolitan Chapter of Korean-American Scientists' Association	400 (800)	No	0	$15,000
Korean Dental Association of Eastern U.S.A.	70 (120)	No	0	$10,000
Korean American Nurses Association	100 (550)	No	0	$3,000
Korean-American Lawyers' Association of New York	50 (100)	No	0	$2,500
Korean Americans in Government	70 (100)	No	0	$3,000

Source: Interviews with Korean trade and professional associations in October 1991.
[a]The figure in parenthesis indicates the total number of Koreans engaged in each occupation in the New York metropolitan area.

tions in New York not listed in the table, including the Korean Apparel Store Owners Association, the Korean Jewelers Association, the Korean Restaurant Owners Association, and the Korean Construction Workers Association. There are also about twelve local Korean business owners' associations, such as the Harlem Korean Merchants Association and the Uptown Korean Chamber of Commerce, that link all Korean store

owners in a particular area. Therefore, the number of Korean merchants affiliated with one or more trade associations is really much
larger than the total number of members given here.

In 1991 the Korean Small Business Service Center had 250 dues-pay-
ing members, to whom it offered free services to resolve any business-
related disputes or problems with government agencies. However, as
noted in the previous chapter, as the central organization protecting Koreans' business interests in New York the KSBSC also helps other
Korean merchants and all Korean trade and local business associations
deal with customers, suppliers, landlords, and government agencies.
Also, local Korean business associations, which are not listed, are usually more likely to take collective actions against customers than are
Korean trade associations. Accordingly, Korean merchants' potential
for collective actions is much greater than the low membership numbers
in table 16 might indicate.

Korean business and professional associations differ fundamentally
in their major objectives. Nonbusiness, professional associations generally serve two major purposes: maintaining friendship among members
and exchanging professional information. Trade associations emphasize
three other objectives: handling business-related intergroup conflicts
collectively, lobbying the government and politicians to protect Korean
business interests, and moderating competition among Korean merchants. In fact, Korean trade associations in New York, as in other metropolitan areas, were originally established mainly to achieve these
three important practical ends. As previously noted, Korean produce
retailers have been involved in many more conflicts with various interest
groups than Koreans in any other type of business. Out of practical
need, most of the 1,800 Korean produce retailers in New York are affiliated with their business association. Korean trade associations usually
have offices and paid employees that focus on intergroup conflicts and
lobbying activities, whereas none of the professional associations has
either.

Korean trade associations have much larger annual budgets than professional associations, mainly because they receive donations from suppliers. Also, their revenues are higher, partly because their members
pay higher annual dues. In the case of the Broadway Korean Businessmen's Association, these are extremely high: $600 for regular members,
but much more for staff members—the president $15,000, each of six
vice presidents $10,000, each ex-president $5,000, and board members
$1,000. Many Korean merchants donate money not only to their

respective business association but also to other Korean ethnic organizations. Korean lawyers, physicians, and accountants earn sizable incomes by serving a largely Korean clientele. Yet it is usually Korean merchants, rather than Korean professionals, who participate in community fund-raising parties. It seems that the merchants' generosity comes partly from their stronger attachment to the community, an attachment formed by their conflicts with outside interest groups.[1] We previously examined some of the major intergroup and lobbying activities undertaken by various Korean trade associations to protect their interests against external forces. Korean trade associations help increase ethnic solidarity in other ways. For example, the Korean Produce Association of New York annually holds the "Korean Harvest and Folklore Festival" just after Choo Seok, the Korean equivalent of Thanksgiving, at Flushing Meadows–Corona Park. Approximately 30,000 Koreans—more than 20% of the Korean population in the New York–New Jersey metropolitan area—attended the 1992 festival to enjoy Korean folk songs, dances, games, and traditional Korean food; that year, the association spent some $250,000 for the festival. The Korean Produce Association thereby assists in retaining the Korean cultural tradition.

The Broadway Korean Businessmen's Association consists of "elite" Korean importers and wholesalers. The president told me that only highly recommended businessmen with "good credit and acceptable personalities" are admitted to the club. By the typology of Korean businesses in table 15, Korean importers and wholesalers are non-middleman merchants who do not face frequent business-related intergroup conflicts. Nevertheless, the Broadway Korean importers and wholesalers have taken a highly collectivistic approach to business for several reasons.

First, Korean importers and wholesalers have needed to cooperate because competition would have hurt them economically more than Korean retailers, especially because of their physical concentration in the Broadway area. Second, the Korean government has encouraged the importers and wholesalers to work collectively because their excessive competition would hurt Korean exports and thus the Korean economy, which has gotten a boost from their distribution of these manufactured goods. The Korean government's influence on Korean importers and wholesalers was particularly strong in the 1970s when Korean suppliers almost entirely depended on Korean-imported items—seen, for example, in the regulation of wig prices by the Korean Wig Importers Association in New York.[2] At present, the Korean government has less sway over the Broadway Korean importers and wholesalers, but still it coordinates many of their activities. Members of the Broadway Korean Businessmen's Association still make annual group trips to Korea, where they meet with high-ranking government officials at the Ministry of Commerce and Industry as well as with business leaders.

Third, Korean importers and wholesalers use a collective strategy because group purchases and group sales reduce costs effectively. Members of the Broadway Korean Businessmen's Association purchase merchandise collectively from South Korea, the Soviet Union, mainland China, and South American countries. They also engage in group sales in the United States and South America through merchandise shows. Many Korean importers and wholesalers are willing to pay high membership dues to belong to the Broadway Korean Businessmen's Association partly because of the benefits they derive from these group activities.

Many Korean women help their husbands at wholesale stores. Nevertheless, as the gendered name of the trade association might suggest, the Broadway Korean Businessmen's Association is an all-male club; only one middle-aged unmarried woman who owns a manufacturing and wholesale business in the Broadway area is affiliated (Min 1997). The Broadway Korean Businessmen's Association established a wives' club as a sister organization in 1990. Its activities include holding seminars on children's education and performing community service. The Broadway Korean Businessmen's Association operates the Broadway Korean-American Bank and the Broadway Korean School (a Saturday Korean-language school). Twenty percent of their budget is spent on providing services to the Korean community, including scholarships for Korean students in need.

In the New York Korean community, the Korean Association of New York (KANY) is the main political organization that represents Koreans to the outside world. It also provides various services, particularly to new Korean immigrants, in the New York metropolitan area. Yet the first four trade associations in table 16 have larger budgets than the Korean Association of New York, and the first three exercise as much power and influence as it does. Because of their important roles inside as well as outside the Korean community, the presidents of those three trade associations—the Korean Produce Association, the Broadway Korean Businessmen's Association, and the Korean-American Grocers Association of New York—seem to enjoy as much prestige in the Korean community as the president of the Korean Association of New York.

Moreover, in recent years, no Korean has been elected the president of KANY without support from major business associations. In fact, eleven of KANY's twelve presidents between 1972 and 1995 were successful businessmen.

We noted in chapter 8 that since the 1992 riots 1.5- and second-generation ethnic organizations have played an increasingly important role in the Korean community in Los Angeles. In New York, by contrast, younger-generation ethnic organizations play a far less significant role, even now. Out of the three 1.5- and second-generation Korean-American organizations in New York—the Coalition of Korean-American Voters, Korean Americans in Government, and Young Korean-American Networks (a young Korean professional organization)—only the Coalition of Korean-American Voters has been active in the Korean community. Yet even this organization, created in 1990, is not truly comparable to any of its Los Angeles counterparts. For example, the 1993 annual budget of the Coalition of Korean-American Voters was only $15,000, against $308,000 for that of the Korean American Coalition, the most influential 1.5- and second-generation ethnic organization in the Korean community in Los Angeles. Compared to trade associations, 1.5- and second-generation ethnic organizations still play a marginal role in the Korean community in New York.

There are several reasons for this difference between the two communities. First, the 1992 riots forced young Koreans in Los Angeles to get involved in the Korean community to protect the economic interests of their parents, while the Korean community in New York has not encountered such a massive crisis. Second, Korean trade and local merchants' associations in New York have been better organized than those in Los Angeles. Therefore, Korean merchants in New York have not needed the help of the second generation to resolve business-related intergroup conflicts successfully. Thus, had there been a long-term Black boycott of Korean stores in Los Angeles similar to the 1990 Brooklyn boycott, the community would have depended in part on second-generation Korean organizations to end the boycott; the Korean business community in New York did not require or desire such intervention. Third, the Korean community in Los Angeles has a longer history of Korean immigration and, accordingly, far more second-generation Korean adults than its counterpart in New York.

Sung Soo Kim, director of the Korean Small Business Service Center, has been widely known as a staunch defender of Korean merchants' economic interests. He earned a master's in political science from the

New School for Social Research and completed his Ph.D. course work at Columbia University before serving as the secretary of the Korean Produce Association in 1985. In that office, he became keenly aware of the many business-related difficulties that Korean merchants faced. In 1986, instead of starting his dissertation, he established the Korean Small Business Service Center to help Korean small business owners.

Since that time, Kim has been active in lobbying government officials, lawmakers, and other community leaders to protect Korean merchants' economic interests. He led the negotiations with African American boycott leaders and city government administrators to resolve the two most recent and longest boycotts of Korean stores. He was also a central figure in creating the Congress of Small Business of New York City, a multiethnic coalition of small business associations. Known as a tough negotiator, he is reportedly the man Mayor Dinkins was most afraid of. During his graduate work in political science, he read extensively in Marx, Habermas, and other critical theorists. Kim has used the critical perspectives derived from these writers in defending Korean small business owners. I have often heard him argue that Korean small business owners are "powerless" and "alienated" in dealing with government bureaucracies and large corporations in a capitalist society.

Sung Soo Kim's face is familiar to *New York Times* readers; several other local newspapers, including *New York Newsday,* have featured stories on his role as the spokesperson for Korean small business owners in New York City. He has also contributed articles defending Korean merchants to many English dailies and weekly magazines. In addition, he has appeared on many English-language talk shows and radio stations. In 1990, he was the only Asian American selected by *New York Newsday* as one of the twenty-nine most influential figures in Queens. Because of his uncompromising personality, he has many critics even in the Korean community. Yet even his critics agree that he has played a key role in protecting Korean merchants from outside interest groups and government agencies.

A content analysis of articles in ethnic newspapers indicates that Koreans' commercial activities and business-related intergroup conflicts have been mainly responsible for demonstrations and boycotts, the more radical forms of ethnic collective actions taken by Koreans in New York against other groups. Korean merchants' conflicts with external interests groups and government agencies have also led to much collective action in less radical forms—fund-raising campaigns, community hearings, and meetings with other interest groups. More important, the content analysis suggests that typical middleman businesses connecting White manufacturers or suppliers and minority customers, such as grocery, produce, and fish retail businesses, have involved more intergroup conflicts than other types of businesses; thus Korean merchants engaged in these middleman businesses have more often acted collectively.

The high level of correlation between the type of business and intergroup conflict helps to explain differences between the Korean community and other Asian communities in New York or between the New York and Los Angeles Korean communities in levels of intergroup conflicts and ethnic solidarity. Because Chinese immigrants in New York heavily concentrate in Chinese restaurants, which depend neither on minority customers nor White suppliers, these restaurant owners have far fewer business-related intergroup conflicts than Korean produce or fish retailers and thus have used ethnic collective actions far less frequently. Because service businesses constitute a much larger proportion of Korean businesses in Los Angeles than in New York, Korean merchants in Los Angeles have used collective actions—a tool more often employed by retailers—against White suppliers far less often than those in New York.

Korean merchants' efforts to resolve business-related intergroup conflicts have made Korean trade associations and business leaders more powerful. A comparison of two types of Korean occupational associations in New York suggests that trade associations have far more influence and power in the Korean community than professional associations. Because of their emphasis on protecting business interests, the trade associations, unlike the professional associations, devote much staff time and money to lobbying and dealing with inter- and intra-group conflicts. Korean trade associations and Korean business leaders have thus been much more active and influential in community politics than Korean professional associations and professionals.

CHAPTER 11

Korean Businesses

Negative Effects

Researchers have pointed out that the concentration of members of an immigrant or minority group in a few or several business specialties increases internal conflicts and thus weakens ethnic solidarity in two different ways. First, it increases intragroup competition and conflicts among co-ethnic business owners; researchers have stressed this outcome, especially among Korean merchants. Second, business owners exploit co-ethnic members as a cheap labor source. Researchers have emphasized the resulting class conflicts between business owners and co-ethnic employees, especially in connection with Chinese immigrant entrepreneurship. To establish the small business basis of Korean ethnic solidarity more convincingly, we need to examine these two arguments with regard to Korean immigrant entrepreneurship.

INTRAGROUP BUSINESS COMPETITION

Because Korean immigrants concentrate in several business lines, strong competition between two or more Korean stores located close to one another is inevitable. Many studies have shown that the competition between those engaged in the same line of business is intense (Chang 1990; I. Kim 1981; K. Kim and Hurh 1985; Min 1988a). For example, a survey of Korean merchants in Atlanta revealed that the vast majority of Korean stores were in competition with their neighboring co-ethnic stores (Min 1988a, 79). Intraethnic business competition means lower profit margins and more stress in operating a business. Sometimes, though it is uncommon, two Korean business owners who engage in the same type of business on the same block do not talk to each other. In other cases, a Korean immigrant will approach a Korean merchant's landlord and offer to pay a higher rent for the property, a practice that has contributed to rent hikes. Furthermore, Korean merchants' excessive competition in pricing sales items causes friction between Korean store owners and African American customers. An African American customer may ask for a refund for the purchased merchandise when he or she is offered a lower price for the same merchandise by another Korean store across the street, which can lead to a merchant-customer dispute. In addition, competition between Korean merchants can turn into physical violence. For example, in 1972 a Korean wig peddler in Jamaica, New York, died after a fight with a Korean retail store owner (I. Kim 1981, 132).

However, intraethnic competition and conflict among Korean merchants, largely limited to the individual level, do not destroy unity on the community level. As Simmel observed (1955, 23), when members of a group encounter threats from the outside world, they will end internal conflict and maintain in-group cohesion to protect the group from the outside threat. Two competing Korean merchants tend to show unity when confronting an outside enemy. This tendency was most clearly exemplified in the 1990–91 Black boycott of two Korean stores in Brooklyn. Before the boycott, long-term business competition led to strong resentment between the two store owners, but the targeting of the two stores by Black boycotters united them. Throughout the boycott (nearly one and a half years), they worked in close cooperation to take concerted actions against the boycotters. However, when I interviewed the two Koreans after the boycott had ended, they were still very critical of each other.

Korean business associations have taken collective actions to moderate competition among Korean merchants. Thus, intragroup business competition and conflict have themselves become a source of ethnic solidarity, particularly for Korean wholesalers. In the late 1960s and early 1970s, when intragroup business competition became fierce, Korean wig importers keenly felt the need to regulate wig prices by establishing an association. In 1972, with the intervention of the Korean government, they established the Korean Wig Union to prevent price dumping and to set a minimum wholesale price for each item (I. Kim 1981, 134). In August 1975, the Korean Wig Union was charged with violating antitrust law and subsequently fined $2,500 by the U.S. fed-

eral court in New York City (I. Kim 1981, 136). Another example
of cooperation is offered by Korean importers and wholesalers in the
Broadway Korean Business District, who were in strong competition
over commodity prices and store hours. In 1979, the Broadway Korean
Businessmen's Association made a rule that Korean wholesale stores in
the Broadway Korean Business District should close at eight in the evening on Tuesday and Thursday, at six on other days (SGT, July 8, 1988).
According to leaders of the association, this rule has been generally observed by most Korean wholesalers in the Broadway area.

Korean retailers and service providers, though less successfully than
wholesalers, have also made efforts to mitigate co-ethnic business competition. In fact, that is a main objective of all major Korean trade
and local merchants' associations in New York. They have tried to reduce competition by regulating prices and preventing Korean stores
from opening too close to others in the same line of business. Through
business owners' meetings and newsletters, they have emphasized that
strong competition between two Korean stores means the destruction
of both. When two Korean store owners are involved in a dispute over
the price of an item or location of a business, they can take their disagreement to a trade or local merchants' association. Each association
provides advice to both parties, sometimes condemning those who do
not follow their recommendations. This type of intervention does not
always resolve disputes, since these associations do not have the legal
authority to sanction the merchants. Nevertheless, these kinds of mediating efforts by Korean merchants' associations are helpful in moderating intragroup business competition.

In the ways described above, Korean merchants have tried to re-
strain business competition over prices, hours, and location. The type
of tragic confrontation already noted—the death of a Korean peddler
in a fight with a Korean retail store owner in 1972—is far less likely
now that Korean merchants are organized. Currently, if there is excessive competition between two Korean merchants in the same business
line, a Korean trade association, a local Korean merchants' association,
and the Korean Small Business Service Center all intervene.

KOREAN OWNER-EMPLOYEE CONFLICTS

Several researchers have studied the class conflict between Chinese business owners and co-ethnic employees in Chinatown (Kwong 1987; Ong
1984; Sanders and Nee 1987; Thompson 1980; B. Wong 1987). They

indicated that Chinese workers employed in co-ethnic firms were subject to high levels of exploitation and that Chinese ethnic employees were very conscious of their class interests, which were opposed to those of their co-ethnic employers. Sanders and Nee (1987) argued that immigrant entrepreneurs make money only by exploiting co-ethnic employees and that this destroys ethnic solidarity. If this conflict hypothesis is applicable to the Korean business community, to what extent does the possible conflict between Korean business owners and co-ethnic employees destroy pan-Korean solidarity?

Zhou (1992) argued that this conflict hypothesis distorts even the economic structure of Chinatown. Using the enclave economy thesis associated with Portes and his colleagues (Portes and Bach 1985), she claimed that Chinese employees working for Chinese businesses attained economic rewards from their investments of human capital comparable to Chinese employees working in the general economy. However, I believe that the hypothesis stressing the exploitative and conflictive relationship between immigrant entrepreneurs and co-ethnic employees seems more applicable to the Chinese community, especially Chinatown, than to the Korean immigrant community. The Korean community differs fundamentally from the Chinese community in its business structure and the socioeconomic background of new immigrants; thus, it lacks the class cleavages of the Chinese community.

On the one hand, Korean immigrants are more entrepreneurial than Chinese immigrants. As noted in chapter 4, there are far more businesses per capita in the Korean community than in the Chinese (see table 7). On the other hand, the Chinese community annually receives a larger number of immigrants than the Korean, and immigrants from mainland China in particular are severely handicapped for employment in the general labor market. Whereas the immigration of people from China, Taiwan, and Hong Kong has increased greatly during recent years, Korean immigration has dropped substantially, falling in 1993 to half of that in 1987, the peak year of Korean immigration (see table 1 in chapter 3). Thus, while there is a great demand for ethnic employees in the Korean community, there is an oversupply of ethnic employees in the Chinese community, especially in Chinatown, where a large proportion of recent immigrants from mainland China settle.

Chinese immigrant workers employed by co-ethnic firms are more vulnerable to exploitation by their employers than are Korean immigrant workers, not only because of the oversupply of ethnic labor but also because of new Chinese immigrants' lack of resources. Most

immigrants from mainland China, especially those settled in Chinatown, come to the United States with almost no resources and thus have
no alternative to low-wage employment in co-ethnic businesses (Kwong
1987). As widely reported by the media, many people have been
brought illegally from mainland China to New York City during recent
years, and they are especially vulnerable. Therefore, the argument that
many Chinese immigrants are more or less permanently trapped in the
working class seems to have an element of truth.

In contrast, as noted in chapter 4, at the time of immigration most
Koreans bring a substantial amount of money, allowing many to start
their own businesses in this country. Thus most Koreans work for co-
ethnic businesses mainly to acquire business experience; their personal
resources enable them to avoid exploitation by their employers and to
move into their own businesses rather quickly, though some Korean
women and illegal residents are trapped in ethnic employment for a
long time. In my 1986 survey of Korean immigrants in Los Angeles,
50% of Koreans employed in Korean-owned businesses reported that
they planned to change their occupations very soon and 66% of them
said they planned to start their own businesses. Many Korean merchants complain that Korean employees do not stay with their jobs long
enough.

Since most Chinese immigrants employed in Chinese-owned businesses are not able to open their own businesses within a short period
of time, they are conscious of their class interests as wage earners. The
vast majority of Chinese workers employed in Chinese-owned garment
factories in New York are unionized (*KCDNY*, September 26, 1989),
and labor organizations are active in Chinatown (Kwong 1987; Light
and Wong 1975). In contrast, most Korean employees who work for
co-ethnic businesses seem to consider business training the major benefit of their employment and thus view labor issues from the standpoint
of their employers. The 1986 Los Angeles survey showed that only 9%
of Korean workers employed in co-ethnic firms were unionized.

Korean workers employed in Korean-owned businesses in New York
have been reluctant to join unions as well. Leaders of White labor unions approached both Korean business leaders and Korean ethnic workers in New York several times, urging them to unionize. Members of the
International Ladies' Garment Workers Union picketed in front of a Korean garment factory in Manhattan in November 1978 (*KTNY*, November 9, 1978); various unions have pressured Korean stores or Korean trade associations in New York City to unionize employees at least

seven times. However, as of July 1989, Korean workers in only four Korean produce retail stores and thirteen garment factories had joined labor unions (*KCDNY*, September 26, 1989). Since most Korean ethnic employees plan to start their own businesses in the near future, they have little interest in the rights of workers.

As noted in chapter 6, Latino workers make up a large proportion of the employees in Korean businesses in New York and Los Angeles. Latinos hired by Korean businesses generally take entry-level jobs such as busing tables in restaurants, stocking shelves in grocery stores, and working as semiskilled laborers in garment factories. This allows Korean employees of co-ethnic firms to avoid the lowest level of the occupational hierarchy. Thanks to highly disadvantaged Latino workers who are willing to take any kind of work, many new Korean immigrants can take managerial and cashiers' positions in Korean-owned businesses. In contrast, Chinese-owned businesses, particularly restaurants and garment factories (the two major sources of employment for Chinese immigrants), usually hire only new Chinese immigrants as employees. Thus, Chinese immigrants and illegal residents employed in these businesses have to take the lowest-level jobs. Their low occupational status is another reason Chinese workers employed in Chinese-owned firms are more vulnerable to exploitation than are their Korean counterparts.

A 1989 survey of Korean businesses in New York conducted by the *Korea Times New York* revealed that Korean businesses paid higher wages to Korean employees than to non-Korean employees. The wage gap ranged from $104 a week for fish retail stores to $19 a week for dry cleaning shops (*KTNY*, December 15, 1989). These differences in pay do not necessarily reflect discrimination against non-Korean employees: Korean employees have received on average more education and, as noted above, hold more skilled jobs. Even Koreans who engage in garment manufacturing in Korean garment factories often hold better-paying positions than the non-Korean employees at the same factories. In September 1993, I interviewed a staff member of the Korean Apparel Contractors Association at his Manhattan factory. He explained that in New York those Korean garment factories that manufacture expensive items such as leather jackets usually hire Korean workers and pay around $10 per hour, whereas those that manufacture inexpensive items entirely depend on Latino workers (usually Mexican and South American immigrants and illegal residents) and pay between $4.25 (then the minimum wage) and $6 per hour. He also disclosed that

Korean garment factories in New York recently hired a substantial number of immigrants and illegal residents from China, India, and Singa-
pore whom they pay between $6 and $7 per hour.

Thus far I have emphasized the differences between Korean and Chinese workers employed in co-ethnic businesses in their financial resources, vulnerability to exploitation, and employment goals. However,
I never forget that not all Korean immigrants are equally fortunate. As
already mentioned, many Korean single women and illegal residents
who work in Korean-owned businesses do not have the financial resources to quickly start their own businesses, and some of them are exploited by co-ethnic employers. The Korean Immigrant Workers Advo-
cates of Southern California (KIWASC), a labor organization in Los
Angeles, was created to help resolve labor-related disputes within the
Korean community. They reported that they received 219 labor complaints between April 1992 and January 1993, and that more than
half of the grievances involved failure to pay wages (KTLA, March 22,
1993). According to my 1990 interview with the director of KIWASC,
some Korean single women employed in co-ethnic firms were also sexu-
ally harassed. New York has no similar ethnic organization to handle
labor disputes. Though labor disputes in New York have not received
media attention, they most likely exist in the Korean community there
as well.

Nevertheless, it seems true that the majority of Korean ethnic employees consider business training the major benefit of their employment, and that the conflict between Korean immigrant entrepreneurs
and co-ethnic employees is not serious enough to weaken pan-Korean
solidarity. This was demonstrated during the Brooklyn boycott of
two Korean stores in 1990. Many Koreans working for co-ethnic businesses participated in the rally in front of City Hall to condemn Mayor
Dinkins for his indifference to boycott organizers.

The concentration of Korean merchants in several types of businesses
leads to strong intraethnic business competition and conflict. However, intraethnic competition and conflict among Korean merchants are
largely confined to the individual level and do not destroy unity on the
community level, as the merchants tend to join together in confronting outside enemies. Competing Korean merchants have shown strong
unity when they have encountered threats from the outside world such
as Black boycotts and the murder of Korean merchants in armed robberies. Also, Korean business associations have taken collective actions

to moderate competition among Korean merchants (more successfully among wholesalers than retailers); thus, intragroup business competition has become a source of ethnic solidarity.

Researchers have found much exploitation of Chinese immigrant workers by co-ethnic employees. One might then expect that conflicts over economic interests between Korean business owners and co-ethnic employees would weaken Korean ethnic solidarity. However, the business structure of Chinatown and the Korean community are very different. There is a greater demand for co-ethnic employees in the Korean community than in the Chinese community, whereas there is an oversupply of new immigrants as cheap labor in the Chinese community. Also, many Korean immigrants bring considerable resources, including capital, with which they can start their own businesses quickly, whereas most immigrants from mainland China lack such resources. Korean immigrants seek employment in Korean businesses mainly to get business training and information and thus are not very conscious of their class interests; ethnic solidarity therefore remains strong.

CHAPTER 12

Conclusion

KOREANS' MIDDLEMAN
ROLE AND ETHNIC SOLIDARITY

Middleman minority theory proposes a triangular relationship involving ethnic solidarity, middleman commercial activities, and host hostility. The theory helps us understand how Koreans' commercial activities lead to intergroup conflicts, which, in turn, contribute to Koreans' ethnic solidarity. However, previous studies of middlemen have not empirically tested the hypothesis concerning the effects of business-related intergroup conflicts on ethnic solidarity, though researchers have shown the impact of middleman commercial activities on host hostility. My study is theoretically significant because it systematically tested this hypothesis relating to ethnic solidarity, using Korean merchants in the United States as a case study.

This study supports the position that Koreans' role as middleman merchants in minority neighborhoods has increased their intergroup conflicts and thereby enhanced their ethnic solidarity. Not all Korean immigrants engage in middleman businesses; conversely, other immigrants, such as Iraqis in Detroit, also play a middleman minority role (Sengstock 1974). Thus, it would be an overgeneralization to simply define Korean immigrants as a middleman minority. Nevertheless, as we noted in chapters 4 and 10, Koreans in Los Angeles and New York concentrate in middleman type businesses more than any other immigrant group. In fact, Korean immigrants control produce, grocery, and fish retail businesses—prototypical middleman trades, which have generated more ethnic solidarity than other types of Korean businesses—in many Black neighborhoods in New York. This is why Korean merchants in New York have encountered more severe intergroup conflicts and have more often used collective strategies to protect their economic interests than any other immigrant group active in small business.

Middleman theory assumes that a middleman group has culturally based ethnic ties that facilitate the group's commercial activities and its solidarity in reacting to external threats. Certainly, Korean immigrants' cultural homogeneity and their common historical shared experiences, such as Japanese colonization and the Korean War, have contributed to their collective efforts to protect their economic interests against outside groups. However, Koreans historically have suffered from factionalism and schism, and thus collectivism has never been a Korean national characteristic. Though Korean immigrants' cultural homogeneity has helped them maintain ethnic identity and ethnic attachment (Min 1991), it is their economic segregation and business-related intergroup conflicts that have galvanized their collective actions; without intergroup conflicts their commercial activities might have been much more individualistic. The mainstream media have often attributed the collectivistic approach of Korean merchants to their culture, a mistaken generalization that prompted me to start this book.

The major findings from this study not only support middleman minority theory but also refine and revise it. The theory posits that middleman merchants encounter conflicts mainly with three outside interest groups—minority customers, native merchants, and workers in the host society—and that these conflicts enhance internal solidarity. Our analysis of the Korean community in New York shows that Korean merchants have conflicts with *White suppliers, White landlords,* and *government agencies,* as well as with *African American customers.* According to middleman minority theory, merchants are often brought to the host society by the ruling group to distribute its products to minority customers. Thus, middleman merchants are almost totally controlled by producers and government agencies. Using the world capitalist system model, Bonacich recently depicted Korean merchants as being used by U.S. corporations, an interpretation that emphasizes the subordination of Korean merchants to powerful forces (Light and Bonacich 1988). However, I have shown that Korean merchants as middlemen have actively responded to White suppliers and government agencies, honing their political skills as they use collective strategies.

Traditional middleman merchants existed in authoritarian, preindustrial, or colonial societies (Blalock 1967, 78–84; Bonacich and Modell 1980; Zenner 1991). The ruling group of the host society usually had no need to pay attention to middleman merchants' demands. This may be why the existing literature has not made any reference to middleman merchants protecting their economic interests with active responses to producers and government agencies. However, the United States differs significantly from the societies in which traditional middleman minorities developed, such as medieval Europe, the Philippines during the colonial period, or South Africa. Contemporary American society, made up of competing interest groups, is far more pluralistic; government agencies and politicians need to respond to demands by Korean and other ethnic merchants if only to promote their own political interests. For example, in the fall of 1993, Mayor Dinkins responded to Korean business leaders' demands by moderating several small business regulations, most likely in the hopes of gaining their support for his reelection.

The difference in social background between traditional middleman merchants and Korean immigrants also partly explains their different behaviors. Traditional middleman merchants, who came from lower-class backgrounds (Bonacich and Modell 1980; Turner and Bonacich 1980), did not have organizational skills necessary to negotiate effectively with suppliers and government agencies. In contrast, Korean merchants, mainly college-educated members of the middle class, do have these skills and can sometimes even manipulate corporations, government agencies, and politicians. Sung Soo Kim, director of the Korean Small Business Service Center in New York, was a doctoral candidate in political science at Columbia University. His great skills at communicating and organizing, the result of long years of graduate education in the United States, have made possible his tough negotiating and lobbying activities.

Though I have emphasized the economic basis of Korean ethnic solidarity, I do not intend to give the impression, as some scholars suggest (Banton 1977, 1979, 1983; Hechter 1987; Hechter, Friedman, and Appelbaum 1982), that Korean immigrants' collective actions are entirely based on "rational choice" and economic interests; their motivation is more complex. For example, as Light and Bonacich pointed out (1988, 326), it would have been rational for Korean merchants to respond to external threats by mobilizing class and pan-Asian solidarity as well as ethnic solidarity. However, as noted throughout this book, Korean merchants have relied on ethnic solidarity far more than class-based or pan-Asian actions. To be sure, Korean merchants did create a coalition with non-Korean merchants to lobby for a law controlling commercial rents, and the Korean Dry Cleaners Association and other Korean trade associations have cooperated with Chinese and White trade associations in lobbying to support their economic interests. Yet in practice, the Korean merchants' class alignment with non-Korean merchants has done little to protect their economic interests. Instead, Korean merchants have mainly depended on intraethnic collective strategies.

Furthermore, Korean merchants' conflicts with outside interest groups have enhanced Korean ethnic solidarity more generally. Many nonentrepreneurial Korean immigrants in New York and Los Angeles have done a number of things to support their co-ethnic merchants: participating in a mass rally to condemn Mayor Dinkins when they believed he was not acting to stop the Brooklyn boycott, donating money to help the victims of the Los Angeles riots, providing free legal services for boycotted merchants, and so on. Thus, this case study proves the validity of the argument that group interests can be effectively served by ethnically based collective actions, mainly because they "combine an interest with an affective tie" (Bell 1975, 169).

Many researchers do not want to consider Korean immigrants a middleman minority, because of the diversity of the Korean immigrant population. They would argue that not all Korean immigrants engage in small business and that of those who do, only a small proportion play the middleman role of distributing products made by corporations to minority customers. However, the Korean immigrant population is occupationally much more homogeneous than other immigrant populations. We can argue persuasively that the vast majority of Korean immigrants are solidly united in defending Korean middleman merchants' economic interests. As shown in chapter 4, the majority of Korean adult immigrants in New York and Los Angeles are self-employed in small business. When two Korean produce stores in a Brooklyn Black neighborhood became the targets of a boycott in 1990, not only all Korean produce store owners but also all other Korean merchants in New York City took it as a threat to their economic survival. Thus, a Black boycott of Korean stores has contributed to solidarity among all Korean merchants. Moreover, Korean employees of co-ethnic businesses, most of whom planned to start their own businesses in the near future, naturally considered the boycott of a Korean store a threat to their economic survival. In addition, Korean nonmerchant professionals—lawyers, accountants, pastors, and the like—took the boycott seriously, partly because they depended on Korean merchants as their clientele and partly because they felt it as a challenge to the Korean community.

Generational divisions are more serious than class divisions in the Korean community. As we have seen, younger-generation Koreans do not agree with Korean immigrant merchants on many issues related to intergroup relations, particularly on the issue of Korean–African American conflicts. Whereas many Korean merchants have taken the position closer to the White group than to the Black in the larger biracial division in the United States, many younger-generation Koreans have emphasized the need for a Korean-Black alliance to fight against the "White system." However, the victimization of Korean merchants during the Los Angeles riots stimulated younger-generation Koreans' ethnic and political consciousness. This is highly significant, for as noted in chapter 4, there is a phenomenal drop in the self-employment rate from foreign-born Koreans to native-born: few second- and third-generation Koreans are likely to run businesses in African American neighborhoods. Thus, in the future defending Koreans' middleman economic interests will not be an important issue in the Korean community. Nonetheless, as a major historical event in Korean American history, the Los Angeles riots will continue to have positive effects on the ethnic identity of native-born Koreans for long years to come. Furthermore, the political skills Korean business leaders have acquired in their efforts to resolve business-related intergroup conflicts will be passed on to second-generation Koreans.

KOREAN–AFRICAN AMERICAN CONFLICTS

The central thesis of this book is that Koreans' concentration in small business enhances ethnic solidarity mainly because it increases intergroup conflicts. Intergroup conflict is therefore theoretically important as a variable mediating ethnic business and ethnic solidarity. However, Korean–African American conflict in itself is a key topic in this book because of its theoretical and policy implications. Korean–African American tensions over the last ten years have been a major social problem in contemporary urban America, affecting not only the Korean community but also relations among ethnic and racial groups more generally in many cities; Korean community leaders, African American civil rights leaders, and government agencies have all tried to reduce these tensions.

In discussing Korean–African American conflicts, we need to distinguish between radical forms of hostility toward Korean merchants, such as boycotts, looting, and arson, and individual disputes between merchants and customers. Korean and African American community leaders, the mass media, and policy makers have emphasized cultural differences, mutual prejudice, and Koreans' language problems as major sources of friction.Undoubtedly, these sociopsychological factors have contributed to the frequent disputes that have occurred on the individual level in Korean stores in Black neighborhoods.

However, Korean-Black conflicts on the collective level, as reflected in Blacks' long-term boycotts and sometimes arson of Korean stores and in Koreans' group responses to these actions, result from broad structural forces that cannot be explained by sociopsychological factors. The deteriorating economic conditions and increasing crime rates in the inner city since the early 1970s pushed large chain stores and independent White-owned businesses out of African American neighborhoods. At the same time, Korean immigrants, who were severely handicapped for employment in the general labor market, were turning to self-employment in small business as an alternative to blue-collar occupations. Despite high crime rates, Korean merchants preferred low-income minority neighborhoods to middle-class White neighborhoods because they could start businesses there with smaller amounts of capital and without competition from large chain stores.

Korean merchants have played a middleman minority role in low-income neighborhoods, distributing the products of White corporations to African American customers. In that role, they were scapegoated by residents who were frustrated with their inability to improve their economic conditions. Korean merchants were easy targets: as new immigrants they did not have political power. They bore the brunt of Black anger, though the larger system was responsible for Blacks' economic problems. This suggests that Korean-Black conflicts are rooted in the racial inequality between Whites and Blacks in general and in the poverty of inner-city Black neighborhoods in particular. Korean and Black community leaders and policy makers who emphasize the sociopsychological reasons for Korean-Black conflict have not paid enough attention to these structural causes.

Though Korean merchants also ran businesses in low-income Latino neighborhoods in large numbers, there they did not encounter boycotts and other forms of anti-Korean violence. This suggests that simple frustration over deplorable economic conditions is not the sufficient condition for organized movements against Korean merchants in Black neighborhoods. The transformation of Black residents' economic frustrations into concerted anti-Korean actions required leaders and an ideology. Black nationalists have played the leading role in organizing anti-Korean activities, and Black nationalism, emphasizing the economic autonomy of the Black community, has served as the needed ideology. Though the ostensible reason for boycotting Korean stores was merchants' disrespectful attitudes toward customers, Black nationalists who organized boycotts emphasized the need for economic control of the community by Blacks.

Middleman minority theory suggests that middleman merchants become scapegoats of both minority customers and the ruling group. Many Korean Americans, especially young Korean Americans, argued that during the Los Angeles riots Korean merchants were used to shield the White majority from African Americans' hostility toward the system. Without doubt, the biased media coverage of Korean-Black conflicts significantly contributed to the victimization of Korean merchants during the riots. However, there is no evidence that the media or the U.S. government intended to use Korean merchants as scapegoats to mitigate African Americans' hostility toward the "White system." By sensationalizing Korean-Black conflicts, the media were irresponsible and unethical, but not malicious. Indeed, it is important that Black, Korean, and mainstream media should be more sensitive to the practical consequences of their coverage. Fair and objective reporting is essential to the ethical code of journalists. Yet, unfortunately, many journalists do not adhere to this code. Federal and city governments should use symposiums and meetings to help sensitize journalists to community issues. Korean and Black media in particular can play a key role in bridging the two communities. In September 1990, when Korean–African American tensions were growing, Los Angeles City's Human Relations Commission brought together the editors of the city's five major ethnic publications to reverse the growing distance between minority populations. Their meetings led to the formation of the Council of Multicultural Publications, an organization comprising twenty publications, in April 1991. Meetings between the editors of ethnic publications contributed to more cautious and objective reporting, particularly by the *Korea Times Los Angeles* (English edition) and the *Los Angeles Sentinel* (Marks 1991). Local governments in New York City and other cities should try to organize similar councils for dialogue.

Much more important than the media in contributing to Korean-

Black tensions are the economic conditions of inner-city neighbor-hoods, which are not likely to substantially improve in the near future. Therefore, Korean merchants in Black neighborhoods will continue to encounter boycotts and other forms of hostility. However, by emphasiz-ing the structural sources of Korean-Black conflicts, I do not intend to suggest that the multifaceted efforts of the Korean community to im-prove social and cultural ties with the African American community, reviewed in chapter 7, are useless. Black boycotts of Korean stores have generally started with individual disputes between store owners and customers. Therefore, by improving their services to customers and by contributing money and merchandise to African American neighbor-hoods, Korean merchants can reduce tensions. As noted in chapter 7, Korean merchants in Jamaica, Queens, have maintained close contacts with the Black neighborhood since they experienced a boycott in 1981. As a result, they have been able to avoid another long-term boycott, though Korean merchants in Brooklyn and Harlem have endured sev-eral. Moreover, establishing communication channels with the Black community through social and cultural ties helps the Korean commu-nity resolve serious conflicts in their early stages. Remember that one reason for the length of the 1990 Brooklyn boycott of two Korean stores—one and a half years—was the lack of any communication and dialogue between the Black community and the Korean community and business leaders.

My stress on Koreans' various efforts to improve relations with the black community as useful and worthwhile is deliberate. Many theo-retically oriented scholars and second-generation Korean Americans ar-gue that the "White system" or "U.S. capitalism" is entirely responsible for Korean-Black conflicts and that therefore Koreans and Blacks can do nothing significant to moderate tensions. Such a position is hardly useful to Korean and Black community leaders and policy makers who wish to address these problems. I remember reading a term paper by a second-generation Korean American doctoral student in which she ar-gued that "if Korean merchants exploit Black customers, U.S. capital-ism is responsible for Korean merchants' behaviors." I believe this type of deterministic thinking is not only useless but harmful and, therefore, irresponsible. To be sure, many intergroup conflicts in the United States, including Korean-Black conflicts, are inseparably tied to the capitalistic economic structure and White power structure. Nevertheless, commu-nity leaders and government agencies can intervene effectively to reduce these conflicts, however limited their interventions might be. We, as social scientists, should provide constructive recommendations rather than pessimistic and cynical conclusions.

In addition, improving relationships with the African American community through cultural and social exchanges is desirable in itself for the future of the Korean American community, regardless of how it affects Korean merchants. Korean immigrants, who are from an ethnically and culturally homogeneous society, are not well prepared to live in a multiethnic society like the United States. They are more isolated from the larger society than any other Asian group. It is an encouraging and positive sign that many Korean individuals and groups have recently participated in the efforts to bridge Korean and Black communities, as described in chapter 7. By learning about other cultures, Koreans will make it possible to live in peace and harmony with other ethnic groups.

Notes

1. INTRODUCTION

1. Nielsen (1985) defines ethnic solidarity as having two important components: goals and mobilization. His definition assumes preexisting ethnic identities but does not presume other structural characteristics of an ethnic group such as a common language, a propensity to endogamy, or a closed network of interactions.

2. In conversations with me, Professors Ivan Light and In-Jin Yoon also observed that the description of Korean immigrants as a middleman minority somewhat distorts the diversity of the Korean immigrant population.

2. HOST HOSTILITY AND MIDDLEMEN'S REACTIONS

1. Since we can measure ethnic attachment with questionnaires, researchers have no difficulty proving the effects of ethnic business on ethnic attachment using surveys. In fact, most of the studies cited above examined the effects of ethnic business on ethnic attachment utilizing survey research. However, we cannot measure ethnic solidarity as defined in this book using questionnaire items; therefore, we need to use other types of data to demonstrate the effects of ethnic business on ethnic solidarity. Here, these include ethnic newspaper articles, interviews with business leaders, and other types of nonsurvey data. This methodological difficulty may have contributed to the paucity of research into the influence of ethnic business on ethnic solidarity.

2. In Light and Bonacich 1988 (chapter 12), Light discussed how Korean merchants' solidarity was affected by various government restrictions of small business activities. But he did not use middleman minority theory as a frame of reference. In a recent conversation with me, Light was reluctant to consider Korean merchants in the United States a middleman minority partly because, unlike Jews or Chinese, overseas Koreans have not traditionally played this role.

3. For this reason, O'Brien and Fugita (1982) argue that the concept of "petite bourgeoisie" is more useful than middleman minority theory in helping us understand commercial activities of Japanese Americans during the prewar period.

4. This view is close to that of Cherry (1989) and E. Wong (1985) that discrimination forced Jews or Chinese in the United States to make occupational adjustment in small business.

5. Stryker had made a similar point in his earlier article (1958) as well.

3. KOREAN COMMUNITIES: NEW YORK AND LOS ANGELES

1. For more detailed information about the earlier Korean immigration, see Chai (1987), Choy (1979), Lyu (1977), Patterson (1988), and L. Shin (1971).

2. The most restrictive immigration laws, commonly known as the national origins quota system, were passed in 1921 and 1924. Although these laws were mainly concerned with reducing immigration from southern and eastern European countries, they completely barred Asian immigration.

3. Whereas in the 1970s Koreans had a too positive image of life in the United States, they have a very negative image in the 1990s. Recently, several movies that exaggerated Korean immigrants' adjustment difficulties—long hours of work, physical danger at the store, language barriers, and family or children's problems—were shown in Korea. Korean immigrants in Los Angeles and New York strongly protested these movies that provided only a one-sided picture of Korean immigrant experiences.

4. Many Korean college graduates who could not find jobs chose immigration to solve their unemployment problem. See Yoon (1993) for an extended discussion.

5. The strong military, political, and economic connections between the United States and South Korea have greatly contributed to the Americanization of Korean metropolitan cities. Several U.S. fast-food franchises, including McDonald's, Burger King, and Kentucky Fried Chicken, have stores in major metropolitan cities in South Korea. South Koreans can also watch American TV programs.

6. More than 80% of Filipino immigrants are Catholics, and the majority of Indochinese refugees are Buddhists. Most of the immigrants from China do not have any religion, while immigrants from India and Pakistan are characterized by religious diversity.

7. Several million Koreans in South and North Korea are separated from family members, whom they are not allowed to visit. However, Koreans in the United States, when they become naturalized citizens, can visit their family members in North Korea. Indeed, the North Korean government has encouraged Korean Americans to visit North Korea, partly because of the U.S. dollars they bring and spend, and many have done so.

8. In fact, many Korean immigrants who were Buddhists in Korea are affiliated with Korean immigrant Christian churches, in part because they have

difficulty maintaining their Asian religion in this country. There are only three Korean Buddhist temples in the New York metropolitan area.

9. One reason Koreatown businesses do not serve many non-Korean customers is that compared to Chinatown or Japan Town, Koreatown is not well known to outsiders. In a marketing survey conducted in Los Angeles, only 11.5% of the respondents reported that they knew the location of Koreatown, whereas 76.9% and 61.7% of them knew the locations of Chinatown and Japan Town, respectively (*SGT,* July 29, 1990). Another reason may be that Korean food is not as popular among Americans as Chinese or Japanese food.

10. According to the Korean census, Kims constitute 22% of the Korean population. Since Kim is a uniquely Korean name and Kims make up such a large proportion of the Korean population, by counting Kims listed in a public telephone directory we can estimate the number of Koreans in a particular city. For this method, see Min (1989) and Shin and Yu (1984).

11. Though Korean immigrant churches have provided many services for their own church members, most have not responded to the needs of the Korean community as a whole. Many community leaders and social workers criticize Korean immigrant churches for failing to pay attention to community-wide issues and problems. They maintain that Korean churches have drained the community's financial resources but have not put this money back into the community.

12. Most medium-sized Korean communities have Korean TV programming for a few hours per day through a local TV channel. Moreover, Koreans who live in small Korean communities can watch Korean TV programs by renting videotapes from Korean grocery stores. Producers in Korea are conscious of overseas Koreans who will watch their programs on videotapes, which are widely distributed.

4. KOREAN IMMIGRANTS' ECONOMIC SEGREGATION

1. The *1992 Survey of Minority Owned Business Enterprises* will be available in 1996.

2. I would like to thank Mehdi Bozorgmehr and Claudia Der-Matirosian at UCLA for analyzing the self-employment rate of native-born Koreans in Greater Los Angeles using 1990 PUMS data.

3. My interviews with leaders of the Broadway Korean Businessmen's Association revealed that for most Korean importers and wholesalers in New York, Koreans make up approximately half of their customers.

4. I. Kim (1981, 121–43) provided an extended discussion of the rise and fall of the Korean wig business in New York.

5. A high level of intragroup business transactions among Korean immigrants is largely the result of Koreans' involvement in strong ethnic networks. However, Korean immigrants have some practical benefits when they buy businesses from co-ethnic members. First of all, they often can take advantage of owner financing when buying businesses from co-ethnics. Second, they feel a business transaction between two Koreans is safer because it is based on mutual trust.

6. Korean owners of garment factories, like other immigrant owners, depend mainly on illegal aliens and new immigrants for garment manufacturing. They usually do not report their employees, paying their wages in cash. Since Korean garment subcontractors get checks, very often postdated checks, from manufacturers for finished goods, they need to get their checks cashed to pay wages and buy raw materials. Several Korean brokers cash these checks, imposing large service charges (usually 1% of the amount in each check).

7. Most Korean restaurants have a Japanese sushi bar established at one corner of the restaurant, mainly because Korean customers like sushi.

8. According to a survey conducted in January 1991, the mean net monthly income of Korean nail salon owners was over $4,000 (see SGT, February 6, 1991).

9. An indoor swap meet has an average of 100 booths, though the number ranges from 15 to 600.

10. Korean swap meet store owners usually do not hire paid employees and thus can save on wages and fringe benefits. Moreover, because they usually use cash in business transactions they often avoid paying sales taxes.

11. The *Korea Times Los Angeles* reported that nineteen Koreans in Los Angeles County were murdered by African Americans between January 1987 and October 1991. My further survey of the *Korea Times Los Angeles* revealed that one more Korean in Los Angeles County was killed by a black gang and another by a Hispanic gang in December 1991.

12. Other immigrant groups are also disadvantaged for employment in the general labor market. But they are probably more reluctant to run businesses in low-income Black neighborhoods than Koreans because they are more averse to the dangers faced by middlemen merchants in Black neighborhoods (i.e., physical violence and armed robbery). In this sense, Korean immigrants' opportunistic attitudes have partly contributed to their concentration in minority-oriented businesses.

5. HOSTILITY TOWARD KOREAN
   MERCHANTS IN BLACK NEIGHBORHOODS

1. David Dinkins defeated the incumbent mayor, Ed Koch, in 1989 partly because many White voters accepted his argument that he could do better in resolving racial conflicts in New York City. However, New York City's White citizens, particularly Jews, were generally dissatisfied with his handling of the Brooklyn boycott of Korean stores and the Black racial violence against Jews in Crown Heights. Their negative evaluation contributed to his loss in the November 1993 mayoral election.

2. The owners of Korean restaurants, bakeries, and other stores in the Flushing area catering to distinctively Korean tastes argue that it does not make a difference whether they put up an English language sign or not, because they depend almost entirely on Korean customers. However, if they improve their services to non-Korean customers by putting up an English commercial sign, preparing English menus, and hiring employees more fluent in English, they are likely to attract some non-Korean customers. Most Korean restaurants in Flush-

ing do not have English menus, which greatly inconveniences non-Korean customers.

3. The other major complaints were Koreans' unwillingness to participate in local community activities and one Korean merchant's attempt to establish a coffee shop near a public park.

4. Interestingly, the Chicano Employees Association, the association of Los Angeles County Hispanic employees, announced that it did not support the boycott, which it argued would only animate racial conflicts in Los Angeles.

5. Asian American community leaders are gravely concerned about any case of anti-Asian violence, particularly because Whites and Blacks who commit hate crimes often have difficulty distinguishing one Asian ethnic group from another. The day after this Japanese woman was beaten, community leaders held a joint press conference and severely criticized the anti-Asian violence.

6. Korean liquor store owners in South Central Los Angeles encountered opposition from African American residents even before the riots (see Fruto 1991).

7. At first, swap meets were included among the businesses that required the permission of the residents to reopen, but following the strong protests of Korean swap meet owners, they were eliminated from this category.

6. SOURCES OF HOSTILITY TOWARD KOREAN MERCHANTS

1. Once Korean immigrants have started their own businesses and established credit, they seem to have less difficulty getting loans from commercial banks. Several Korean merchants in my Atlanta survey reported that American banks with which they opened business checking accounts offered them commercial loans. American lending institutions are willing to deal with Korean merchants mainly because of the general perception that Korean immigrants are successful in small businesses. Some American banks located inside or near Koreatown in Los Angeles or Flushing in New York have hired Korean managers to attract Korean business customers.

2. Korean alumni members, trade association members, and church members usually organize a *kye* to maintain friendships by meeting regularly. When they participate in a *kye,* they need to meet with members at least once a month. A *kye* meeting is usually held in a restaurant and the person who draws money pays for food for all members.

3. Based on their survey of Korean garment subcontractors in Los Angeles, Light and his associates (Light, Kwuon, and Zhong 1990) argue that between 11% to 36% of Korean garment manufacturers used *kye* funds for business capitalization. However, their sample seems to be biased. Many Korean garment manufacturers in Los Angeles as well as in New York are remigrants from Brazil and Argentine, where nearly half the Korean immigrants engage in garment manufacturing or sales of garment goods (wholesale or retail). As "twice minorities," Korean remigrants from South American countries are extremely likely to maintain strong ties and participate in rotating credit associations. Therefore, I suspect that a higher proportion of Korean garment manufacturers than other Korean merchants in the United States participate in a *kye*.

4. The main problem with both is the use of a metropolitan area rather than

a Black neighborhood as the unit of analysis. Though the increase in Korean immigrants' business ownership in a particular metropolitan area may not lead to a decrease in Black business ownership in the same area, the increase in the number of Korean-owned businesses in a specific Black neighborhood may lead to a decrease in Black business ownership there.

5. For example, in the Church Avenue–Flatbush Avenue neighborhood where the 1990 boycott of Korean stores occurred, only thirteen of sixty-seven stores were owned by Blacks (H. Lee 1993).

6. Yusuf Hawkins, an African American visiting the Bensonhurst section of Brooklyn, was murdered by a gang of Italian American youths in 1989. Black nationalists organized several marches to protest the murder.

7. At least in Koreatown in Los Angeles, where Koreans and Mexicans constitute the majority of the population, the two groups are involved in two other types of economic conflict: as landlords and renters, and as store owners and customers. According to Oliver and his associates (Oliver, Johnson, and Farrell 1993), these three dimensions of conflict explain why a large number of Mexican residents participated in looting Korean stores in Koreatown during the Los Angeles riots.

8. Whereas many White Americans who have conservative attitudes toward child socialization and family life are interested in traditional Korean customs, many other White Americans, particularly those who are liberal minded and young, are critical of some of these customs. Many White students in my class on Asian Americans criticized Korean merchants for being rude.

7. KOREANS' EFFORTS TO IMPROVE RELATIONS WITH AFRICAN AMERICANS

1. The Coca-Cola Company's interests in joining were mainly economic, that is, to advertise their products to Korean grocery retailers.

2. The church was established in 1921 largely by Korean students at Columbia University. It was the center of the Korean independence movement in the 1920s and 1930s when Korea was colonized by Japan. During the period of military dictatorship in South Korea (1961 to 1987), the church was the center of the overseas antigovernment, democratic movement.

3. For example, Black rap music is very popular among Korean teenagers. According to the Rev. Hong, young Blacks and Koreans like rap music because they are emotional, which is one important cultural commonality between the two groups.

4. For a detailed discussion of the background of the formation and the role of this organization, see Chang 1990, chapter 6.

5. As previously noted, just prior to the riots representatives of Korean and Black chambers of commerce were looking for a site to construct apartments in African American neighborhoods, a project that the riots halted. Given the skepticism of Korean business leaders after the riots, there is little possibility that the Korean Chamber of Commerce will resume the program in the near future.

6. Korean merchants in Los Angeles were fearful of another race riot and

more destruction of their stores if the grand jury should reach a verdict of not guilty in the second trial. Thus, the merchants were as satisfied with the guilty verdict as Blacks were.

8. KOREAN–AFRICAN AMERICAN CONFLICTS: POSITIVE EFFECTS

1. Park sued the picketer who beat his wife and caused her to have an abortion to counteract a $6 million lawsuit filed by a Haitian woman made against Bong Jae Jang for allegedly beating her.

2. This address was prompted by a Brooklyn judge, Jerald Held, who on May 11 attacked Mayor Dinkins for failing to intervene personally in the fifteen-week-old boycott.

3. Not only Korean but also many White Americans in New York City were disappointed with Dinkins's handling of the boycott. Many White citizens voted for Dinkins in the 1989 mayoral election, hoping that he could do better than Ed Koch in moderating racial tensions in the city. However, they felt the Black mayor did not act speedily to resolve the impasse at the Brooklyn stores. In the 1993 mayoral election, the Republican Party candidate, Rudy Giuliani, used Dinkins's "inadequate handling" of the Brooklyn boycott as a major election issue. When the Korean community's supporting group held a fund-raising party for Giuliani in October 1993, he invited Bong Jae Jang, one of the victims of the 1990 Brooklyn boycott, to attack Mayor Dinkins for failing to intervene to end the boycott quickly.

4. Representatives of the NAACP and CORE, participating in the rally as guest speakers, severely attacked the "racial bigotry" of boycott leaders.

5. Unfortunately, financial difficulties and lack of leadership have kept the committee from functioning effectively.

6. Koreans' unwillingness to use the technique of protest is deeply rooted in their Confucian cultural tradition. Confucianism puts great emphasis on the individual's conformity to society and discourages individuals from challenging any authority, whether it be parents, teachers, or the government.

7. The democratization in South Korea also contributed to the shift in Korean immigrants' political interest from their home country to the United States. When South Korea was under military rule before the popular election in 1987, there were many antigovernment political organizations in the Korean American community. These political organizations, which focused on homeland politics, have since gradually disappeared.

8. I interviewed a staff member of the Korean American Coalition in the summer of 1994 and asked about the progress of the national Korean American Alliance. He told me that because of its lack of financial resources, the association had not undertaken any significant activities.

9. In the summer of 1993, Stanley Karnow, a freelance journalist, visited the Korean community in Los Angeles and interviewed several second-generation Korean community leaders, including Angela Oh, for an article on the Korean American community. He told me that the younger-generation Koreans whom he interviewed initially refused to accept that Black rioters shared responsibility

for victimizing Korean merchants during the riots, but that when pressed hard they reluctantly agreed that Blacks bore some blame.

9. KOREAN MERCHANTS' COLLECTIVE RESPONSES TO SUPPLIERS, LANDLORDS, AND GOVERNMENT AGENCIES

1. A boycott of a produce wholesale business is particularly damaging because vegetables and fruits spoil quickly.

2. Many Korean store owners signed leases without knowing the terms and later found that they were responsible for these expenses.

3. During the 1990–91 boycott of two Korean stores in Brooklyn, one Jewish Brooklyn resident sent a letter to President Bush, asking him to take an action quickly to stop the "unjustifiable boycott."

4. My observations suggest that younger-generation Korean girls at prestigious universities often date and marry Jewish American boys. Cultural similarities between the two groups seem to contribute to these frequent intermarriages.

5. According to representatives of the Korean Garment Contractors Association, immigration officers arrest illegal workers in garment factories but release them soon after their arrest. They defend their hiring of illegal aliens by pointing out that the illegal aliens are always available.

6. The main impetus for creating the Congress of Small Business came from the city: to increase their revenues, New York City government agencies began to enforce small business rules and regulations more aggressively in 1991.

10. COLLECTIVE ACTIONS AND POWER IN THE KOREAN COMMUNITY

1. Their generosity also seems linked to the titles given to large contributors—president, vice president, and board members—which are more useful to merchants than to professionals, who enjoy the high social positions associated with their occupations.

2. As discussed in chapter 4, in the early 1970s Korean importers in New York were concentrated in the wig business. But beginning in the mid-1970s, when the wig demand fell, Korean wig importers began to import other manufactured items from South Korea, such as handbags, costume jewelry, and clothing. The Korean Wig Importers Association became the Broadway Korean Businessmen's Association.

References

SECONDARY SOURCES

Abelmann, Nancy, and John Lie. 1995. *Blue Dreams: Korean Americans and the Los Angeles Riots.* Cambridge: Harvard University Press.

Ahn, Chong Sik. 1991. "An Alternative Approach to the Racial Conflict between Korean-American Small Business Owners and the Black-American Community in the New York Metropolitan Area." In *The Korean-American Community: Present and Future,* edited by Tae-Hwan Kwak and Seong Hyong Lee, pp. 49–55. Seoul, Korea: Kyung Nam University Press.

Aldrich, Howard, and A. Reiss. 1976. "Continuities in the Study of Ecological Succession: Changes in the Race Composition of Neighborhoods and Their Businessmen." *American Journal of Sociology* 81: 846–66.

Aldrich, Howard, John Carter, Trevor Jones, and David McEvoy. 1983. "From Periphery to Peripheral: The South Asian Petite Bourgeoisie in England." In *Research in the Sociology of Work,* edited by I. H. Simpson and R. Simpson, 2:72–93. Greenwich, Conn.: JAI Press.

Allport, Gordon. 1958. *The Nature of Prejudice.* Garden City, N.Y.: Doubleday.

Auster, Ellen, and Howard Aldrich. 1984. "Small Business Vulnerability, Ethnic Enclaves, and Ethnic Enterprise." In *Ethnic Communities in Business,* edited by Robin Ward and Richard Jenkins, pp. 39–58. New York: Cambridge University Press.

Banks, Sandy. 1985. "Korean Merchants, Black Customers–Tensions Grow." *Los Angeles Times,* April 15.

Banton, Michael. 1977. "Rational Choice: A Theory of Race and Ethnic Relations." Working Papers on Ethnic Relations, no. 8, SSRC Research Unit on Race Relations, University of Aston, Birmingham, England.

———. 1979. "Two Theories of Racial Discrimination in Housing." *Ethnic and Racial Studies* 2: 416–27.

———. 1983. *Racial and Ethnic Competition.* New York: Cambridge University Press.

Barringer, Felicity. 1992. "Census Reveals a City of Displacement." *New York Times,* May 15.

Bell, Daniel. 1975. "Ethnicity and Social Change." In *Ethnicity: Theory and Experience,* edited by Nathan Glazer and Daniel Moynihan, pp. 141–74. Cambridge: Harvard University Press.

Bhachu, Parminder. 1993. "Twice vs. Direct Migrants: East African Sikh Settlers in Britain." In *Immigration and Entrepreneurship,* edited by Ivan Light and Parminder Bhachu, pp. 163–84. New Brunswick, N.J.: Transaction Publishers.

Blake, Robert, and Jane Mouton. 1962. "The Inter-Group Dynamics of Win-Lose Conflict and Problem-Solving Collaboration in Union Management Relations." In *Inter-Group Relations and Leadership,* edited by Muzafer Sherif, pp. 94–100. New York: John Wiley.

Blalock, Herbert. 1967. *Toward a Theory of Minority Group Relations.* New York: John Wiley.

Bogardus, Emory. 1968. "Comparing Racial Distance in Ethiopia, South Africa, and the United States." *Sociology and Social Research* 52: 149–56.

Bonacich, Edna. 1973. "A Theory of Middleman Minorities." *American Sociological Review* 35: 583–94.

———. 1980. "Middleman Minorities and Advanced Capitalism." *Ethnic Groups* 2: 211–19.

———. 1987. " 'Making It' in America: A Sociological Evaluation of the Ethics of Immigrant Entrepreneurship." *Sociological Perspectives* 30: 446–66.

———. 1993. "Asian and Latino Immigrants in the Los Angeles Garment Industry: An Exploration of the Relationship between Capitalism and Racial Oppression." In *Immigration and Entrepreneurship: Culture, Capital, and Ethnic Networks,* edited by Ivan Light and Parminder Bhachu, pp. 51–73. New Brunswick, N.J.: Transaction Publishers.

Bonacich, Edna, Ivan Light, and Charles Choy Wong. 1976. "Small Business among Koreans in Los Angeles." In *Counterpoint: Perspective on Asian America,* edited by Emma Gee, pp. 437–49. Los Angeles: Asian American Studies Center, UCLA.

Bonacich, Edna, and John Modell. 1980. *The Economic Basis of Ethnic Solidarity: Small Business in the Japanese American Community.* Berkeley: University of California Press.

Boyd, Robert. 1990. "Black and Asian Self-Employment in Large Metropolitan Areas: A Comparative Analysis." *Social Problems* 37: 258–74.

Bozorgmehr, Mehdi. 1992. "Internal Ethnicity: Armenian, Bahai, Jewish, and Muslim Iranians in Los Angeles." Ph.D. diss., University of California, Los Angeles.

Bozorgmehr, Mehdi, Georges Sabagh, and Claudia Der-Martirosian. 1993. "Beyond Nationality: Religio-Ethnic Diversity." In *Irangeles: Iranians in Los Angeles,* edited by Ron Kelley, Jonathan Friedlander, and Anita Colby, pp. 59–80. Berkeley: University of California Press.

Bozorgmehr, Mehdi, Claudia Der-Martirosian, and Georges Sabagh. 1996. "Middle Easterners: A New Kind of Immigrants." In *Ethnic Los Angeles,* edited by Roger Waldinger and Mehdi Bozorgmehr. New York: Russell Sage Foundation Press.

Breznick, Alan. 1991. "City Squeezing Business for Fees." *Crain's New York Business,* July 22.

Canaan Publishing Company. 1992. *The 1992–93 Korean Business Guide.* New York: Canaan Publishing Company.

Capeci, Dorminic, Jr. 1985. "Black-Jewish Relations in Wartime Detroit: The Marsh, Loving, and Wolf Surveys and Race Riots of 1943." *Jewish Social Studies* 5: 221–42.

Caplan, Nathan. 1970. "The Negro Ghetto Man: A Review of Recent Empirical Studies." *Journal of Social Issues* 26: 56–73.

Carmichael, Stokely, and Charles Hamilton. 1967. *Black Power: The Politics of Liberation in America.* New York: Vintage Books.

Chai, Alice. 1987. "Freed from the Elders But Locked into Labor: Korean Immigrant Women in Hawaii." *Women's Studies* 13: 223–34.

Chan, Janet, and Yuet-Wah Cheung. 1985. "Ethnic Resources and Business Enterprise: A Study of Chinese Business in Toronto." *Human Organization* 44: 142–54.

Chang, Edward. 1990. "New Urban Crisis: Korean-Black Conflicts in Los Angeles." Ph.D. diss., University of California, Berkeley.

———. 1993a. "From Chicago to Los Angeles: Changing the Site of Race Relations." *Amerasia Journal* 19 (2): 1–3.

———. 1993b. "Jewish and Korean Merchants in African American Neighborhoods: A Comparative Perspective." *Amerasia Journal* 19 (2): 5–21.

Cheng, Lucie, and Yen Le Espiritu. 1989. "Korean Business in Black and Hispanic Neighborhoods: A Study of Intergroup Relations." *Sociological Perspectives* 32: 521–34.

Cherry, Robert. 1989. "Middleman Minority Theories: Their Implications for Black-Jewish Relations." *Journal of Ethnic Studies* 17 (4): 117–38.

Chin, Ku-Sup, In-Jin Yoon, and David Smith. 1996. "Immigrant Small Business and International Economic Linkage: A Case of the Korean Wig Industry in Los Angeles, 1968–1977." Forthcoming in *International Migration Review.*

Cho, Mindy. 1993. "Farewell America, Good-Bye Shattered Dreams." *Korea Times Los Angeles* (English edition), March 31.

Cho, Sumi K. 1993. "Korean Americans vs. African Americans: Conflict and Construction." In *Reading Rodney King/Reading Urban Uprising,* edited by Robert Cooding-Williams, pp. 196–211. New York: Routledge.

Choy, Bong-Youn. 1979. *Koreans in America.* Chicago: Neilson Press.

Chung, Philip W. 1993. "Broadcast by Atlanta News Station Outrages KAs." *Korea Times Los Angeles* (English edition), July 14.

Chung, Suzie. 1992. "300 KAs Rally for Justice at UCLA." *Korea Times Los Angeles* (English edition), May 18.

Clifford, Frank, and Sheryl Stolberg. 1991. "Blacks and Koreans, with Bradley's Aid, Make Truce." *Los Angeles Times,* October 4.

Cohen, Abner. 1969. *Custom and Politics in Urban Africa: A Study of Hausa Migrants in Yoruban Towns.* Berkeley: University of California Press.

Cohen, Nathan. 1970. *The Los Angeles Riots: A Sociological Study.* New York: Praeger.

Coser, Lewis. 1964. *The Functions of Social Conflict.* 2d ed. Glencoe, Ill.: Free Press.

Council of Korean Churches of Greater New York. 1992–93. *Korean Churches Directory of New York.* New York: Council of Korean Churches of Greater New York.

Creaver, James. 1983. "Black Agenda Hosts Korean Dialogue." *Los Angeles Sentinel,* September 15.

Cronon, Edmond David. 1969. *Black Moses: The Story of Marcus Garvey and the Universal Negro Improvement Association.* Madison: University of Wisconsin Press.

Dart, John. 1985. "Korean Immigrants, Blacks Use Churches as Bridge to Ease Tensions." *Los Angeles Times,* November 9.

Desbarats, Jacqueline. 1985. "Indochinese Settlements in the United States." *Annals of American Association of Geographers* 75: 522–38.

Deutsch, Morton, and Mary Evans Collins. 1951. *Interracial Housing.* Minneapolis: University of Minnesota Press.

Dollard, J. L., L. Doob, N. E. Miller, D. H. Mowrer, and R. R. Sears. 1939. *Frustration and Aggression.* New Haven: Yale University Press.

Drake, St. Clair, and Horace R. Cayton. 1945. *Black Metropolis: A Study of Negro Life in a Northern City.* New York: Harcourt, Brace.

Eitzen, Stanley. 1971. "Two Minorities: The Jews of Poland and the Chinese in the Philippines." In *Ethnic Conflicts and Power: A Cross-National Perspective,* edited by Donald Gelfand and Russell Lee, pp. 140–56. New York: John Wiley and Sons.

Elazer, Daniel, and Murray Friedman. 1976. *Moving Up: Ethnic Succession in America.* New York: Institute on Pluralism and Group Identity.

English, Merle, and Ji-Yeon Yuh. 1990. "Black-Korean Conflict Simmers." *Newsday,* February 13.

Espiritu, Yen Le. 1989. "Beyond the 'Boat People': Ethnization of American Life." *Amerasia Journal* 15 (2): 49–67.

———. 1992. *Asian American Panethnicity: Bridging Institutions and Identities.* Philadelphia: Temple University Press.

Foner, Nancy. 1987. "The Jamaicans: Race and Ethnicity among Migrants in New York City." In *New Immigrants in New York,* edited by Nancy Foner, pp. 195–217. New York: Columbia University Press.

Ford, Scott. 1972. *Interracial Public Housing in Border City: A Situational Analysis of the Contact Hypothesis.* Lexington, Mass.: Heath.

———. 1973. "Interracial Public Housing in Border City: Another Look at the Contact Hypothesis." *American Journal of Sociology* 78: 1426–47.

Forster, Arnold, and Benjamin Epstein. 1974. *The New Anti-Semitism.* New York: McGraw-Hill.

Friedmann, Georges. 1967. *The End of the Jewish People,* translated by Eric Mosbacher. New York: Doubleday.

Fruto, Richard Reyes. 1991. "Supermarket, Union at Odds." *Los Angeles Times,* September 8.

Fugita, Stephen, and David O'Brien. 1991. *Japanese American Ethnicity: The Persistence of Community.* Seattle: University of Washington Press.

Geist, William. 1985. "The Deli on Park Avenue Is Starting to Fit In." *New York Times,* February 20.

Gilbert, G. M. 1951. "Stereotype Persistence and Change among College Students." *Journal of Abnormal and Social Psychology* 46: 245–54.

Gold, Steven. 1992. *Refugee Communities: A Comparative Field Study.* Newbury Park, Calif.: Sage Publications.

Goren, Arthur. 1982. *The American Jews.* Cambridge: Harvard University Press.

Ha, Julie. 1992. "Reactions from KA Students at UCLA." *Korea Times Los Angeles* (English edition), May 11.

Hacker, Andrew. 1992. *Two Nations: Black and White, Separate, Hostile, Unequal.* New York: Scribner's.

Harber, Alan. 1969. "Economic Development: Liberation and Liberalism." *New Generation* 50: 18–21.

Hartocollis, Anemona. 1990. "Little Support across Races for Boycott." *New York Newsday* June 15.

Hechter, Michael. 1987. *Principles of Group Solidarity.* Berkeley: University of California Press.

Hechter, Michael, D. Friedman, and M. Appelbaum. 1982. "A Theory of Ethnic Collective Action." *International Migration Review* 16: 212–34.

Hornung, Rick. 1990. "The Making of a Revolutionary: Coltrane Chimurenga and the Struggle for Black Leadership in New York." *Village Voice,* October 9.

Hunt, Chester, and Lewis Walker. 1974. *Ethnic Dynamics: Patterns of Intergroup Relations in Various Societies.* Homewood, Ill.: Dorsey.

Hunt, Dennis. 1991. "Outrageous as He Wants to Be." *Los Angeles Times,* November 3.

Hurh, Won Moo, and Kwang Chung Kim. 1984. *Korean Immigrants in America: A Structural Analysis of Ethnic Confinement and Adhesive Adaptation.* Madison, N.J.: Fairleigh Dickinson University Press.

———. 1988. "Uprooting and Adjustment: A Sociological Study of Korean Immigrants' Mental Health." Final report submitted to National Institute of Mental Health.

———. 1990. "Religious Participation of Korean Immigrants in the United States." *Journal of the Scientific Study of Religion* 29: 19–34.

Hwangbo, Kay. 1991. "Koreans Shift to Republican Party." *Korea Times Los Angeles* (English edition), September 8.

———. 1992. "Korean Americans Organize and Mobilize." *Korea Times Los Angeles* (English edition), May 11.

Immigration and Naturalization Service. 1950–1978. *Annual Reports.* Washington, D.C.: U.S. Government Printing Office.

———. 1979–1993. *Statistical Yearbook.* Washington, DC.: U.S. Government Printing Office.

Jameson, Sam. 1992. "L.A. Losing Allure for South Korean Immigrants after the Riots." *Los Angeles Times,* May 23.

Jamison, Harold. 1988. "Vann's Try to Settle Korean Fights Hits Snag." *Amsterdam News,* October 8.

Jo, Moon H. 1992. "Korean Merchants in the Black Community: Prejudice among the Victims of Prejudice." *Ethnic and Racial Studies* 15: 395–411.

Johnson, James H., Jr., and Melvin Oliver. 1989. "Interethnic Minority Conflict in Urban America: The Effects of Economic and Social Dislocations." *Urban Geography* 10: 449–63.

Kang, K. Connie. 1993. "Fear of Crime Robs Many of Dreams in Koreatown." *Los Angeles Times,* June 21.

———. 1994. "A Cause for Korean American Celebration—and Controversy." *Korea Times Los Angeles* (English edition), June 1.

Karwatch, Rob. 1990. "Crash of Cultures Is More Than Just Skin Deep." *Chicago Tribune,* July 15.

Katz, Daniel, and Kenneth Braly. 1933. "Racial Stereotypes of One Hundred College Students." *Journal of Abnormal and Social Psychology* 28: 280–90.

Kaufman, Jonathan. 1988. *Broken Alliance: The Turbulent Times between Blacks and Jews in America.* New York: Scribner's.

Keys Ad. and Printing Company. 1990. *The Korean Directory of Southern California (1990–91).* Los Angeles: Keys Ad. and Printing Company.

Kim, Bok-Lim. 1978. *Asian Americans, Changing Patterns, Changing Needs.* Montclair, N.J.: Association of Korean Christian Scholars in North America.

Kim, Dexter. 1992. "Las Vegas Store Owners Suffer through Riots on Their Own." *Korea Times Los Angeles* (English edition), June 8.

Kim, Hyun Sook, and Pyong Gap Min. 1992. "Post-1965 Korean Immigrants: Their Characteristics and Settlements." *Korea Journal of Population and Development* 21: 121–43.

Kim, Illsoo. 1981. *New Urban Immigrants: The Korean Community in New York.* Princeton: Princeton University Press.

———. 1987. "Korea and East Asia: Premigration Factors and U.S. Immigration Policy." In *Pacific Bridges: The New Immigration from Asia and the Pacific Islands,* edited by James Fawcett and Benjamin Carino, pp. 327–45. Staten Island, N.Y.: Center for Migration Studies.

Kim, Kwang Chung, and Won Moo Hurh. 1985. "Ethnic Resources Utilization of Korean Small Businessmen in the United States." *International Migration Review* 19: 82–111.

Kim, Nam-Jun. 1992. "Black Seoul: Koreans Are the Wrong Target for Black Anger." *Korea Times New York* (English edition), January 11.

Kim, Sophia Kyung. 1991. "Black Community Hunt for Gunman." *Korea Times Los Angeles* (English edition), October 28.

———. 1992a. "Ice Cube the Peacemaker." *Korea Times Los Angeles* (English edition), May 4.

———. 1992b. "Lloyd Honored as the Trial Lawyer of the Year." *Korea Times Los Angeles* (English edition), June 8.

Kirschenman, Joleen, and Cathryn M. Neckerman. 1991. " 'We'd Love to Hire Them, But . . . ': The Meaning of Race for Employers." In *The Urban Underclass,* edited by Christopher Jencks and Paul Peterson, pp. 203–32. Washington, D.C.: Brookings Institution.

Kitano, Harry. 1976. *Japanese American: The Evolution of A Subculture.* 2d ed. Englewood Cliffs, N.J.: Prentice Hall.

Korean-American Grocers Association of Southern California. 1990. "Understanding Korean-American Retailers." Pamphlet prepared for a Sensitivity Training Program for American Sales and Marketing Professionals.

Korean Association of New York. 1985. *The History of the Korean Association of New York.* New York: Korean Association of New York.

Korean Businessmen's Association of New York. 1987. *A Ten Year History of Korean Businesses in New York.* New York: Korean Businessmen's Association of New York.

Korean Central Daily Los Angeles. 1994. *The 1994–95 Korean Business Directory of Southern California.* Los Angeles: Korean Central Daily Los Angeles.

Korean National Bureau of Statistics. 1977. *Population Composition by Surnames: A Report on the Data from the 1970 Census of Population.* Seoul: Economic Planning Board, Republic of Korea.

———. 1987. *Social Indicators of Korea.* Seoul: Economic Planning Board, Republic of Korea.

Korean Youth and Community Center. 1990. "The Mission."

Kwong, Peter. 1987. *The New Chinatown.* New York: Noonsday Press.

Lee, Felicia. 1988. "Brooklyn Blacks and Koreans Forge Pact." *New York Times,* December 21.

Lee, Heon Cheol. 1993. "Korean-Black Conflict in New York City: A Sociological Analysis." Ph.D. diss., Columbia University.

Lee, Julie. 1994. "Defining 1.5 Generation." *Korea Times Los Angeles* (English edition), April 6.

Light, Ivan. 1983. *Cities in World Perspectives.* New York: Macmillan.

———. 1984. "Immigrant and Ethnic Enterprise in North America." *Ethnic and Racial Studies* 7: 195–216.

Light, Ivan, and Edna Bonacich. 1988. *Immigrant Entrepreneurs: Koreans in Los Angeles, 1965–1982.* Berkeley: University of California Press.

Light, Ivan, Hadas Har-Chvi, and Kenneth Kan. 1994. "Black/Korean Conflict in Los Angeles." *Managing Divided Cities,* edited by Seamus Dunn, pp. 72–87. Newbury Park, Calif.: Sage Publications.

Light, Ivan, Im Jung Kwuon, and Deng Zhong. 1990. "Korean Rotating Credit Associations in Los Angeles." *Amerasia* 16 (1): 35–54.

Light, Ivan, and Elizabeth Roach. 1996. "Self-Employment: Mobility Ladder or Economic Lifeboat?" In *Ethnic Los Angeles,* edited by Roger Waldinger and Mehdi Bozorgmehr. New York: Russell Sage Foundation Press.

Light, Ivan, and Carolyn Rosenstein. 1995. *Race, Ethnicity, and Entrepreneurship in Urban America.* New York: Aldine de Gruyter.

Light, Ivan, Georges Sabagh, Mehdi Bozorgmehr, and Claudia Der-Martirosian. 1994. "Beyond the Ethnic Enclave Economy." *Social Problems* 41: 65–80.

Light, Ivan, and Angel Sanchez. 1987. "Immigrant Entrepreneurs in 272 SMSA's." *Sociological Perspectives* 30: 373–99.

Light, Ivan, and Charles Choy Wong. 1975. "Protest or Work: Dilemmas of the Tourist Industry in American Chinatowns." *American Sociological Review* 80: 1342–67.

Lim, H. 1982. "Acceptance of American Culture in Korea: Patterns of Cultural Contact and Koreans' Perception of American Culture." *Journal of Asiatic Studies* 25: 25–36.

Liu, Mini. 1988. "Asians against Afro-Americans: Who Benefits?" *Amsterdam News,* October 29.

Loewen, James. 1971. *The Mississippi Chinese: Between Black and White.* Cambridge: Harvard University Press.

Lovell-Troy, L. A. 1981. "Ethnic Occupational Structure: Greeks in the Pizza Business." *Ethnicity* 8: 82–95.

Lucas, Lawrence. 1990. "Seeing through Smoke Screen of the Boycott." *Amsterdam News,* October 6.

Lyman, Stanford M. 1974. *Chinese Americans.* New York: Random House.

Lyu, Kingsley K. 1977. "Korean Nationalist Activities in Hawaii and the Continental United States, 1900–1945, Part I: 1900–1919." *Amerasia Journal* 4 (1): 23–90.

Marks, Mariene Adler. 1991. "Discriminating Gestures: Building Ethnic Bridges in Los Angeles." *Korea Times Los Angeles* (English edition), April 24.

Marx, Gary. 1969. *Protest and Prejudice.* New York: Harper and Row.

Maynard, Robert. 1970. "Black Nationalism and Community Schools." In *Community Control of Schools,* edited by Henry M. Levin, pp. 100–111. Washington, D.C.: Brookings Institution.

McFadden, Robert D. 1990. "Blacks Attack Three Vietnamese; One Hurt Badly." *New York Times,* May 14.

Merton, Robert. 1949. "Discrimination and the American Creed." In *Discrimination and National Welfare,* edited by H. I. MacIver, pp. 99–126. New York: Harper and Row.

Miller, Jack David, and Reed Coughlan. 1993. "The Poverty of Primordialism: The Demystification of Ethnic Attachments." *Ethnic and Racial Studies* 16: 183–202.

Min, Pyong Gap. 1984a. "From White-Collar Occupations to Small Business: Koreans' Occupational Adjustment." *Sociological Quarterly* 25: 333–52.

———. 1984b. "A Structural Analysis of Korean Businesses in the United States." *Ethnic Groups* 6: 1–25.

———. 1987. "Factors Contributing to Ethnic Business: A Comprehensive Synthesis." *International Journal of Comparative Sociology* 23 (3–4): 195–218.

———. 1988a. *Ethnic Business Enterprise: Korean Small Business in Atlanta.* New York: Center for Migration Studies.

——. 1988b. "Korean Immigrant Entrepreneurship: A Multivariate Analysis." *Journal of Urban Affairs* 10: 197–212.

——. 1989. "Some Positive Functions of Ethnic Business for an Immigrant Community: Koreans in Los Angeles." Final report submitted to the National Science Foundation. Department of Sociology, Queens College of CUNY, Flushing, N.Y.

——. 1991. "Cultural and Economic Boundaries of Korean Ethnicity: A Comparative Analysis." *Ethnic and Racial Studies* 14: 225–41.

——. 1992a. "Korean Immigrant Wives' Overwork." *Korea Journal of Population and Development* 21: 23–36.

——. 1992b. "The Structure and Social Functions of Korean Immigrant Churches in the United States." *International Migration Review* 26: 352–67.

——. 1993. "Korean Immigrants in Los Angeles." In *Immigration and Entrepreneurship: Culture, Capital, and Ethnic Networks,* edited by Ivan Light and Parminder Bhachu, pp.185–204. New York: Transaction Publishers.

——. 1995. "Technological Advances and Ethnic Attachment." Paper presented at the annual meeting of the American Sociological Association, Washington, D.C., August.

——. 1997. "Korean Immigrant Wives' Labor Force Participation, Marital Power, and Status." In *Women and Work: Race, Ethnicity, and Class,* edited by Elizabeth Higginbotham and Mary Romero. Newbury Park, Calif.: Sage Publications.

Miracle, Andrew, Jr. 1981. "Factors Affecting Interracial Cooperation: A Case Study of a High School Football Team." *Human Organization* 40: 150–54.

Mirak, Robert. 1980. "Armenians." In *Harvard Encyclopedia of American Ethnic Groups,* edited by Stephen Thernstrom, pp. 136–49. Cambridge: Harvard University Press.

Moritz, Owen. 1982. "In the Korean Shadow of Yankee Stadium." *New York Daily News,* July 25.

Morokvasic, Mirjana, Roger Waldinger, and Annie Phizacklea. 1990. "Business on the Ragged Edge: Immigrant and Minority Business in the Garment Industries of Paris, London, and New York." In *Ethnic Entrepreneurs: Immigrant Business in Industrial Societies,* edited by Roger Waldinger, Howard Aldrich, and Robin Ward, pp. 157–76. Newbury Park, Calif.: Sage Publications.

Morris, Aldon. 1984. *The Origin of the Civil Rights Movement: Black Communities Organizing for Change.* New York: Free Press.

Murphy, William. 1990. "Prevent Racial Bigotry." *New York Newsday,* May 12.

Myrdal, Gunnar. 1944. *An American Dilemma: The Negro Problem and Modern Democracy.* New York: Harper.

Nakanishi, Don T. 1993. "Surviving Democracy's 'Mistake': Japanese Americans and the Enduring Legacy of Executive Order 9066." *Amerasia Journal* 19 (1): 7–36.

Navarro, Armando. 1993. "The South Central Los Angeles Eruption: A Latino Perspective." *Amerasia Journal* 19 (2): 69–86.

New York City Department of City Planning. 1992. *Demographic Profiles: A*

Portrait of New York City's Community District from the 1980 and 1990 Censuses of Population and Housing. New York: New York City Department of Planning.

Nielsen, François. 1985. "Toward a Theory of Ethnic Solidarity in Modern Societies." *American Sociological Review* 50: 133–49.

Njeri, Itabari. 1989. "Cultural Conflict." *Los Angeles Times,* November 8.

Noel, Donald. 1968. "A Theory of the Origin of Ethnic Stratification." *Social Problems* 16: 157–72.

O'Brien, David, and Stephen Fugita. 1982. "Middleman Minority Concept: Its Explanatory Value in the Case of the Japanese in California Agriculture." *Pacific Sociological Review* 56: 458–74.

Oliver, Melvin, and James Johnson. 1984. "Inter-Ethnic Conflict in an Urban Ghetto: The Case of Blacks and Latinos in Los Angeles." *Research in Social Movements, Conflict, and Change* 6: 57–94.

Oliver, Melvin L., James H. Johnson, and Walter C. Farrell. 1993. "Anatomy of a Rebellion: A Political-Economic Analysis." In *Reading Rodney King/ Reading Urban Uprising,* edited by Robert Cooding-Williams, pp. 117–41. New York: Routledge.

Olzak, Susan. 1986. "A Competition Model of Ethnic Collective Action in American Cities, 1877–1889." In *Competitive Ethnic Relations,* edited by Susan Olzak and Joane Nagel, pp. 17–46. New York: Academic Press.

———. 1989. "Labor Unrest, Immigration, and Ethnic Conflict in Urban America, 1880–1914." *American Journal of Sociology* 94: 1303–34.

Olzak, Susan, and Joane Nagel, eds. 1986. *Competitive Ethnic Relations.* New York: Academic Press.

Olzak, Susan, and Elizabeth West. 1991. "Ethnic Conflicts and the Rise and Fall of Ethnic Newspapers." *American Sociological Review* 56: 458–74.

Omni, Michael. 1993. "Out of the Melting Pot and Into the Fire: Race Relations Policy." In *The State of Asian Pacific America: Policy Issues to the Year 2020,* edited by LEAP Asian Pacific American Public Policy Institute and UCLA Asian American Studies Center, pp. 199–214. Los Angeles: LEAP Asian Pacific American Public Policy Institute and UCLA Asian American Studies Center.

Omni, Michael, and Howard Winant. 1986. *Racial Formation in the United States: From the 1960s to the 1980s.* New York: Routledge.

Ong, Paul. 1984. "Chinatown Unemployment and the Ethnic Labor Market." *Amerasia Journal* 11 (1): 35–54.

Ong, Paul, and Suzanne Hee. 1993. *Losses in the Los Angeles Civil Unrest.* Los Angeles: Center for Pacific Rim Studies of the University of California.

Ong, Paul, Kye Young Park, and Yasmin Tong. 1994. "The Korean-Black Conflict and the State." In *The New Asian Immigration in Los Angeles and Global Restructuring,* edited by Paul Ong, Edna Bonacich, and Lucie Cheng, pp. 264–94. Philadelphia: Temple University Press.

Page, Stanley. 1992. "One Man's Comment." *Korea Times Los Angeles* (English edition), May 23.

Palmer, Mabel. 1957. *The History of Indians in Natal.* Natal Regional Survey, vol. 10. Cape Town: Oxford University Press.

Pannell, Creed. 1989. "The Korean Invasion: A New Threat to Black Business." *Metro Atlanta,* March.

Park, In-Sook Han, and Lee-Jay Cho. 1995. "Confucianism and the Korean Family." *Journal of Comparative Family Studies* 26: 117–35.

Park, In-Sook Han, James Fawcett, Fred Arnold, and Robert Gardner. 1990. *Korean Immigrants to the United States: A Pre-Departure Analysis.* Papers of the East-West Population Institute, no. 114. Hawaii: Population Institute, East-West Center.

Patterson, Wayne. 1988. *The Korean Frontier in America: Immigration to Hawaii, 1896–1910.* Honolulu: University of Hawaii Press.

Philips, Chuck. 1991. "Wiesenthal Center Denounces Ice Cube's Album." *Los Angeles Times,* November 2.

Piore, Michael. 1979. *Birds of Passage: Migrant Labor and Industrial Societies.* New York: Cambridge University Press.

Porter, Jack N. 1981. "The Urban Middleman: A Comparative Analysis." *Comparative Social Research* 4: 199–215.

Portes, Alejandro. 1984. "The Rise of Ethnicity: Determinants of Ethnic Perceptions among Cuban Exiles in Miami." *American Sociological Review* 49: 389–97.

Portes, Alejandro, and Robert Bach. 1985. *Latin Journey: Cuban and Mexican Immigrants in the United States.* Berkeley: University of California Press.

Portes, Alejandro, and Robert Manning. 1986. "The Immigrant Enclave: Theory and Empirical Examples." In *Competitive Ethnic Relations,* edited by Susan Olzak and Joane Nagel, pp. 47–68. New York: Academic Press.

Portes, Alejandro, and Rubén Rumbaut. 1990. *Immigrant America: A Portrait.* Berkeley: University of California Press.

Proffitt, Steve. 1992. "Seeking to Coalesce the Korean American Community." *Los Angeles Times,* May 24.

Purdum, Todd. 1990. "Dinkins Supports Shunned Grocers." *New York Times,* September 22.

"Race-Baiting in Flatbush." 1990. *New York Post,* February 18.

Ravitch, Diane. 1974. *The Great School Wars: New York City, 1805–1973.* New York: Basic Books.

Reddick, L. D. 1942. "Anti-Semitism among Negroes." *Negro Quarterly* 1: 114–15.

Reiss, Albert, and Howard Aldrich. 1971. "Absentee Ownership and Management in the Black Ghetto: Social and Economic Consequences." *Social Problems* 18: 319–39.

Reitz, Jeffrey G. 1980. *The Survival of Ethnic Groups.* Toronto: McGraw-Hill.

Rinder, Irwin. 1958–59. "Stranger in the Land: Social Relations in the Status Gap." *Social Problems* 6: 253–60.

Rumbaut, Rubén. 1991. "Passages to America: Perspectives on the New Immigration." In *America at Century's End,* edited by Alan Wolfe, pp. 208–57. Berkeley: University of California Press.

———. 1994. "Origins and Destinies: Immigration to the United States Since World War II." *Sociological Forum* 9: 583–621.

Saito, Leland. 1993. "Asian Americans and Latinos in San Gabriel Valley, California: Ethnic Political Cooperation and Redistricting 1990–92." *Amerasia Journal* 19 (2): 55–68.

Sanders, Jimmy, and Victor Nee. 1987. "Limits of Ethnic Solidarity in the Enclave Economy." *American Sociological Review* 52: 745–67.

Sengstock, Mary. 1974. "Iraqi Christians in Detroit: An Analysis of an Ethnic Occupation." In *Arabic Speaking Communities in American Cities,* edited by B. Aswad, pp. 21–37. Staten Island, N.Y.: Center for Migration Studies.

Shannon, Edward. 1988. "Let's Tone Down Anti-Korean Rhetoric." *Amsterdam News,* October 8.

Sherif, Muzafer, O. J. Harvey, and B. J. White. 1961. *Intergroup Conflict and Cooperation: The Robbers Cave Experiment.* Norman: Institute of Group Relations, University of Oklahoma.

Sherif, Muzafer, and Carolyn Sherif. 1953. *Groups in Harmony and Tension.* New York: Harper and Row.

Shibutani, T., and Kian Kwan. 1966. *Ethnic Stratification: A Comparative Approach.* New York: Macmillan.

Shin Chey, Youn-Cha. 1992. "Media Commentary: The Enemy This Time." *San Francisco Chronicle,* May 8.

Shin, Eui-Hang, and Eui-Young Yu. 1984. "Use of Surname in Ethnic Research: The Case of Kim in the Korean-American Population." *Demography* 21: 347–59.

Shin, Linda. 1971. "Koreans in America, 1903–1945." In *Roots: An Asian American Reader,* edited by Amy Tachiki, Eddie Wong, and Franklin Odo, pp. 201–6. Los Angeles: Asian American Studies Center, UCLA.

Silberman, Charles. 1985. *A Certain People: American Jews and Their Lives Today.* New York: Summit Books.

Simmel, Georg. 1955. *Conflict and the Web of Group Affiliations.* Glencoe, Ill.: Free Press.

Sinden, Peter G. 1980. "Anti-Semitism and the Black Power Movement." *Ethnicity* 7: 34–46.

Sleeper, Jim. 1990. *The Closest of Strangers: Liberalism and the Politics of Race in New York.* New York: W. W. Norton.

Stryker, Sheldon. 1958. "Social Structure and Prejudice." *Social Problems* 6 (4): 340–54.

———. 1974. "A Theory of Middleman Minorities: A Comment." *American Sociological Review* 38: 281–82.

Sunoo, Paik Brenda. 1992. "Out of Ashes, Solidarity." *Korea Times Los Angeles* (English edition), May 11.

Tabor, Mary. 1992. "Unfulfilled Promises." *New York Times,* October 26.

Tait, George Edward. 1988. "ANPM Responds to 'Buy Black' Critics." *Amsterdam News,* October 29.

Thomas, William, and Florian Znaniecki. 1927. *The Polish Peasant in Europe and America.* New York: Knopf.

Thompson, R. H. 1980. "From Kinship to Class: A New Model of Urban Overseas Chinese Social Organization." *Urban Anthropology* 9: 265–93.

Tsukashima, Ronald T., and Darrel Montero. 1976. "The Contact Hypothesis:

Social and Economic Contact and Generational Changes in the Study of Black Anti-Semitism." *Social Forces* 55: 149–65.

Turner, James. 1973. "The Sociology of Black Nationalism." In *The Death of White Sociology,* edited by Joyce Ladner, pp. 232–52. New York: Random House.

Turner, Jonathan, and Edna Bonacich. 1980. "Toward a Composite Theory of Middleman Minorities." *Ethnicity* 7: 144–58.

U.S. Bureau of the Census. 1972. *1970 Census of Population, Subject Reports, Chinese, Japanese, and Filipinos in the United States.* Washington, D.C.: U.S. Government Printing Office.

———. 1983. *1980 Census of Population, General Population Characteristics, United States Summary* (PC80-1-B1). Washington, D.C.: U.S. Government Printing Office.

———. 1990. *Census of Population and Housing.* Public Use Microdata Sample. Washington, D.C.: U.S. Bureau of the Census.

———. 1991. *1987 Economic Censuses,* MB87-3. Washington, D.C.: U.S. Government Printing Office.

———. 1993a. *1990 Census of Population, General Population Characteristics, United States* (CP-1-1). Washington, D.C.: U.S. Government Printing Office.

———. 1993b. *1990 Census of Population, General Population Characteristics, California* (CP-1-5). Washington, D.C.: U.S. Government Printing Office.

———. 1993c. *1990 Census of Population, General Population Characteristics, New York* (CP-1-34). Washington, D.C.: U.S. Government Printing Office.

———. 1993d. *1990 Census of Population, Asians and Pacific Islanders in the United States* (CP-3-5). Washington, D.C.: U.S. Government Printing Office.

U.S. Commission on Civil Rights. 1986. *Recent Activities against Citizens and Residents of Asian Descent.* Washington, D.C.: U.S. Government Printing Office.

———. 1992. *Civil Rights Issues Facing Asian Americans in the 1990s.* Washington, D.C.: U.S. Government Printing Office.

Waldinger, Roger. 1985. "Immigrant Enterprise and the Structure of the Labor Market." In *New Approaches to Economic Life: Economic Restructuring, Employment, and the Social Division of Labor,* edited by Bryan Roberts, Ruth Finnegan, and Duncan Gallie, pp. 213–27. Manchester: Manchester University Press.

———. 1986. *Through the Eye of the Needle: Immigrants and Enterprise in New York's Garment Trades.* New York: New York University Press.

———. 1989. "Structural Opportunity or Ethnic Advantage? Immigrant Business Development in New York." *International Migration Review* 23: 48–72.

———. 1996. "Conclusion: Ethnicity and Opportunity in the Plural Society." In *Ethnic Los Angeles,* edited by Roger Waldinger and Mehdi Bozorgmehr. New York: Russell Sage Foundation Press.

Waldinger, Roger, and Howard Aldrich. 1990. "Trends in Ethnic Business in the United States." In *Ethnic Entrepreneurs: Immigrant Business in Industrial Societies,* edited by Roger Waldinger, Howard Aldrich, and Robin Ward, pp. 49–78. Newbury Park, Calif.: Sage Publications.

Waldinger, Roger, and Mehdi Bozorgmehr. 1996. "Introduction: The Making of a Multicultural Metropolis." In *Ethnic Los Angeles,* edited by Roger Waldinger and Mehdi Bozorgmehr. New York: Russell Sage Foundation Press.

Waldinger, Roger, Robin Ward, and Howard Aldrich. 1985. "Trend Report: Ethnic Business and Occupational Mobility in Advanced Society." *Sociology* 19: 586–97.

Ward, Robin. 1985. "Minority Settlement and Local Economy." In *New Approaches to Economic Life: Economic Restructuring, Employment, and the Social Division of Labor,* edited by Brian Roberts, Ruth Finnegan, and Duncan Gallie, pp. 198–212. Manchester: Manchester University Press.

Weisbord, Robert, and Arthur Stein. 1970. *Bittersweet Encounter: The Afro-American and the American Jew.* Westport, Conn.: Negro Universities Press.

Williams, Robin. 1964. *Strangers Next Door.* Englewood Cliffs, N.J.: Prentice Hall.

Wilson, Kenneth, and Allen Martin. 1982. "Ethnic Enclaves: A Comparison of the Cuban and Black Economies in Miami." *American Journal of Sociology* 88: 135–60.

Wilson, Kenneth, and Alejandro Portes. 1980. "Immigrant Enclaves: An Analysis of the Labor Market Experiences of Cubans in Miami." *American Journal of Sociology* 86: 295–319.

Wilson, William. 1987. *The Truly Disadvantaged: The Inner City, The Underclass, and Public Policy.* Chicago: University of Chicago Press.

Wong, Bernard. 1987. "The Chinese New Immigrants in New York's Chinatown." In *New Immigrants in New York,* edited by Nancy Foner, pp. 243–72. New York: Columbia University Press.

Wong, Eugene. 1985. "Asian American Middleman Minority Theory: The Framework for an Ethnic Myth." *Journal of Ethnic Studies* 3 (1): 51–86.

Wurdinger, Victoria. 1992. "The Korean Influence." *Nails,* December.

Yarrow, Marian Radke, John Campbell, and Leon Yarrow. 1958. "Acquisition of a New Norm: A Study of Racial Desegregation." *Journal of Social Issues* 14: 8–28.

Yeon, Bong Won. 1986. "Koreans in Brazil." In *The Current Status and Future Prospectus of Overseas Koreans* (in Korean), edited by the Center for Studies of World Affairs, pp. 102–10. New York: Center for Studies of World Affairs.

Yim Lee, Kapson. 1992. "Civil Rights Commission Hears Community Criticism of Media." *Korea Times Los Angeles* (English edition), May 18.

Yinger, Milton. 1985. "Ethnicity." *Annual Review of Sociology* 11: 151–80.

Yoon, In Jin. 1993. *The Social Origin of Korean Immigration to the United States, 1965–Present.* Papers of the East-West Population Institute, no. 121. Honolulu: East-West Center.

Yu, Eui-Young. 1983. "Korean Communities in America: Past, Present, and Future." *Amerasia Journal* 10 (2): 23–52.

———. 1985. "Koreatown, Los Angeles: Emergence of a New Inner-City Ethnic Community." *Bulletin of Population and Development Studies* 14: 29–44.

Zenner, Walter. 1980. "Theory of Middleman Minorities: A Critical Review." In *Sourcebook on the New Immigration,* edited by R. S. Bryce-Laporte, pp. 419–25. New Brunswick, N.J.: Transaction Publishers.

———. 1982. "Arabic-Speaking Immigrants in North America as Middleman Minorities." *Ethnic and Racial Studies* 4 (4): 457–76.

———. 1991. *Minorities in the Middle: A Cross-Cultural Analysis.* Albany: State University of New York Press.

Zeul, Carolyn, and Craig Humphrey. 1971. "The Integration of Black Residents in Suburban Neighborhoods: A Reexamination of the Contact Hypothesis." *Social Problems* 18: 462–74.

Zhou, Min. 1992. *Chinatown: The Socioeconomic Potential of an Urban Enclave.* Philadelphia: Temple University Press.

Zhou, Min, and John Logan. 1989. "Returns on Human Capital in Ethnic Enclaves." *American Sociological Review* 54: 809–20.

KOREAN LANGUAGE DAILIES AND MAGAZINES

Korea Central Daily New York (KCDNY).

2/16/1985. "New York City Government Has Intervened in the Harlem Boycott."

8/31/1988. "A Boycott of a Korean Store Likely to Last Long."

12/16/1988. "Koreans and Blacks Had a Dinner for Racial Harmony."

4/10/1989. "Coco Market about to Be Closed by a Harlem Boycott."

4/12/1989. "Anti-Korean Sentiment Strong among Sunnyside-Woodside Residents."

4/14/1989. "Korean-Language Signs Encounter Protest."

4/15/1989. "Opening a Communication Channel with Blacks."

9/26/1989. "The First Asian Labor Festival."

10/27/1989. "Boycott of a Korean Store in Harlem Came to an End."

2/16/1990. "Korean-Black Cultural Activities for Dialogue."

5/16/1990. "A Vietnamese, Mistaken for a Korean, Severely Beaten by Black Youths."

5/19/1990. "Asian American Community Leaders Discussed Common Measures against the Black Boycott."

5/22/1990. "Supporters from Chinatown Toured Korean Stores in Brooklyn."

5/25/1990. "Black Students Rallied for an End of the Boycott."

5/30/1990. "Stop Boycotting Korean Stores."

6/16/1990. "Collective Responses to Landlords."

8/1/1990. "Church Fruit Is Closed for Repair Work."

8/3/1990. "A Tentative Decision to Hold a Demonstration on September 18th."

8/8/1990. "A Rockaway Korean Store Got No Police Protection."

8/24/1990. "Picketers Beat Bong Jae Jang."

8/28/1990. "Black Boycott Spread to Belmont Avenue."

9/25/1990. "Why Korean-Black Conflicts?"

11/3/1990. "A Bill to Restrict Foreign Language Signs Encountered Criticisms."

11/14/1990. "There Is No Korean-Black Conflict in Los Angeles."

7/29/1991. "Commercial Waste Disposal Fee Lowered."

11/6/1991. "New York Korean Grocery Leaders Visited a Korean Wholesale Store in Ontario."

11/9/1991. "The Korean Community Considers a Number of Measures against 'Black Korea.' "

12/13/1991. "The Nostrand Event Is a Hate Crime."

1/9/1992. "The Korean-American Grocers Association of New York Ready to Establish a Wholesale Store."

5/20/1992. "Korean Merchants Should Get out of Black Neighborhoods by All Means."

6/25/1992. "KAGRONY Asked the Department of Health to Revise Laws to Regulate Street Food Vendors."

7/18/1992. "Korean Victims in Washington Heights Given Another Chance to Start Their Businesses."

8/10/1992. "An Unknown American Citizen Donated $25,000 to Mrs. Hong."

4/25/1994. "We Will Achieve Korean-Black Interracial Harmony."

Korea Times Los Angeles (KTLA).

3/20/1991. "Korean-Black Joint Statement Is Issued."

3/22/1991. "Blacks Attacked Korean Merchants in Retaliation."

3/28/1991. "Blacks Announced a Plan to Undertake Troublesome Korean Markets and Directly Operate Them."

3/30/1991. "Blacks' Assaults on Korean Stores Have Increased."

3/31/1991. "Black Police Officers Arrested Koreans Beaten by a Black Truck Driver."

4/11/1991a. "Korean-Black Merchant Leaders Visiting Korea."

4/11/1991b. "A Black Customer Slapped a Korean Liquor Store Owner on the Face Saying 'Go Back to Korea.' "

8/9/1991/ "Visitors from Korea Doing Luxury Shopping at Koreatown."

8/17/1991. "Black Muslims Threaten to Boycott All Korean Stores."

8/19/1991. "Arson on Two Korean Stores at the Same Time."

9/7/1991. "A Korean Clothing Store Owner Won in a Court Battle with His Landlord."

9/13/1991. "KARE Plans to Stop Giving Financial Support to the Store in Late September."

9/18/1991. "Korean Churches Contributed Greatly to Improving Korean-Black Relations."

9/27/1991. "LA County Black Employees Support the Boycott of John's Market."

10/6/1991. "Too Many Concessions to Blacks."

10/23/1991. "700 Korean Businesses Housed in 27 Koreatown Shopping Malls."

10/25/1991. "Let's Resolve Conflicts through Christian Love."

10/26/1991. "Please Give Du a Fair Sentence."

10/30/1991. "19 Koreans Murdered by Blacks over Four Years."

11/4/1991. "Jewish Organizations Also Boycott Ice Cube's Album."

11/16/1991. "100 Low-Income Black Children to Receive Vocational Training for Employment in Korean Stores."

11/17/1991. "Du Given Five-Year Probation."

11/20/1991. "Koreans' Anger against 'Black Korea' Spread Quickly."

11/23/1991. "500 Black Demonstrators Condemned Judge Karlin's Sentence."

11/27/1991. "A Korean Created a Song Encouraging Korean-Black Harmony."

11/28/1991. "African/Korean-American Christian Alliance Held a Mass Parade."

12/12/1991. "A Korean Merchant Arrested and Charged with Beating A Black Girl."

12/15/1991. "Cardinal Mahoney Actively Intervened in Korean-Black Conflict."

12/18/1991. "Blacks Destroyed Nine Korean-Owned Cars."

12/20/1991. "A Japanese Woman, Mistaken for a Korean, Battered with a Baseball Bat."

12/21/1991. "Boycott of Don's Market Ended."

1/1/1992. "Korean Businesses in South Central Los Angeles."

1/7/1992. "Donations to the Black Community Need More Publicity and Organization."

3/3/1992. "Korean and Black Catholics Had a Meeting for Racial Harmony."

5/23/1992. "Special Issue on the 4/29 Race Riots."

5/26/1992. "Koreans and Black Gangs Discussed Ways to Reduce Korean-Black Tensions."

5/31/1992. "Korean-American Grocers Association and Black Gangs Had Their Second Meeting."

6/11a/1992. "Korean Stores Selectively Targeted for Arson."

6/11b/1992. "Koreatown Businesses Have Reached 3,000."

6/15/1992. "Preparing Law Suits against Governments."

6/17/1992. "Korean Victims of the Riots Will Continue Their Demonstration for Three Months."

6/22/1992. "A Radio Station Encouraged Arson and Looting of Korean Stores."

6/25/1992. "Legal Restriction for Reopening of Liquor Stores Threatens Koreans' Economic Survival."

7/2/1992. "Korean Immigrants in Isolation."

7/12/1992. "One-Month-Old City Hall Rally Ended."

7/15/1992. "Conflict over Distribution of the Donated Money."

7/23/1992. "$4,752,571 Was Raised in the U.S."

7/25/1992. "Korean-American Legal Advocacy Foundation to Be Established Soon."

7/28/1992. "Riot Damages on Asian-Owned Businesses."

7/29/1992. "Conflict over Use of Funds Settled."

8/14/1992. "Korean Riot Victims Demonstrated against Korean Consul General and Mr. Ki Hwan Ha."

10/2/1992. "Korean American Democratic Committee Established."

10/8/1992. "An Opportunity to Find Harmony and Similarities between Koreans and Blacks."

10/25/1992. "Black Pastors and Students' Visits to Korea."

10/28/1992. "Korean-Black Friendship Golf Tournament."

10/31/1992. "2,400 Koreans in Orange Country Registered for Voting in 1992 Alone."

11/10/1992. "Black Students Who Visited Korea Had a Press Conference."

11/5/1992. "The New Era in the 100-Year Korean American History."

11/7/1992. "Payment to 200 Additional Riot Victims Is Inevitable."

11/15/1992. "The Meaning of Jay Kim's Election to the U.S. House of Representatives."

11/22/1992. "Six Months after the Riots."

12/11/1992. "Half of Korean Riot Victims Planning to Leave Black Neighborhoods."

1/1/1993. "Korean-Black Adolescents Enjoy Friendships with Fishing and Basketball Games."

1/4/1993. "Koreatown Security Patrol Team to Be Created in February."

1/9/1993. "The Liquor Business: Problems and Prospects."

2/12/1993. "Koreatown Security Patrol Team Established."

2/22/1993. "A Concert for Interracial Harmony."

3/3/1993. "Korean-Black Children's Mutual Visit and Study Program."

3/9/1993. "No Hope for Reconstruction."

3/14/1993. "Good-Bye, America."

3/22/1993. "Failure to Pay Wages Contributed to the Largest Proportion of Labor Disputes."

3/28/1993. "Interview with Angela Oh."

4/3/1993. "Post-riot Survey on Mutual Understanding."

4/11/1993. "Riot Stress and Riot Victims' Mental Health."

4/22/1993. "Seoul to Soul: Dance."

4/30/1993. "Results of the Audit of Donations for Riot Victims Disclosed."

7/21/1993. "The Watts Foundation Prepared Various Racial Harmony Programs."

7/28/1993. "The National Korean-American Alliance Established."

8/7/1993. "16 Black Students Come Back from Their Visit to Korea."

8/21/1993. "Korean Ethnic Organizations Undergoing a Generational Transition."

10/4a/1993. "The Entire Amount of Korean Government's Financial Support Turned Over to the Korean American Scholarship Foundation."

10/4b/1993. "Korean and Black People Are Running for Interracial Harmony."

7/30/1994. "An Unused Korean Riot Victims Fund to Be Used for Construction of the Korean Community Center."

8/11/1994. "My Trip to Korea Provided an Opportunity to Correct My Anti-Korean Biases."

Korea Times New York (KTNY).

11/9/1978. "ILGWU Pressures a Korean Garment Business to Unionize Workers."

7/30/1981. "A Boycott of a Jamaica Korean Grocery Store."

8/4/1981. "A Korean Grocery Owner Asked the Court to Stop Boycotting."

8/6/1981. "Black Boycott Stopped."

2/8/1982. "Black Youngsters Demonstrated Demanding Employment."

6/29/1982. "Anti-Korean Pamphlets in Harlem."

8/2/1982. "Planning a Demonstration in Front of *Daily News.*"

5/19/1983. "New York Korean Businessmen's Association Plan to Send a Proposal for Rent Regulation."

5/24/1983. "New York Korean Businessmen's Association Started a Petition Drive for Rent Regulation."

6/15/1984. "Black Youngsters Pressured a Korean Store to Hire Black Workers."

10/31/1984. "Blacks Started Boycotting Korean Stores in Harlem."

12/13/1984. "Korean Community Leaders Visited City Hall to Discuss Harlem Boycott."

1/5/1985. "Korean-Black Relations Likely to Be Improved."

5/14/1985. "A Proposal for a Law for Rent Regulation Gained Strong Support."

6/2/1985. "A White Wholesaler Surrendered to Unity of Korean Producer Retailers."

7/24/1985. "A Hearing on Need for a Rent Regulation Law."

5/8/1986. "Uptown Korean Merchants' Association Participated in a Rally for a Rent Regulation Law."

12/12/1988. "Korean-Black Conflict Should Be Solved within the Framework of Racial Harmony."

12/15/1989. "Results of a Survey of 441 Korean Business Owners in New York."

8/6/1990. "Most Koreans Support the Idea of Holding a Mass Rally."

4/8/1991. "Korean Dry Cleaners Number 1,100."

5/4/1991. "24 Illegal Residents Arrested While Working at Korean Garment Factories."

7/26/1991. "The Congress of Small Business Created."

1/29/1992. "Hong's Song: A Green Light for Korean-Black Conflict."

2/29/1992. "Let Us Help Mr. Tong Kwang Kim."

3/26/1992. "Korean Seafood Retailers Association Requested a Fair Judgment on the Freshness of the Market Fish."

5/16/1992. "It's Time We Second-Generation Koreans Work for the Protection of Korean American Interests."

6/17/1992. "Koreans Who Took the Citizenship Test Greatly Increased after the Riot."

7/6/1992. "Residents Visited a Korean Victim of the Riots in New York City."

Sae Gae Times (SGT).

7/8/1988. "History of the Broadway Korean Businessmen's Association."

7/29/1988. "Korean Fish Retailers Shook Fulton Fish Market."

9/9/1988. "Blacks Planning a Large-Scale Anti-Korean Demonstration."

9/14/1988. "Produce Supplier Apologized for Racial Discrimination against Korean Merchants."

10/6/1988. "Korean and Black Negotiation Teams Had Their First Meeting."

10/25/1988. "Korean Fish Retail Stores Everywhere in New York."

12/2a/1988. "Black Peddlers Caused Trouble to Korean Stores."

12/2b/1988. "Slavins Ultimately Yielded to Koreans' Boycott."

12/6/1988. "Blacks Trying to Recapitulate Boycotts in Jamaica and Harlem."

12/29/1988. "Korean Merchants Opened Business Accounts with a Black Bank."

4/8/1989. "Altercation in a Korean Store Ultimately Gone to Court."

6/6/1989. "The Background of the Establishment of the Korean-American Grocers' Association and the Future Prospects."

8/22/1989. "Koreans Support Dinkins."

8/26/1989. "One Year after the Brooklyn Boycott."

1/30/1990. "Black Organizations outside of the Neighborhoods Intervened in the Boycott."

2/8/1990. "The Groups Who Control the Brooklyn Boycott Unveiled."

3/26/1990. "Both Candidates Focus on Effective Operation of the Korean Association and Improvement of Intergroup Relations."

5/22/1990. "Now Is the Time for Korean and Black Communities to Be United."

5/24/1990. "Man Ho Park Responded to Boycotters with a $6 Million Law Suit."

5/25/1990. "Let's Participate in the Buy-Merchandise Campaign to Help the Koreans Suffering from Racial Prejudice."

6/19/1990. "A Korean Victimized by a Hate Crime."

7/5/1990. "Korean Garment Contractors' Leaders Protested Frequent Raids by Department of Labor."

7/29/1990. "Koreatown Is Not Known to LA Residents."

8/16/1990. "LA Korean Stores Become Targets of Attack by Black Youths."

8/17/1990. "Mr. Jang Visiting LA for an Interview."

8/18/1990. "A Pamphlet Instigating Blacks to Boycott Korean Stores Spread."

8/23/1990. "Mr. Jang Battered by Picketers."

9/4/1990. "Joint Venture for Prevention of Korean-Black Conflict."

9/19/1990. "9/18 Rally Shook City Hall Plaza."

10/2/1990. "300 Koreans and Blacks Participated in a Festival for Racial Harmony."

11/3/1990. "A Measure to Restrict Foreign Language Signs Needs More Discussion."

1/29/1991. "Korean Nail Salon Owners' Association Proposed a Compromise Bill."

1/31/1991. "Arson of Two Korean Stores in South Central LA."

2/1/1991. "Bong Ok Chang Declared Innocent."

2/6/1991. "Results of Survey of Korean Nail Salon Owners."

2/9/1991. "City Government Issued Violation Tickets Recklessly."

2/25/1991. "Settlement of Korean Merchants' Lease Conflict."

3/16/1991. "Mr. Chang Applied for a Small Business Loan."

5/4/1991. "INS Raided Korean Garment Factories."

6/26/1991. "Blacks' Picketing in Front of a Korean Market Lasts One Week."

6/29/1991. "58 Garment Businesses Caught Violating Labor Laws."

8/15/1991. "The Congress of Small Business Is Established."

9/4/1991. "Korean Merchants Gave a Block Party for 1,000 Black Residents in Brooklyn."

9/16/1991. "Bronx Korean Merchants' Association Gave a Block Party."

9/29/1991. "40 Black Pastors Plan to Visit Korea."

10/11/1991. "We Cannot Work with First-Generation Koreans."

11/14/1991. "St. Ice Beer Company Asked to Stop Supporting Ice Cube."

11/20/1991. "Plan for Employment of Black Youths for Racial Harmony."

12/7/1991. "The Libraries in Korean and Black Communities Initiated Cultural Exchange Programs."

3/11/1992. "New York City Department of Business Development Listened to Korean Garment Contractors' Complaints."

4/15/1992. "Demonstration Demanding 'Give Blacks Jobs.' "

4/25/1992. "Korean-Black Conflict in Brooklyn Getting Worse Again."

4/28a/1992. "Du's Lawyer Selected as the Defense Lawyer of 1991."

4/28b/1992. "Result of Korean-Black Joint Project Coming Soon."

5/12/1992. "Mindan Contributed $200,000 for Riot Victims."

5/15/1992. "1.5- and 2d-Generation Koreans Actively Participating in the Korean Community."

6/8a/1992. "The Korean Produce Association Donated Money to Teacher McCray."

6/8b/1992. "New York Supermarkets Getting Out of Poor Black Areas."

6/16/1992. "Korean Stores in South Chicago Attacked by Black Rioters."

6/17/1992. "Korean Stores Suffered $7 Million Loss in the Bulls Riot."

6/20/1992. "KAGRO Received Financial Support from Several Grocery Manufacturers."

7/7/1992. "The Los Angeles City Government Owes an Apology to Koreans."

7/9/1992. "Korean Stores in Washington Heights Attacked."

7/11/1992. "Du Agreed to a $300,000 Compensation Settlement."

8/15/1992. "A SBA Loan Helped Mr. Hong Establish His Business at the End of August."

9/2/1992. "Korean Riot Victims Suffering from Posttraumatic Stress Symptoms Have Rapidly Increased."

9/12/1992. "Du's Shooting of a Black Girl Contributed to the Occurrence of the 4/29 Riot."

9/15/1992. "A Campaign for Helping the Black Homeless Gradually Becoming Active."

9/29/1992. "LA Koreans' Citizenship Applications Have Rapidly Increased."

10/24/1992. "Koreans Moving Out of LA Have Increased."

10/27/1992. "LA Korean Consul General Took a Large Proportion of Donations from Korea."

11/25/1992. "700 Love Turkeys Donated to New York City."

11/27a/1992a. "American Citizens Who Helped Koreans Were Recognized."

11/27b/1992. "A National Korean-American Civil Rights Organization Is Being Established."

12/1/1992. "Dinkins Plans to Increase Financial Support and Contract to Small Business Owners."

12/22/1992. "Korean Merchants in Harlem Struggling to Compete with Illegal Peddlers."

1/4/1993. "New York City Will Eradicate Illegal Peddlers."

1/8/1993. "Korean Garment Subcontractors Harassed by Immigration Officials' Raids."

2/18/1993. "New York City Government Loosened Various Small Business Regulations."

2/23/1993. "KAGRONY Established a Springboard for Development."

4/28/1993. "Sidewalk Stand Extended to 5 Feet Beginning July."

5/13/1993. "Let's Do Away with the Old-Generation Prejudice and Open a Dialogue."

5/28/1993. "Stocks Will Be Sold to KAGRONY Members for Establishment of a Korean Cooperative Company."

9/10/1993. "First Korean Bill of Rights Declared."

10/4/1993. "Dinkins Refused to Respond to Korean Merchants' Specific Requests."

1/8/1994. "Fulton Street Fish Market Wholesalers Urged to Stop Cheating on Weights."

7/30/1994. "A Building for the Korean Community Center Bought with the Remaining Fund Donated for the Riot Victims."

Index

Compositor:	J. Jarrett Engineering, Inc.
Text:	10/13 Sabon
Display:	Sabon
Printer and Binder:	Data Reproductions Corporation